LEGALIZING SEX

Legalizing Sex

Sexual Minorities, AIDS, and Citizenship in India

Chaitanya Lakkimsetti

NEW YORK UNIVERSITY PRESS
New York

NEW YORK UNIVERSITY PRESS
New York
www.nyupress.org

References to Internet websites (URLs) were accurate at the time of writing. Neither the author nor New York University Press is responsible for URLs that may have expired or changed since the manuscript was prepared.

Library of Congress Cataloging-in-Publication Data
Names: Lakkimsetti, Chaitanya, author.
Title: Legalizing sex : sexual minorities, AIDS, and citizenship in India / Chaitanya Lakkimsetti.
Description: New York : New York University Press. [2019] | Includes bibliographical references and index. | Also available as an ebook.
Identifiers: LCCN 2019012039 | ISBN 9781479810024 (cl. ; alk. paper) | ISBN 1479810029 (cl. ; alk. paper) | ISBN 9781479826360 (pb. ; alk. paper) | ISBN 1479826367 (pb. ; alk. paper)
Subjects: LCSH: Sexual minorities—Legal status, laws, etc.—Social aspects—India. | Sexual minorities—Political activity—India. | Transgender people—Legal status, laws, etc.—Social aspects—India. | Transgender people—Political activity—India. | Sex workers—Legal status, laws, etc.—Social aspects—India. | Sex workers—Political activity—India. | AIDS (Disease)—Patients—Legal status, laws, etc.—Social aspects—India. | AIDS activists—India.
Classification: LCC KNS2107.G38 L35 2019 | DDC 342.5408/7—dc23
LC record available at https://lccn.loc.gov/2019012039

New York University Press books are printed on acid-free paper, and their binding materials are chosen for strength and durability. We strive to use environmentally responsible suppliers and materials to the greatest extent possible in publishing our books.

Manufactured in the United States of America

10 9 8 7 6 5 4 3 2 1

Also available as an ebook

CONTENTS

Introduction: Contemporary Politics of Sex   1

1. "HIV Is Our Friend"   29

2. Challenging "Bare Life"   53

3. Empowered Criminals   76

4. Tolerable Identities, Intolerable Sex Acts   101

5. Interconnected Rights   127

Acknowledgments   147

Appendix A. Abbreviations   153

Appendix B. Timeline for Anti-Sodomy-Law Contestations   155

Notes   157

References   175

Index   187

About the Author   199

Introduction

Contemporary Politics of Sex

"*We want employment, we want jobs, we want welfare.*" This was a main slogan at a daylong *dharna* (protest) organized by a South India–based transgender and *hijra* group one humid summer afternoon in the city of Hyderabad in July 2015. The main goal of the dharna was to demand that the state government recognize transgender rights as recommended by India's Supreme Court (SC). In 2014, for the first time in India's history as an independent nation, the SC had recognized nonnormative gender identities as legal. It had also recommended that the government implement corresponding affirmative action policies in employment and education. There was a significant media presence and great interest in the dharna, whose organizers had mobilized a surprisingly large number of progressive groups to support their cause. It had been previously unthinkable that one of the most marginalized and stigmatized groups in the country could make demands of the state. When the day was over, the gathering had been a huge success that increased the visibility of the community while also showcasing its newfound political power.

Despite this success, at the time of this dharna the transgender community was under threat from the anti-sodomy law Section 377, a colonial-era statute that criminalizes "unnatural" sex acts. Although the SC had granted transgender individuals rights based on gender identity, by retaining Section 377 the same court had also reduced them to criminals. This contradiction was vocalized very poignantly by Laxmi Narayan Tripathi, a transgender activist: "Over here the ministry is saying that I have a right to choose my own bathroom. But tomorrow if I choose to go to the men's bathroom, will I be safe there? And if I get raped in the men's bathroom, does the rape law cover me? Today I am in a live-in relationship or I may be having an affair. If the police walk into my bedroom and arrest me under Section 377, will my dignity be protected?"[1] Laxmi's quote captures the paradoxical ways in which sexual and gender minorities experienced rights until 2018, when Section 377 was ruled unconstitutional. Nonnormative gender identities were legal, but nonnormative sex *acts* were not. Laxmi could choose a bathroom of her preference, but she could not choose sexual partners without concerns that Section 377 might compromise her safety and privacy. Whereas Section 377 is often perceived as a law that criminalizes homosexual sex, Laxmi's comments also show that it is a central component of the repression faced by gender-nonnormative groups, who are often labeled by the Indian state as being sexually deviant. Transgender individuals (especially trans women) who are hypervisible in public spaces are firsthand witnesses to the police harassment and extortion facilitated by such laws. As a result, transgender individuals like Laxmi were forced to experience their rights in a bifurcated way.

Laxmi's quote not only gets at the contradictory ways in which marginalized groups experience rights but also reveals that in contemporary India the rights-based struggles of previously marginalized and stigmatized groups have gained prominence in social discourse. The most recent decision of the SC on Section 377, in September 2018—decriminalizing same-sex sex between consenting adults—opens up the opportunity for these groups to demand further basic rights from the state, including antidiscrimination protection and marriage and adoption rights. These developments offer an opportunity to understand how marginalized groups found their voices and successfully mobilized for their rights in contemporary India. This book engages with the politics of the marginalized by comparatively examining three different (but overlapping) rights-based struggles undertaken by gay activists, transgender groups, and sex workers. How are previously marginalized groups able to appeal to the Indian state for legal recognition, and what political opportunities are available for these groups to make these appeals? How do these political opportunities shape the way groups assert their rights and demand social recognition? How does the Indian state respond to these demands?

To understand how previously marginalized groups have come to occupy an important place in the contemporary political landscape, I begin the journey of this book in the late 1980s, when HIV/AIDS brought sexual minorities to the state's attention for the first time.

While the state's initial response toward the epidemic was denial and blame, national and international pressure forced it to implement policies focusing on prevention rather than suppression. AIDS policies incorporated minority groups—sex workers, MSM (men who have sex with men), and transgender groups—into state and transnational biopower projects for the first time. While the state initially targeted the behavior of these "high-risk" groups, it later sought community partnerships *with* them. These were vital in helping the state respond to the epidemic more effectively.

Before HIV/AIDS became an issue, sexual minorities were not treated as populations or political communities with the moral standing to approach the state with demands to improve their lives. Sexual minorities have not been even peripherally part of any developmental programs of the Indian state.[2] However, they *were* subject to the state's juridical surveillance. In fact, the state was a pervasive presence in their lives as they constantly negotiated stigmatization and the illegality of their identities with the police and other state actors. These interactions with the state often took the form of bribing officials, complying with coercive sexual demands to avoid arrests, and shifting areas of operation to avoid extended police surveillance.[3] Thus, it is remarkable that the visibility of these groups as capable of negotiating life and livability with the state is happening precisely at the moment when their bodies are under intense surveillance.

The HIV/AIDS epidemic marks a shift in the relationship between the state and sexual minorities in contemporary India. The shift from juridical power to biopower allows previously marginalized groups to function for the first time as subjects (rather than objects) of state and transnational projects. Juridical power is often seen as synonymous with legal power and law, but Foucault describes it as an arrangement and representation of power *apart* from the law.[4] Juridical power is a negating, repressive, and prohibitive force associated with refusal, limitation, obstruction, and censorship. Such power "is what says no."[5] In contrast, biopower is decentralized, diffused, capillary, and omnipresent. Individuals are subjected to complex, multiple, shifting relations of power in their social field and at the same time are enabled to take up the position of a subject in and through those relations. For Foucault, "biopower is a condition for the possibility of individual subjectivity."[6]

HIV/AIDS biopolitics not only marks a new relationship between the Indian state and marginalized groups but also enables the proliferation of subjectivities produced through this complex and shifting relation of power. The new political subjectivities formed through these projects give marginalized groups the power to speak back to the state as well as fight back against repressive state power. The visibility of sexual minorities in India's public sphere since the 1990s has resulted in challenges to the criminalization of sodomy and prostitution, as such laws are seen as impeding HIV/AIDS work. Since the question of criminalization also impacts a broad spectrum of sexual minorities (including lesbians and queer women), these struggles against criminalization also become broadly based, moving beyond HIV and health concerns. These contemporary sexual rights politics provide an opportunity to think about biopolitics, the state, and citizenship in a new light, as well as helping us to understand the connection between the state and marginalized groups in the era of globalization.[7]

While scholars have focused on the politics of sexually marginalized groups in India as well as their legal mobilization in opposition to the colonial-era anti-sodomy law, this book adopts a comparative approach that examines how sex workers, gay individuals, and transgender/hijra activists are reshaping biopolitics, state power, and citizenship in contemporary India.[8] Much of the scholarly attention to HIV/AIDS prevention in India focuses on health outcomes, often overlooking the power dynamics that make these outcomes politically interesting.[9] Scholarly critiques that do focus on such dynamics tend to frame HIV/AIDS projects as a form of state surveillance and regulation that benefits only the state.[10]

The incorporation of sexually marginalized groups into state programs requires an analysis of state power that goes beyond a negative or instrumental understanding of the relationship between state and marginalized communities. Instead of looking at HIV/AIDS politics and rights as separate, I approach them as a continuum that helps us to understand the shifting power relationship between the state and marginalized groups, changed subjectivities, political opportunities, and social movement strategies.[11]

The transformations in subject formation that are forged by HIV/AIDS projects are not unique to marginalized sexual groups in India.[12]

HIV/AIDS activism and public health interventions have significantly impacted sexual subjectivities and the identities of sexual minorities in other parts of the world as well. For example, in *Sex Work in Southeast Asia* Lisa Law examines the emergence of a sex worker subject through AIDS education activities in Asia. Law argues that the global discourse on HIV/AIDS and the introduction of peer education in Southeast Asia have significantly shifted official attitudes regarding prostitution, offering a foundation on which a new sex worker subjectivity has been built.[13] Accounts from activists focused on including sex workers in HIV/AIDS prevention programs that target the everyday negotiations among sex workers, clients, and social agencies corroborate this.[14] Indeed, there is a broad sense that there is a connection between the AIDS epidemic and sex workers' renewed subjectivities in the Global South. But not just sex worker subjectivities have changed. The fact that HIV/AIDS-associated work has significantly impacted the subjectivities of people living with AIDS as well as gender and sexual dissidents in different parts of the world is also highlighted by other scholars. Vinh-Kim Nguyen's work on West Africa shows how for the disenfranchised West African AIDS population, sometimes the only way to survive is by having a fatal illness. The "therapeutic" forms of sovereignty and citizenship in the context of AIDS can ensure life itself as well as varying degrees of opportunity beyond health. Similarly, Audrey Yue's scholarship on gay Asian Australians shows how governance of the HIV/AIDS pandemic in Australia has validated and affirmed gay Asian sex by giving it a public profile. The Indian case illuminates similar processes as it illustrates how AIDS becomes a context where previously disenfranchised and marginalized groups begin to negotiate their livability. Furthermore, it adds to this conversation by showing how social movements representing marginalized communities enlarge their sphere of cultural and political engagement and transformation by engaging with the state.

This generative politics of HIV/AIDS compels a close examination of the connection between citizens' rights and the biopolitical agendas of the state. The book's main argument is that in order to be effective, biopolitical projects need the participation of the governed. Thus the governed can also make demands of the state. By focusing on how regulation and resistance work in relation to one another, this book also shows how political identities and social movements can be propelled by the state's interest in governing sex. Hence the need to pay attention to complex and strategic decisions sexual minority activists make in their interactions with the state.

Researching Sexual Minority Politics in India

In order to understand how previously marginalized groups have been able to appeal to the Indian state for their rights, I undertook twenty months of qualitative research in India over a period of eight years, 2007 to 2015. I conducted interviews with members of national and transnational HIV/AIDS organizations as well as LGBTKQHI (K is for *kothi* and H is for *hijra*) and sex worker organizations, in addition to participating in national-level meetings and advocacy around legal changes.

While New Delhi was my research home base, I also traveled to Mumbai, Bengaluru, Kolkata, Chennai, Hyderabad, and Rajahmundry to meet with groups from outside the national capital in order to include voices that may not make it into the national debates. In these cities, I conducted eighty-five in-depth interviews with activist groups, national nongovernmental organizations (NGOs), community-based organizations (CBOs), lawyers, transnational NGOs working on HIV/AIDS and human rights, and representatives of the National AIDS Control Organization (NACO; the national body that designs and executes policies around HIV/AIDS).

I also draw on ethnographic observations from transgender and kothi support group meetings in New Delhi, sex worker national meetings, legal and policy consultations, parliamentary debates, pride marches, and community meetings. I also analyzed legal documents (including petitions, minutes of court proceedings, and judgments), materials generated by activist groups (pamphlets, statements, and reports), policy documents (the HIV/AIDS policies of NACO, policy briefs on transgender issues), and legislative debates.

The project began as a comparative study of the state's regulation of sex work and homosexuality. I was particularly focused on struggles to reform anti-sodomy and prostitution laws. When I first began this project in 2007, HIV/AIDS was not part of my analysis. But during my first research visit (2007–2008), I realized how salient HIV/AIDS-related arguments were for demanding legal rights and recognition. My immersion in the field also helped me to go beyond thinking of the state simply as antagonistic toward sexual minorities. By paying attention to the Indian state's investment in these communities, I have complicated my view of this relationship. This reality in the field has helped me to rethink my conception of the state as well as the indelible link between HIV/AIDS politics and rights-based struggles.

While my conception of the state and the connection between health politics and rights-based struggles changed, my focus was still on two groups—LGBQK and sex worker groups. My interaction with hijra and transgender-identified peer educators during my time at the Naz Foundation in New Delhi helped to expand my research to the third group; they educated me on the impact of Section 377 on their everyday lives. With the incorporation of transgender groups as a separate "high-risk" category in NACO's programmatic agenda in 2007, it became very evident to me that shifts in state power and legal and political recognition are also salient for transgender/hijra groups. Moreover, the 2014 SC judgment on transgender rights makes the comparison more compelling as it shows how the state went from strict criminalization to limited recognition and the legalization of marginalized sex/gender identity groups.

Researching sexual minorities also means paying attention to the construction of identity categories as well as the circulation of these categories within the health and human rights arena. I broadly use the term "sexual minorities" to include both LGBTKQHI individuals and sex workers as well as to indicate the social and legal marginality they face. Usually "sexual minorities" designates marginalized gender identities and sexual orientations, but I have made the choice to include sex workers as well. Sex workers challenge the normative expectation that sex, which should be available for free in marriage or a committed relationship, ought not to be commodified outside of these relationships. As a result, sex work poses a challenge to the norm of monogamous heterosexuality. With the hierarchical ordering of sex, sex work is placed outside what Gayle Rubin calls the "charmed circle" (accepted and privileged sexual practices) of sexuality, hence attracting stigma and criminalization.[15] Including sex workers in the "sexual minority" category also expands sexual politics beyond identity and/or orientation to questions of labor, including the struggle for recognition of sex work as labor.

This comparative study also helps illustrate that sexual politics in India are not confined to urban, middle-class gay subjects but are also equally propelled by challenges posed by individuals who are at the margins of these struggles.

While there are regional terms in some Indian languages for "sex worker" (such as *yonikaarmi* in Bengali), the terms "sex work" and "sex worker" have wide resonance across various sex worker groups in India. Furthermore, it is not uncommon for women in prostitution to introduce themselves in English as "sex workers" on national and international platforms. Claiming the term "sex worker" is a way of challenging the stigma and taboo associated with the terms "prostitute" and "prostitution" (and associated terms in Indian languages). It is also a means of establishing a positive collective identity rooted in claims about their labor.

Within the epidemiological context, the term "MSM" signals non-identity-based sexual experiences as well as an acknowledgment that not all same-sex inclinations fit under the strict binary of homo/hetero.[16] In the Indian context, MSMs include kothis, *panthis* (masculine partners of kothis), and double-deckers (people who identify as both penetrated and penetrating partners). Often incorporated under the aegis of MSM, kothis are largely described as feminine-identified males. While they express sexual desire toward men, some feel social and familial compulsion to marry women, and while some cross-dress occasionally or often, others don't.[17]

Kothi is not only a sexual/gender identification but also a class designation.[18] Kothis largely belong to the non-English-speaking lower-middle class and feel their marginalization in terms of language, education, and socioeconomic status, as well as sexuality.[19] *Hijras* are biological males who reject their "masculine" identity to identify as women, "not men," "in-between man and woman," or "neither man nor woman." While hijras are often seen as playing a fixed gender role, kothis alternate between the masculine role of the husband demanded in the marriage relationship and the feminine role in the same-sex relationship outside marriage. Kothi, as a category, is often used in an expansive sense to designate nonmasculine homosexual males, including cross-dressers and hijras (especially those who have not undergone ritual castration). There is a symbiotic relationship between kothis and hijras that has been strengthened due to the lack of support systems for kothis in urban spaces and small towns. This has led kothis to depend upon hijra subcultures for support. Despite the symbiotic relationship between these communities, since the mid-2000s and within the HIV/AIDS programmatic agenda there has been a separation of kothi and hijra as distinct categories. Where kothi is seen as a designation based on sexuality, hijra is seen as a gender designation with separate needs and, as a result, separate interventions.[20]

Unlike the terms kothi, hijra, and MSM, which are circulated within the global health arena, LGBTQ is often used to designate human rights and rights-based struggles derived from global human rights campaigns. Despite the fact that categories such as "lesbian," "gay," "bisexual," "transgender," and "queer" are often considered global identities and kothi and hijra are local ones, I consider both as "translocal" categories. As "indigenous" categories such as kothi and hijra become widely circulated by global health projects, the supposedly global terms "lesbian," "gay," "queer," and "transgender" also take on national/local/regional meanings. Thus, when I refer to Section 377 struggles, I prefer to use the umbrella term LGBTKQHI instead of LGBTQI, even though this is how it is commonly referred to in legal documents and public discourse. This is to indicate both the transnational dimension as well as the particularly Indian inflection of these struggles.

Despite the fact that these terms emerge from particular discursive sites, such as public health interventions and human rights activism, these are not fixed designations confined to specific spaces or individuals. In 2007 Raju, who was working at the Naz Foundation India, provided a striking description of the fluidity and permeability of these terms. During an informal conversation at a kothi support group meeting, I asked Raju about the difference between kothi and gay; his response was, "Gay is an English-speaking kothi." Even though Raju's remarks reveal the underlying class dimension of these terms (where gay stands for middle-class English-speaking subjects and kothi stands for working-class subjectivity), he did not privilege "gay" as a reference point for same-sex-desiring men in India. Had he done so he would have responded, "Kothi is a Hindi-speaking gay." Similarly, Jessie, who identifies as gay and often hangs out with Raju and other kothis at the Naz Foundation, told me that while he prefers to call himself gay, the kothis around him insist that he is not gay but rather kothi; he does not mind this. The fluidity between these categories was further evident to me when Rahul (also from the Naz Foundation) shared these remarks with me during a conversation we were having about terms: "When kothis take public transportation they become hijras, and when they talk to the media they become gay. These categories are very fluid." These comments suggest that even though the terms "kothi," "hijra," and "gay" have particular class connotations, they are not fixed categories. This does not mean that movement between these categories is easy, especially given that kothis and hijras report transphobia within LGBTQ spaces, where they often feel unwelcome and excluded. The conversation about terms indicates not only the richness of sexual politics in India but also the limits and possibilities of forging alliances across class-, region-, and caste-based identities.

Biopolitics and Belonging

Sexuality scholars have already emphasized that sexuality is central to the idea of the state.[21] In *Sexual States*, Jyoti Puri argues that sexuality impacts the state as much as the state impacts sexuality "as states seek to define sexual normality, discipline bodies, and control populations."[22] Puri emphasizes that by turning to sexuality we can see that, contrary to popular belief, in the contemporary neoliberal era the state is shrinking. She argues that the state continues to modify, expand, and justify its power by promoting itself as a "check upon sexuality's potential to disrupt social order."[23] Through her specific focus on the struggles against the Indian anti-sodomy law, she shows that state power not only is produced through state discourses and institutions but also is collectively shared and imagined in activist accounts. I build on Puri's insightful analysis of the state as fragmented and internally inconsistent, extending her theoretical framework to also account for how different social movements act as state appendages. Turning attention to state governance in the context of HIV/AIDS means focusing on community organizations and individuals who also take on the role of the state. As the state itself is dispersed throughout its governmental functions, communities become its extensions as they participate in these complex and shifting power relationships. Focusing on the strategic and complex negotiations and decisions that gender and sexual minorities and sex worker rights activists make, I ask how and why the state becomes central to struggles over sexuality. What kinds of state imaginaries are being expanded in these struggles over sexuality? And how might these imaginations propel or prevent social change and demands for social justice?

To understand the complex and shifting power relationships that sexual minorities navigate, I use the analytics of biopolitics and governmentality. Michel Foucault's biopolitics provides a useful framework for understanding the shift in state interest vis-à-vis sexual minorities, the emergence of new political subjectivities, and the proliferation of discourses around sexual rights in contemporary India. I deploy these concepts to connect the interests that state and transnational/national actors have in regulating and disciplining bodies in order to encourage safe sexual practices among "high-risk" groups in the era of AIDS.[24] Biopolitics helps us to understand not only the state's entrenched interest in sex but also how the political subjectivities of marginalized groups coalesce into strategic bids for increased shared power and rights.

Foucault introduced the idea of biopower to analyze a historical shift in modern states' exercise of power.[25] He argues that new modalities of power began to emerge in Europe in the eighteenth century, when the state shifted its emphasis from controlling territory to controlling populations. Once birth rates became important to the functioning of modern states, sex became an object of state interest both as a means to control territory and sovereignty and as an object of regulation in its own right. Foucault presents sex as a site for the elaboration of state power.[26] Through biopower, individual bodily discipline is combined with the regulation of biological processes, such as maternity, mortality, sickness, and health. Biopolitics is the "entry of phenomena peculiar to the life of [the] human species into the order of knowledge and power, into the sphere of political techniques."[27] Biopolitics fosters life and works at the level of population.

Governmentality is Foucault's term for the ensemble of institutions, procedures, calculations, and tactics that allow the modern state to exercise power outside its formal structures.[28] Governing modern societies involves a multitude of actors and entities, including politicians, philanthropists, state bureaucrats, and medical experts. HIV/AIDS biopolitics ties together the priorities of state actors, transnational donors, scientific and expert communities, national NGOs, and "targeted" communities. Communities not just are targets of rule but are "increasingly entangled within the webs of governance as instruments."[29] State power is dispersed as non-state actors take on the role of governance by participating in the sexual governance of themselves and their communities. These projects also impact formal state structures, as state agencies share powers with non-state actors. The state does not disappear but rather uses its power to appear as a structure that stands apart from, and above, society. Focusing on governmentality also calls into question the very distinction insisted on by the term "nongovernmental organization," emphasizing instead the similarities of governance across domains.

Governmentality is often tied to the more recent rise of transnational projects with economic power and social authority. Intergovernmental compacts, transnational NGOs, multinational humanitarian organizations, and grassroots groups extend governance both above and below the level of the state.[30] They suggest that manifestations of "the local" that are shaped through transnational networks claim a wider spatial and moral purview than that of the merely national state. The transnational governmentality approach as taken by Ferguson and Gupta argues that its central effect "is not so much to make states weak (or strong), as to reconfigure states' abilities to spatialize their authority and stake their claims to superior generality and universality."[31] The framework of transnational governmentality thus considers how state policies are structured by (but not reduced to) globalization formations. I use these insights to ask how new ways of regulating the sexual conduct of sexually marginalized communities through transnational governmentality projects reconfigures the Indian state's role in regulating nonnormative sex and gender. Feminist accounts of the state often view this shift from state to transnational governmentality as a shift in the state's role as welfare provider to the state's relinquishing of these roles and their attendant burdens to communities and individuals.[32] While it is true that communities are increasingly asked to be responsible for their own "empowerment" as the state relinquishes its responsibility for the health and welfare of its citizens, the impact of these transnational governmentality projects cannot be assessed without understanding how communities and individuals participate in and engage with them. Taking my cue from anthropologist Aradhana Sharma's work on transnational governmentality and women's empowerment in India, I emphasize that biopolitical projects can also shape the politics of the governed in a new and unexpected way.

Feminist and postcolonial critiques of Foucault have significantly challenged and extended Foucault's work to consider specific gendered subjectivities and non-Western and postcolonial contexts.[33] Scholars use biopolitics to analyze the modern state's role in managing life and death together.[34] They argue that marginalized populations, in particular, face a biopolitics of death. In the context of the HIV/AIDS epidemic, Butler, Biehl, and Comaroff argue that modern states not only do not foster life but also do away with life, either through silently withdrawing resources or by explicitly endorsing death for groups who are not seen as worth protecting. They show how "states of exception" are created, whereby states withdraw key resources from stigmatized groups in the name of promoting and preserving life for the rest of society. Butler emphasizes how the meaning of "sex," which Foucault constructs as an activity in the service of life, becomes associated with death in the context of HIV/AIDS so that medical and juridical discourses can separate "innocent victims" from those who "deserve it" and, as a result, are left to die. In this way, Butler argues that under the pretext of administrating life, modern states target some of their own populations for death (through withdrawing key resources) and produce a dialectical relationship between "letting die" and "letting live."[35]

necropolitical

Partha Chatterjee's work on India has also emphasized that "governmentality always operates on a heterogeneous social field, on multiple population groups, and with multiple strategies."[36] In postcolonial India, most residents are only tenuously and contextually considered rights-bearing citizens, Chatterjee argues, and hence are only marginally drawn into the disciplinary projects of the state. These subjects are not completely ungoverned, but Chatterjee claims that their relationship with the state falls outside the formal practices of law characteristic of civil society. Instead, urban squatters, landless people, refugees, and others have been negotiating with the state from a position of political dependence, citing the government's obligation to look after the poor and needy, making a moral appeal as communities that are striving to build a decent social life. These negotiations by marginalized groups through informal and extralegal means, as Chatterjee indicates, make them po-

litical communities in contrast to mere populations, which are enumer-
ated for the bureaucratic functions of the state. Chatterjee's framework
offers a way to think about the democratic struggles of marginalized and
deprived groups that are usually not visible in the realm of civil society.

Sexual minorities have not been considered as populations or political communities who have the moral authority to approach the state to
improve their lives. Their sexuality and gender place them outside both
this moral realm and state projects that are intended to promote life. On
one hand, because of their status as criminal subjects, sexual minorities
are placed outside the formal governance structures of civil society and
thus also outside of projects that promote life. Tellingly, these groups
have not been even peripherally part of any welfare programs of the Indian state.[37] On the other hand, because of their criminal status they are
also subject to the state's juridical surveillance. It is thus remarkable that
the visibility of sexual minorities as groups that are capable of negotiating life and livability with the state is happening precisely at the moment
when their bodies are under intense surveillance. By using biopower
as a way to think about the politics of both life and death, I emphasize
the construction of an embodied subjectivity that responds to the state's
processes of inclusion and exclusion. The initial response of the Indian
state toward the AIDS epidemic was to endorse the death of subjects
who were deemed to be the cause of the epidemic by withholding key resources from them and allowing them to die. Yet the management of the
epidemic also demanded that the state claim the responsibility of nor-
malizing and fostering life. Sexual minorities, who were earlier deemed
worthy of juridical exclusion from citizenship and life-promoting attention, were brought into the state's projects of managing (worthy) life.

Whereas sexual minority groups in India were not part of the state's
generative politics of life before HIV/AIDS, it is because of the concern
about the health of the nation that these populations were brought into
explicit governance of the state for the first time since the mid-1980s.
The HIV/AIDS epidemic has mobilized sex workers and MSM and
transgender/hijra groups at various stages of the national AIDS policy
as "high-risk" groups. They are incorporated into these programs not
only as subjects whose sexual behavior needs to be changed but also as
partners whose active participation is seen as important for the success
of these programs. Because of the need to manage sexual behavior down

to the minutest detail, "high-risk" groups are responsible for managing not only their own behavior but also that of their peers and communities. The result is that the relationship between the state and sexually marginalized groups has changed from damning them as unimportant to accepting them as critical agents of change. These biopower projects enable shifts in the regulatory power of the state, vis-à-vis sexually marginalized groups, from strictly juridical power to biopower, where marginalized groups also share power with the state.

In addition to biopower projects becoming a basis for fostering life, they can also form the basis for claiming citizenship. Nikolas Rose introduces the concept of "biological citizenship" to explain identity-based movements where subjectivity is shaped around illnesses and disease, such as breast cancer, nuclear radiation, psychiatric illness, and HIV/AIDS.[38] Thus claims of citizenship have expanded to biology, and aspects of life once placed on the side of fate have become subjects of deliberation and decision. In this new space of hope and fear established around genetic and somatic individuality, new subjectivities and new politics emerge. Biological citizenship claims, made in the context of environmental disasters like Chernobyl or epidemics such as HIV/AIDS, serve as exemplars of such new subjectivities and citizenship claims based in biology.[39]

HIV/AIDS activism may be the first social movement in the United States that accomplished the mass conversion of disease "victims" into activist-experts, thus creating the conditions for the production of new subjectivities and identities out of the traumatic experiences of illness and stigmatization.[40] However, the networks forged between gay activist groups and medical experts in the context of HIV/AIDS in the United States differ in important ways from the AIDS prevention programs in India. An important difference is that rather than arising from years of political organizing, as in the gay community in the United States, Indian AIDS prevention programs were started with transnational funding and participants were recruited as "high-risk" groups without prior organizing as a self-conscious community.[41]

Among non-Western states, both Brazil and South Africa offer examples of effective mobilization for AIDS-related biological citizenship. Treatment action campaigns (TACs) in both countries forged alliances with governmental, nongovernmental, and marginalized groups and individuals to reach "people living with HIV/AIDS" and make life-enhancing drugs available for millions of people.[42] The TACs not only campaigned for inclusive policies and effective coverage of HIV-positive populations but also were concerned with creating "empowered citizens" as well as using international funding to advance their goals. As people with AIDS learned scientific terms and navigated treatment regimes, they constituted themselves as biomedical citizens and forced their own inclusion in treatment programs. The processes of claiming citizenship that these studies portray are focused on the biotechnological innovations and pharmaceutical activism that give former noncitizens—female sex workers, *travestis*, and intravenous drug users—an opportunity to claim a new identity as citizens worthy of life.[43] And for these stigmatized groups HIV/AIDS programs often represent the only official doorway to "claim citizenship and social rights, especially the right to healthcare, through a curious intermingling of a politics of recognition, subjectification and optimization."[44] My work builds on these studies to offer an account of citizenship in the context of HIV/AIDS in India as well as how previous noncitizens strategically deploy the rationalities of illness and health to demand rights and citizenship.

In India, law- and rights-based struggles have been central to the politics of sexual minorities. Furthermore, sexual minorities are fighting for basic civil and political rights (such as the right to life, equal treatment before law, protection against arbitrary state violence), as well as social and economic rights (to welfare, employment, education, and work). These rights-based struggles are grounded not only in identity politics but also in class struggles where sex is also articulated as labor and work.

Following political philosopher Ben Golder's interpretation of Foucault's later work, I understand rights as instruments in the sense that they are particular tools used in the service of political projects. For Foucault rights are instrument effects in a double sense: "Whilst rights function as tools, nevertheless the very contours of those rights are themselves the effect of pre-existent and re-produced power relations (capital, discipline, patriarchy, racial and sexual oppression) which themselves effect the subject of rights."[45] And rights claims, whether they are aimed at extending rights to previously excluded groups or intended to create new "relational rights" between subjects, are frequently deployed to contest and broaden the boundaries of community.

There is a general skepticism around rights among critical feminist and queer scholars, as the rights discourse is often seen as an endorsement of state power even as these projects seek to challenge the state.[46] In this understanding, formal rights regimes simultaneously mask and enable the state's disciplinary power. Furthermore, rights regimes do not stand apart from social relations of power but are fundamentally implicated in them, facilitating, transmitting, and naturalizing relations of domination even as—indeed especially as—they claim to emancipate. In this perspective, the political mobilization of the rights discourse appears to not only be ineffective but, more crucially, reinforce state power, which they claim to limit, contest, or displace.

While this skepticism about rights-based projects is important, it often comes at the cost of completely rejecting rights. I move beyond thinking of rights regimes as just another way through which the state manages to take hold of communities and fold them back into its power. I also think of rights regimes as tactics and strategies that are deployed by marginalized groups in order to broaden their own political agenda.[47] In this sense, rights are a means to further political goals—not an end in themselves. It is telling that the law is an important site in India for political debates on the inclusion and belonging of sexual minorities in the country and "has come to define the interface between state and sexuality."[48] Hence, I focus on which political visions these rights discourses enable and/or obstruct.

"Unapprehended Criminals": The Law's Treatment of Sexual Minorities

Law occupies a significant place in the regulation and ordering of sex and sexuality. Law does not work separately from society, as it reflects dominant social norms.[49] This is especially true in the case of sex and sexuality, where dominant norms are imposed as "natural" and "normal," whereas deviation from the norm is seen as "unnatural" and in need of being regulated through law. In India, laws that criminalize "unnatural sex" and prostitution, along with public indecency and public nuisance laws, play a major role in ordering and regulating nonnormative sex and gender.[50] These laws establish nonnormative sex acts not only as deviant and but also as criminal. Moreover, the criminal laws to which sexual minorities are subjected create a class of permanently targeted people who are subjected to state surveillance and policing. As Amar Wahab points out, the legal frameworks that institutionalize nonnormative sexualities as a crime and declare them as offenses against the nation-sate "also organizes these registrations into a 'matrix of power; that generates the state's capacity to coerce on behalf of the 'moral' collective."[51] In India, the legal regulation of sodomy and prostitution give the state the power to coerce nonnormative subjects on behalf of the "moral" collective.

The British colonial state introduced the anti-sodomy law in India in 1860 under Section 377 of the Indian Penal Code (IPC). The law defines "unnatural" sexual acts (carnal intercourse "against the order of nature" with any man, woman, or animal) as punishable with life imprisonment.[52] By designating punishments for consensual, nonprocreative sexual acts, the law established such acts as abnormal and deviant. The anti-sodomy law is neutral in its wording, as it targets both homosexual and heterosexual acts that are deemed against the "order of nature." In India, the number of recorded cases prosecuted under Section 377, especially those of consensual sexual acts, is miniscule. Rather, in the long history of its presence, the law has often been used to bridge the lacunae in rape laws.[53] Because until 2012 Indian law defined rape strictly as penovaginal penetration, Section 377 was often used as a supplement.[54] As Jyoti Puri points out, even though Section 377 was intended to regulate "unnatural" sexual acts, in practice it is mostly used to prosecute heterosexual rapes.[55]

Despite the fact that prosecution under Section 377, especially for consensual same-sex acts, is miniscule, it has become a point of contention since the mid-1990s. By the mid-2000s it had become a flash point for sexual minorities to rally and struggle against. The initial accusation was that Section 377 impedes HIV/AIDS prevention by driving same-sex sex underground, making it difficult for the state and NGOs to identify "high-risk" groups for HIV/AIDS prevention efforts. However, over the course of eighteen years, marked by a number of legal battles, this position on Section 377 transformed into a struggle that brought a broad range of sexual minorities (including lesbians and queer women) to a common platform, providing a space for these groups to contest the state. In order to do so, activist groups focused on the persecution of sexual minorities under Section 377 and highlighted the extralegal ways in which criminal laws function. In India, police actions against sexual minorities, including physical violence, blackmail, extortion, rape, threatened arrest, and illegal detention, frequently occurred "under the cover of legitimacy provided by the criminal law framework."[56] This is even more so for multiply marginalized groups, including kothis and hijras, whose gender and sexual nonconformity, combined with the public nature of their acts, make them vulnerable to police abuse and violence.[57] The social movement against Section 377 brought an awareness that unless adult same-sex acts were decriminalized, it would not be possible to demand other civil and political rights, including antidiscrimination laws, marriage, and adoption rights.

Nonnormative sex acts are regulated not only through anti-sodomy law; prostitution laws also play an important role. The legislative and legal framework for the regulation of prostitution in India is contained in the Immoral Traffic Prevention Act (ITPA) of 1986. The Indian statutory approach claims to balance the views that sex work is immoral, that the sex trade is exploitative, and that sex workers need to be rescued and rehabilitated. ITPA does not prohibit prostitution per se but rather criminalizes third parties benefiting from prostitution (such as procuring women for brothels), punishes adults over eighteen for living off the income of a prostitute, and punishes any person who solicits or seduces for the purpose of prostitution or engages in prostitution in public places. It also allows police to conduct raids on brothels without a warrant on the mere suspicion that an offense under ITPA is being committed on the premises. The act also established correctional institutions in which women offenders are to be detained and reformed as well as special police officers to enforce the law. Existing research on ITPA indicates that police rarely use it against brothel keepers, traffickers, and customers and that sex workers are punished disproportionately.[58] Even when ITPA is not enforced, the criminal status of sex work fundamentally skews the bargaining potential of sex workers, who cannot enforce contracts with brothel keepers, landlords, or customers. It has been reported by human rights groups that police proceed against the sex workers merely on suspicion and without any evidence of solicitation. This produces an underclass of permanently targeted people who at any time are liable to be assaulted in public merely because of their presence, taken away to the police station and wrongfully confined, subjected to humiliating treatment, and robbed of their earnings. Sometimes false cases are lodged against them, which serves the double purpose of "solving" an existing case and keeping the accused off the street.[59] As Prabha Kotiswaran argues, the "law embodies a mix of the policies of suppression of promiscuous sexual activity on one hand and the toleration of prostitution on the other."[60] Hence, despite the limited use of the ITPA, its ambiguity, coupled with the constant threat of its invocation, renders it extremely powerful.[61]

Even though much of this debate around ITPA centers on cisgender women sex workers and was generated in the context of the mobilization of this population, since ITPA is a gender-neutral legislation it applies to male and transgender sex workers as well. With the amendment of ITPA in 1986, transgender sex workers became criminal subjects, giving the police the legal basis for their arrest and intimidation. As a result, the decriminalization of adult consensual sex work concerns sexual minorities broadly. However, ITPA has not received as much attention as Section 377, which became central to the struggles of sexual minorities in India.

    While there are no separate laws that criminalize gender variance, the criminal legal frames of Section 377, ITPA, and public nuisance and indecency laws are often used to police hijra and transgender groups. The gender identity, sexual preference, and occupation (sex work and seeking alms) of transgender people and especially hijras place them under everyday surveillance by police. Moreover, the history of the criminalization of gender variance from colonial times is residually present in the imagination of the public as well as the criminal justice system.[62] In 1871, the British colonial state introduced the Criminal Tribes Act, under which hijras were regulated. The act mandated registration of hijras and their property and imposed a penalty on registered hijras appearing in female clothes or dancing in public or for hire. It gave power to magistrates to remove male children under sixteen who were living with registered hijras and to prosecute them. The act's property registration component aimed to interfere with hijra inheritance and succession patterns and prohibited them from making wills or offering gifts. Moreover, this legal history etched into the public imagination the dominant colonial view of hijras as sodomites, kidnappers, and castrators.

However, these laws and legal frameworks began to be contested in the 1990s when HIV/AIDS became an issue and as peer educators and NGOs reported that these statutes interfered with biopower projects, making it impossible for them to reach out to impacted communities. Moreover, they also reported widespread violence against peer educators and NGOs implementing their programs. The violence against HIV/AIDS workers indicated the beginning of tension between the juridical (exclusion through violence) and biopolitical modes of state regulation. The state itself became more obviously fragmented, as its different agencies and actors aligned with separate interests. Because of the need to involve sexually marginalized groups in the state's health management projects, agencies like the Health Ministry and NACO have been supportive of the decriminalization of adult same-sex sex and sex work. However, other state agencies, such as the Ministry of Home, have focused more on criminal law, attempting to hold onto juridical power that denies rights to marginalized groups. These differences among state agencies also produce conflict and disjuncture within the state, revealing that, in the light of HIV/AIDS, sexual governance can simultaneously transform (both internally and externally) and destabilize the state. Furthermore, marginalized groups have strategically used this disjuncture within the state to challenge state legitimacy and/or leveraged these differences to serve their political goals.

Sexuality Struggles in Contemporary Social Context

While sexuality had been central to the social reform movement in India during British colonial rule and the autonomous feminist movement in India during the 1970s, since the 1990s questions around nonnormative sex and gender have figured prominently for the first time in the postcolonial public sphere.[63] However, the contemporary politics of sexual minorities has to be situated within transnational human rights frameworks as well as increasing Hindu right-wing politics that violently and virulently suppress any sexual expression perceived as a threat to the "nation."

Within the transnational civil society, there is more tolerance toward gender- and sexual-identity-based rights at the same time that there is increasing intolerance toward sex workers' rights. The story about transnational involvement is not just one of opportunity alone but is also about constraints. In the "global" fight against trafficking, transnational advocates propose underlying approaches to sex work and trafficking in local contexts as a strategy to combat human rights abuses. They also propose stringent laws to curb the demand for sex work. This position defines sex work as violence against women and conflates "voluntary" sex work with "involuntary" trafficking. Critical feminist scholarship in this area notes that the increased "moral panic" around trafficking and sex work is rooted in anxieties about migration and the cross-border movement of people.[64] Also at issue is the fact that sex workers' rights movements "have been undercut by a bevy of new federal, state, and international laws that equate all prostitution with the crime of 'human trafficking' and which imposes harsh criminal penalties against traffickers and prostitute's customers."[65] The result is the promotion of carceral agendas that focus on criminal justice responses rather than social justice interventions.

This has led to an increase in the number of raids and attempted "rescues" of sex workers as well as the withdrawal of funding for HIV/AIDS organizations that support the recognition of sex work as a legitimate form of labor. There is also a "global industry" of rescue and raid premised on the idea that sex workers need to be saved from the "illegal trade." Organizations such as VAMP (Veshya Anyay Mukti Parishad) in Western India have been fighting against rescues and raids and the invasive policing of prostitutes, arguing that these agendas are grounded not in human rights frameworks but in practices that revictimize sex workers. They have also noted that police who conduct rescue-and-raid operations often terrorize women through the wholesale rounding up of sex workers regardless of age, taking away their livelihoods, as well as through rape.[66] Within these carceral feminist articulations, sexuality figures mostly as a danger to women, needing protection from sexual predators. Furthermore, sex workers' issues are looked at only from the perspective of violence against women, thereby undermining the labor-rights arguments put forward by sex worker groups in India and elsewhere. This tendency to collapse sex work and trafficking is also reflected in the transnational communities' "concern" over India's standing in the Trafficking in Persons Report and in the pressure put on the Indian state to reform its trafficking laws.[67]

In contrast, the transnational human rights approaches to sexual and gender minorities are somewhat uniform. Transnational civil society actors are well aware that social and criminal sanctions against homosexuality suppress HIV/AIDS education and prevention programs designed for MSM and other persons of diverse sexual orientations and gender identities.[68] Gay men mobilized strongly in the wake of AIDS deaths in the 1980s to fight stigma and discrimination and seek civil and political rights. Furthermore, the links between HIV/AIDS and gay men's sexual rights are established in the process of fighting stigma and discrimination. The emerging understanding is that anti-sodomy laws infringe on LGBTQ civil rights and that repealing these laws is a first step toward achieving other citizenship rights (economic, political, and cultural) for sexual minorities.

In addition, a growing transnational jurisprudence establishes rights for diverse sexual orientations. The landmark ruling by the United Nations Human Rights Committee in *Toonen v. Australia* in 1994 was one of the earliest developments in this area.[69] There is also growing transnational legal precedence for the repeal of anti-sodomy laws in countries around the world, including but not limited to the United Kingdom, the United States, Canada, South Africa, Nepal, and Brazil. Furthermore, human rights principles around diverse sexual orientations are also disseminated through various UN treaties and bodies including UNESCO, the UN High Commission for Refugees, and UNAIDS. And most recently, the 2007 enactment of the Yogyakarta Principles has brought sexual orientation and gender identity into the transnational human rights arena.[70] LGBTKQHI groups in India have used this international legal precedent to argue against the Indian state's continuing support of anti-sodomy laws.

The increasing visibility of sexual minorities in contemporary India has to be situated in the context of growing right-wing political discourses seeking to impose majoritarian values over the constitutionally guaranteed rights of equality and liberty. Since the 1990s, there has also been an increase in right-wing assertions that focus on suppressing any sexual desire that is expressed outside heterosexual monogamy. The release of the film *Fire* (dir. Deepa Mehta, 1996) brought issues of same-sex desire—especially women's—into contestation with Hindu right-wing politics. It became controversial when Hindu right-wing groups attacked the film as an affront to Indian culture and tradition.

Despite the fact that the film was approved by the Central Board of Film Certification, widespread violence broke out in different parts of India, with cinema halls vandalized. As a result, the film was returned to the censor board for reexamination. This right-wing intolerance is further manifested in attacks on freedom of speech, as when these groups attacked the book *One Part Woman* by the South Indian writer Perumal Murugan, decrying it as an affront on Indian culture.[71] Murugan's book depicts a practice in South India where consensual sex with strangers is permitted and not considered taboo during the chariot festival of the god Ardhanareeshwara. Historically, this practice has been used by childless couples as recourse in a social context where childlessness invites social stigma and exclusion from the community, especially for women. In depicting this practice, Murugan's book came under attack from Hindu right-wing forces that claimed that it defamed women and attacked religious sentiments.

The right-wing anti-sex position also takes the form of "public vigilantism," including attacks on women who are seen donning Western clothing or attending pubs. These self-appointed protectors of Indian culture have also been known to attack unmarried heterosexual couple in parks and public spaces. And there have been instances in which Muslim men have been attacked for having romantic relationships with Hindu women; these cross-religious romances are labeled a part of a larger conspiracy called "love jihad," wherein Muslim men are accused of converting Hindu women to Islam by luring them in the name of love. Through their violent acts, right-wing forces try to establish that sexuality can be expressed only within endogamous, monogamous marriages. Additionally, religious groups have also challenged the decriminalization of adult consensual homosexuality and continue to articulate homosexuality as foreign to Indian culture and traditions. Yet the conservative response to sexual minorities is not uniform and should not be considered a priori. While there is visible and open contestation from Hindu right-wing groups to the decriminalization of consensual adult same-sex sex, there is no such open resistance to the recognition of transgender rights.

Thus, contemporary Indian sex and gender rights and politics have to be situated within the simultaneous opening and closing of sexuality debates. Where HIV/AIDS and transnational human rights discourses advocate for a liberalization of sexual politics, right-wing groups advance anti-sex and anti-sexuality sentiments. In doing so, they violently and virulently try to establish India as an inherently heteropatriarchal, monogamous space that is rooted in caste and religious order. These opportunities and constraints also shape how sexual minorities experience rights and citizenship in contemporary India.

Journey of the Book

Since the book is about the connection between the state, social movements, and citizenship, it moves between these registers as it unfolds how marginalized groups have been able to claim space in the Indian state and challenge stigma and discrimination. Chapters 1 and 2 delve into how HIV/AIDS biopower projects incorporate "high-risk" groups as managers of their own sexual behavior as well as how they have brought attention to contradictory mandates of the Indian state vis-à-vis sexually marginalized groups. Chapters 3 and 4 focus on how biopower projects have provided an opportunity for these groups to seek legal recognition as well as to resist state violence. Finally, the conclusion discusses the social justice and rights visions these projects advance.

Chapter 1, "'HIV Is Our Friend,'" provides an overview of HIV/AIDS policies as well as how sexually marginalized groups are drawn into biopower programs as "high-risk" groups. In 1983, when HIV/AIDS was first detected among sex workers in India, the state's initial response was to blame the sex workers themselves as well as to forcefully test them and confine them in prison. However, it proved impossible to incarcerate every sex worker and to stop the spread of the epidemic. Instead, I argue, ultimately a consensus formed that supported giving marginalized groups a leadership role in tackling the epidemic. Drawing on ethnographic observations and HIV/AIDS policy of NACO, this chapter also highlights how these biopower projects deepened the involvement of high-risk groups as they moved from simple prevention to behavioral change. Ultimately, communities became extensions of biopower projects as they implemented these programs at the day-to-day level.

Chapter 2, "Challenging 'Bare Life,'" draws on Giorgio Agamben's concept of "bare life" to show how prior to HIV/AIDS sexual minorities experienced the state only through "raw power," where rampant violence and abuse were the norm and the state freely consigned individuals to death by depriving them of resources. The management of "risk" in light of the HIV/AIDS epidemic brought attention to the violence faced by sexual minorities, especially arbitrary police violence supported by criminal laws. During the earlier phases of the epidemic, peer educators and outreach workers—who were drawn from "high-risk" groups themselves—faced challenges and even violence in reaching out to their peers. Even carrying condoms for outreach purposes was seen as evidence of "criminal" sexual activity. This tension between peer educators and police reveals internal contradictions in the state; peer educators, who are at the cusp of state juridical and biopower, bring this contradiction in the state to the foreground.

Chapter 3, "Empowered Criminals," compares the mobilization of sex workers and MSM and gay groups around two separate legal campaigns: the fight to decriminalize adult consensual same-sex sex (Section 377 activism) and the crusade to stop new amendments to ITPA. Through advocacy and sustained campaigning, sex worker and MSM/kothi groups were able to not only mobilize against these laws but also use their role in HIV/AIDS prevention programs to argue that these laws undermined the state's health mandate. Through protests and lobbying, they gained the crucial support of HIV/AIDS groups as well as the federal Ministry of Health (which is primarily responsible for implementing HIV/AIDS policy). Furthermore, sex workers successfully stalled ITPA amendments in 2007, and LGBTKQHI groups had brief success with the reform of Section 377 in 2009. I argue that despite these successes, sex workers and LGBTQKHI groups still remained "empowered criminals." They were empowered to make claims on the state based on their shared responsibility in preventing HIV/AIDS, and yet they were still classified as criminals because the laws that criminalize sex acts remain intact.

Chapter 4, "Tolerable Identities, Intolerable Sex Acts," comparatively focuses on the rights struggles of gay groups and transgender/hijra groups by analyzing two seemingly contradictory judgments of the Indian SC: the Koushal judgment of 2013, which declared Section 377 constitutional, and the same court's 2014 National Legal Services Agency (NALSA) decision, which granted rights to transgender groups, in order to discuss the impact of these legal decisions on the rights and recognition of LGBTQKHI groups. While the NALSA judgment made nonnormative gender identities legal, the Koushal judgment retained

Section 377 and therefore upheld the idea that sexual acts considered to be against the "order of nature" were criminal. The chapter illustrates that while years of social activism have led to the tolerance of multiple identities (today LGBTQKHI groups regularly organize pride marches and rally their political identities in public), nonnormative sexual acts remained criminal until 2018. The legal dichotomization of acts and identities has very important implications for the struggles of sexually marginalized groups.

Finally, chapter 5, "Interconnected Rights," focuses on the relationship between rights-based struggles and the social transformation goals of sexual minorities. In September 2018, the SC of India reversed the Koushal judgment and declared Section 377 unconstitutional. This marked a huge success for sexual minorities who rallied against the law for almost two decades and saw it as a symbol of state-sponsored homophobia. The two decades of sexual minority politics in India have not only foregrounded sexual orientation and gender identity as important constitutional rights but also strengthened the idea of constitutional morality. Constitutional morality, defined as respecting diversity and protecting the most marginalized sections of society, has helped sexual minorities to fight a growing populist morality that quintessentially defines India as Hindu and heteronormative. These successes also indicate that biopolitical mandates can be strategically used to fight popular morality and norms. In addition, by articulating sexual rights as interconnected with other social justice goals, sexual minorities in India also showcase the importance of intersectional struggles. The conclusion also touches on challenges and opportunities for alliance building across sexual minority groups.

Despite these recent successes, the split state and split nature of rights represented by the complex and shifting interaction between state and marginalized groups offer a rich opportunity for the study of social movements, sexuality rights, the Indian state, and the international health crisis. It is this empirical and theoretical richness that makes the Indian case so fascinating.

1

"HIV Is Our Friend"

> I remember we once used to do an exercise with sex workers in West Bengal, Kolkata, and other parts as well. We would ask them to map who their friends are and who their enemies are. And most sex workers would say, "HIV is our friend." That was quite startling to me, and they would say, "Without HIV you wouldn't be here. You wouldn't even talk to us." So, HIV is the first pretext, first excuse, where sex workers could claim to be part of the development discourse. They have been policed, and cleansed, and rescued and rehabilitated. But they have never even been targeted for say, a welfare program.

The above quote was shared with me by Nandinee Bandyopadhyay—a sex worker rights advocate and public health expert associated with a project in the state of West Bengal—as she reflected on the role that HIV/AIDS played in sex worker mobilization in India. Her quote raises some important questions: How can a disease that causes stigma, death, and discrimination be anyone's friend? How does this friendship benefit sex workers and other groups included in state-run HIV/AIDS programs? What motivates the state to extend such friendship to groups that, until their inclusion in these programs, are excluded and pushed to the margins of society?

The quote shared with me by Ms. Bandyopadhyay gets to the heart of changes in the state's approach to regulation vis-à-vis sexually marginalized groups. This changing nature of state regulation must also indicate a change in the nature of political power. Whereas previously sexually marginalized groups were treated only as stigmatized subjects who needed to be disciplined and even excluded, this new mode of power draws them in as subjects and even partners in sexual governance.

This chapter begins by delving into the stigma and marginalization faced by sexual minorities before HIV/AIDS became an issue where they were mostly subjected to juridical power. While the Indian state's initial response to the HIV/AIDS epidemic was one of denial and suppression, due to national and international pressure the state was forced to implement a national AIDS policy that focused on prevention rather than suppression. Drawing on ethnographic insights from my field work in New Delhi, where I shadowed a peer educator from an HIV/AIDS awareness program, and from policy documents, I illustrate the changing relationship between state and sexually marginalized groups. As transnational governmentality projects aim to optimize life, optimal "high-risk" individuals for these governmentality projects are also those who understand prevention, can negotiate safe sex, and exert active agency in their social environments. At a theoretical level, this chapter makes the argument that HIV/AIDS marks a decisive shift in the Indian state's relationship with previously marginalized groups from strictly exercising juridical power to more nuanced operations of power where their partnership is also sought.

Marginalized and Stigmatized

As the epigraph to this chapter indicates, before the HIV/AIDS epidemic sex workers were visible to the Indian state only as criminals. Sex work in India is not a monolithic sector. Its organization and structure vary depending on the form it takes, such as brothel-based, home-based, street-based, and so forth. Regardless of these differences in the organization of sex work, there is a shared experience of marginality among sex workers that stems not only from criminalization but also from the extreme stigma attached to paid sex. Because of the stigma and criminalization, sex workers often don't find any redress to the violence they face from clients and intermediaries, such as pimps and brothel owners. Moreover, criminalization places sex workers at the mercy of police, who often engage in practices such as extortion and forced sex. In several sex workers' accounts, police are seen as a bigger problem than clients and other intermediaries.[1]

In addition, as sex workers lack a state-issued identity, they often cannot avail themselves of any state services such as subsidized food or housing or, for elderly sex workers, old age pensions. They also lack access to banks and credit institutions, which further pushes them into the hands of loan sharks. It is also reported that this lack of access to banks puts them further at risk of losing substantial portions of their hard-earned income when clients and police rob them. In addition to criminal frameworks, the framework of rescue and rehabilitation leads to the forceful detention of women in "correction" and "rehabilitation" homes. As noted in a recent study of a sex workers' collective in southern and western India, this culture of criminalization and police abuse "sends a message to other groups in society that sex workers can be abused with impunity."[2]

Along with sex workers, MSM groups also face extreme vulnerability and precarity. The HIV/AIDS programs operate under the assumption that in countries like India, focusing only on sexual identities would exclude large numbers of people whose same-sex sexual behavior might put them at risk for HIV/AIDS. While the umbrella of MSM is large, kothis and panthis (masculine partners of kothis) are the largest groups whose sexual risk is addressed by these programs.[3]

Due to the stigma around same-sex sexual activities, kothis are secretive about their sexual preferences. Since kothis often seek sexual partners in public places, such as cruising sites and public bathrooms, they are vulnerable to violence, especially from gangs and the police. There are reports of violence and even murder when kothis refuse to part with their money or to offer sex to thugs and local gangs. Police not only take no notice of this violence but also threaten kothis and other MSM groups. These communities report that police violence (including extortion, forced sexual encounters, physical and verbal abuse) is one of the biggest issues that they face. Kothis also come from lower socioeconomic and educational backgrounds and often lack an awareness of the legal system and the law, which puts them at risk for further police abuse and violence. In my conversations with kothis in the cities of Lucknow and New Delhi, they shared that when they report violence and abuse to the police, they are themselves interrogated about their activities in public places instead of having their complaint investigated. Moreover, kothis are afraid that reporting a crime to the police will mean revealing their addresses and identities, which could be used to out them to their families. Police inaction and abuse send a loud message to the nation: MSM lives are dispensable and worthless. Similar to the situation for sex workers, treating MSM as criminals signals that these groups can be abused with impunity.

The final groups that were violently marginalized before HIV/AIDS prevention programs extended state friendship are transgender people and hijras. Even though hijras are famously referred to as India's third gender and are more visible than other sexual and gender minority groups in India, their visibility does not guarantee them rights. Hijras play an important cultural role, especially in North India, because their in-between status of being neither a man nor a woman is seen as conferring them power to grant fertility to newly married couples. Hijra presence at weddings and births is seen as auspicious, and *tholi badhai* (blessings) is one of the primary sources of income for community members. This occasional inclusion and respect does not guarantee them any protection; instead hijras face widespread verbal and physical abuse. This contradiction was explained to me by Rudrani, a prominent hijra activist in New Delhi:

> One of my friends [a hijra] went to tholi badhai to bless a newborn baby girl. The family where she went to bless has two grown-up sons. During the tholi badhai every member of the family came and touched my friend's feet and treated her as a goddess. But a week later, my friend was out shopping and one of the sons from the same family passed a comment at her and called her a whore. A week ago, when she visited the house she was a goddess; after a week you are seeing her buying lingerie from a store and she becomes a whore for you? Because they have this perception that hijras are supposed to be inside their homes and hijras who are outside in the public after dark are considered doing wrong and illegal activities.

In addition to tholi badhai, hijras often seek alms in public places in addition to their sex work. During my conversations with hijras, even those who have advanced degrees reported discrimination in employment. The discrimination against hijras in education and employment further compels them to take up begging and sex work. Along with sex workers and MSM groups, hijras also report police abuse as a major issue. Since hijras' mere public presence is seen as an act of transgression, verbal and physical abuse is an everyday fact of life. Laws against vagrancy and public indecency further establish their criminality. Hijras are not included in any state welfare programs because their civil identity itself is in question. Until recently, most forms of civil identification (passport, identity cards, and others) recognized only male and female sex categories, thus excluding them from participating in state welfare programs, such as pension and housing policies for the elderly and the poor, public food distribution, and entry into public schools and hospitals. Because of the stigma around hijra communities, there are reports of hijras being denied essential medical services in state-run hospitals. Along with hijras, other transgender groups also report high instances of violence and sexual and physical abuse in India.

Stigma, ridicule, and systematic neglect are what these groups have experienced and continue to experience. And the most stunning fact is that these groups were approached by the state only as unwanted and as communities to be cleansed, rehabilitated, and disciplined. This was the primary stance of the Indian state until HIV/AIDS became an issue in the 1980s. Despite these extreme forms of criminalization and marginalization, sexual minorities have put up with everyday forms of resistance against police and the state and have devised ways to challenge their criminalization. But collective challenges to law did not emerge in the public sphere until the mid-1990s.

Blaming the Victims of HIV

When HIV was first detected in 1986 among sex workers in the city of Chennai, the Indian state claimed that it was a Western disease spread because of Western attitudes toward sexuality. Women engaged in sex work were vilified for importing the disease by having sex with foreigners and were identified as a potential reservoir of infection that threatened the general population.[4] The first law passed in India pertaining to AIDS was very punitive. The 1989 AIDS Prevention Bill provided health authorities with invasive policing powers in the form of forcible testing and the power to isolate members of so-called high-risk groups (particularly sex workers at that time).[5] The bill also required registered medical practitioners to report to the government the identity of any person they knew to be HIV-positive. In Mumbai, Delhi, and Kolkata, incidents of the forceful confinement of sex workers in prisons and forceful testing were reported during this period.[6] The state's approach toward sexually marginalized groups strengthened the stigma attached to already-stigmatized groups since they were perceived as vectors of disease. Moreover, at this stage the Indian state denied the presence of homosexuality and same-sex activities because they were considered Western practices that did not exist in India, thus withholding essential services from these communities.[7]

Due to national and international pressure, the Indian state eventually shifted its AIDS control policies toward prevention and control—rather than suppression—of the epidemic.[8] In 1994 India's first National AIDS Control Program (1994–1999) was launched and NACO was created to implement the program. Although NACO is technically under the Ministry of Health and Family Welfare, it was created as an autonomous body with freedom to design its own policy. NACO also established State AIDS Control Societies (SACS) in most states to carry out the national mandate of the program as well as interface with local and grassroots organizations, overseeing funding and implementation.

India is home to the third largest HIV epidemic in the world.[9] According to NACO estimates, in 2015 the overall HIV prevalence rate was estimated to be 0.26 percent, with an adult prevalence rate estimated at 0.3 percent among men and 0.22 percent among women. While these rates are low when compared to the prevalence rates in countries in sub-Saharan Africa (9 percent), because of India's huge population, they equate to 2.1 million people living with HIV/AIDS. In 2015 an estimated 67,600 people died of AIDS-related causes nationally. In general, the Indian epidemic is seen as showing a declining trend at the national level, with a 32 percent decline in new infections and a 54 percent decline in AIDS-related deaths in 2015.[10]

It is estimated that in India the epidemic is primarily transmitted through heterosexual sex (87 percent of the prevalence). This is different from the United States, where it is seen as a homosexual disease, as well as sub-Saharan African, where it is seen as a generalized disease (not confined to a few groups, although sex workers are more at risk). In epidemiological terms, this difference marks India as a country with a concentrated epidemic in a few "high-risk" populations. NACO's interventions operate on the premise that in a low-prevalence country such as India the epidemic can be contained efficiently by focusing prevention efforts on core high-risk groups (MSM, transgender people, female sex workers, injecting drug users [IDUs]) and bridge populations.[11]

During the initial phases, female sex workers and IDUs were targeted as high risk.

A significant amount of HIV/AIDS funding in India comes from international donor agencies such as the World Bank, USAIDS, the Department for International Development, the Global Fund, the Bill & Melinda Gates Foundation, and the United Nations Development Programme (UNDP), all of which donate money to NACO to implement HIV/AIDS programs and design the national policy on AIDS. NACO statistics indicate that while the Indian government's budget for preventing HIV/AIDS until 2016 was 28.61 billion rupees, the amount received from foreign donors was significantly more, 41.48 billion rupees.[12] Governing sex in the context of AIDS involves an ensemble of actors, including but not limited to national and transnational national NGOs, CBOs, public health experts, state agencies, and individual members belonging to high-risk groups. Not only do these agencies provide funding, but they are also involved in policy design and provide technical guidance and support to NACO. Hence the technologies of sexual governance are carried out not only by the state alone but through an ensemble of institutions, procedures, calculations, and tactics that allow the state to exercise power outside its formal structures, which Foucault terms as "governmentality."[13]

The Switch to Awareness

NACO's programs are implemented in five-year periods, and each phase reflects not only the changing direction of the program but also the shifts in the technologies of governance. While NACO has not indicated the rationale for why its programs are organized in phases, it is not hard to infer that these phases correspond to the five-year plans of the federal government.[14] Since 2005, these policies have been designed with extensive consultations with transnational donors, national and international donors, civil society organizations, and community members.

The first national policy, the National AIDS Control Program (NACP) I (1994–1999), focused on generating awareness, disseminating information, setting up a surveillance system, and providing preventive services for high-risk groups.[15] During these initial phases, awareness and education became the main goals of these programs, which meant that high-risk groups were merely seen as needing information and services, and the state took responsibility for providing these services.

While sex workers (along with bridge populations, including migrant men and truck drivers) were initially targeted as a high-risk group, this did not translate into respect for them. On the contrary, during the initial phases the state approached sex workers as unenthusiastic subjects of these programs who needed to be educated about the importance of prevention. This initial approach was apparent to me when I spoke with Meena Seshu, the general secretary of SANGRAM (Sampada Gramin Mahila Sanstha), an organization that works to claim rights for sex workers and people living with HIV/AIDS in Maharashtra and Karnataka, in the western and southern India. In a 2007 interview about the role of HIV in sex worker mobilization Seshu stated,

> It was in 1992—the story starts there. The main issue was that people who had no experience working with sex workers were asked to work with them. If at all we had any experience, it was mostly negative experience. And the message we were receiving from the government is that sex workers cannot be made change agents and that it is very tough to work with them. We were even told that if we want people to use condoms we should be working with clients not sex workers. And we [people actually implementing these programs at the grassroots] didn't agree with the government's approach that sex workers are vectors of HIV/AIDS. I couldn't work in a situation where the sex workers had no say on condoms and negotiation around condom use.

Seshu's comments reveal the way in which state agencies completely denigrated sex workers and even tried to absolve themselves of any responsibility of educating themselves about the issues of sex workers. Seshu continued to share some of the earlier challenges SANGRAM faced in getting these programs to respect sex workers while also providing quality services. One such obstacle was the fact that neither the state nor the implementers of these programs had any clue about how sex workers negotiated with their clients:

> As outsiders who were approaching sex workers we often faced resistance! The brothel owners told us that we had no clue about how sexual

transactions take place. That is true—we knew nothing. They [sex workers and brothel owners] were the one with knowledge, we had the condoms. They taught us everything about sex work, they taught us about how the system works. The government has this document about how to negotiate with clients and how to make men use condoms. Later on, when I looked at the manual, I was stunned about how it did not include the knowledge of sex workers at all, and these women have generations of experiences with men.

Seshu worked to challenge the top-down approach of the state and get sympathetic organizers to realize that without sex workers' voices and active involvement in these programs, they would not be successful.

Representatives of DMSC (Durbar Mahila Samanwaya Committee), a sex workers' collective in one of the largest red-light districts (Sonagachi, in the city of Kolkata, West Bengal), shared similar insights. What started as a 1992 research study on Kolkata's red-light districts funded by the World Health Organization (WHO) later developed into a major HIV prevention project with sex workers. Dr. Smarajit Jana, a public health expert who headed the study and was later instrumental in forming DMSC, reflected on how this initial experience evolved to shape the overall approach of many sex worker projects:

The first problem we had to face in the beginning was that people in and around the red-light areas looked at us suspiciously. They didn't like anyone who is an outsider to be walking in and around the red-light district, and they did not want to talk with us. So, we felt that until and unless we established some sort of rapport in the sex workers' community, we will not be able to carry on this research. It took around three months to just gather the most basic information on the red-light district.

This lack of knowledge about the organization of the sex trade and the lives of women in this sector posed problems for public health experts, similar to the experiences shared by Seshu. Because the population is highly stigmatized and criminalized, access to sites and individuals is limited. As a result, leaders of this intervention project and others realized that without involving the communities, these health programs would not be successful. According to Dr. Jana,

To run an intervention program there is a need to know much about the community and their perspective, issues within the sex trade, and its relationship with the mainstream society. See, when WHO gave us funding, they had this view that HIV/AIDS interventions should have three basic elements. You give education, you give condoms, and you provide STI services. Those are important things, technically speaking, but whether a person is able to access or utilize the services is dependent on many factors. How [do] they prioritize issues? To what extent are they able to enforce decisions? To what extent will we be able to communicate with the community?

For Dr. Jana, a prerequisite to the effective implementation of the projects in communities that were closed to and suspicious of outsiders was mutual accommodation, which he also called friendship:

We started recognizing that [sex workers'] priority issue is neither HIV [nor] health; their priority issues that came up through interaction with them were police violence and violence they face from local hooligans. We felt that we had to address those so that they can feel that we are their true friends. Frankly speaking, it was clear that HIV is our agenda, not their agenda, so it was very clear, how to make our agenda theirs. And it cannot be done until and unless we accept their agenda.

In this process, public health programs that targeted sex workers as a high-risk group were challenged to address issues of marginalization, violence, stigma, and criminalization. The Sonagachi project not only included sex workers in the programs as peer educators but also saw collective mobilization as a way to increase the sex workers' bargaining power with clients and brothel owners. Originating in these interventions, "respect, recognition, and rights" became both a way to approach stigmatized and criminalized groups and a popular demand the groups raised in turn. A booklet published by DMSC spells out the connection in a way that is more politicized than Dr. Jana's explanation: "Because the practice of safer sex, we felt, cannot be dealt with in isolation, we adopted the strategy of understanding the power structure, and combining empowerment with the enhancement of negotiating skills of the sex workers, for the sex workers, and by the sex workers."[16]

The Sonagachi project's social experiment of including sex workers as peer educators, partners, and even owners of this program was recognized by donors and the Indian state as a best practice to be emulated by HIV/AIDS intervention programs elsewhere in the country and globally. As early as 1999, sex workers were implementing, running, and overseeing HIV/AIDS programs. A 2000 UNAIDS report described the project's effects as follows: "Gradually, what started as a narrowly-conceived HIV prevention project has become a social movement in West Bengal of no mean importance and is drawing sex workers and women's rights organizations from all over India and beyond. The essential difference between the process that has taken place in Sonagachi and elsewhere in the developing world is that the sex workers themselves, including their families and friends, haven't taken the lead to carry out the work of the intervention."[17] By the early 2000s the idea that high-risk groups should take an active role was consolidated into NACP II, and sex worker initiatives became key to this understanding, which is not limited to only a few organizations like DMSC but has become part of NACO's approach and is often cited as a best practice for scaling up and reaching out to the communities:

> On many occasions, community-based organizations (CBOs) are found to be most effective in scaling up HIV prevention programs. The Sonagachi project started in 1992 and was subsequently handed over to the FSW [female sex workers] CBO Durbar Mahila Samanwaya Samiti (DMSC) in 1999. Soon after that, this organization was able to expand to fifteen red-light Districts in the State of West Bengal in a span of two years, increasing the coverage of the FSW population in the state to a level of 75%–80%.[18]

Once these programs realized that without the active participation of sex workers success couldn't be ensured, they included high-risk groups as active participants and implementers of these programs. NACP II (1999–2006) incorporated these lessons from the success of DMSC and focused on behavior change and including high-risk groups as active agents in the program.

Another important goal during this period was scaling up targeted interventions with high-risk groups in high prevalence states. In fact,

NACO considers the targeted intervention (TI) program to be one of the most important prevention strategies. TI projects provide a package of prevention, support, and linkage services to high-risk groups through a model that emphasizes outreach and service delivery, which includes screening for and treatment of sexually transmitted infections (STIs), free condom and lubricant distribution among high-risk groups, and integrating counseling and testing centers for HIV. However, the core of TI programs is peer educators who are essential links between the community and the programs.

Peer-to-Peer HIV Interventions: Everyday Management of Risk

During my conversation with DMSC representatives, I was told that the idea of peer-to-peer intervention was pioneered by their organization. Peer-to-peer interventions have become key to HIV/AIDS programs, and peer educators connect the communities and intervention programs through decentralized distributions of power. During my research trips to New Delhi, I observed several intervention groups, including Savera, which works on HIV/AIDS interventions with sex workers and MSM in the areas of South and Southwest Delhi and was running an intervention program with the help of sex workers. It was through Savera that I was able to shadow a peer educator.

Savera's outreach office is adjacent to one of the biggest truck depots in Southwest Delhi. Hundreds of trucks wait there to be loaded and unloaded. The trucks give the neighborhood a transient feel, and the diesel emissions add more dullness and gray to the landscape. The office itself is in an unremarkable single-story building, comprising one big room with educational posters on HIV/AIDS, condoms, and other health messages; it looks like any other NGO space. While my conversations with Savera representatives took place here, this was actually where the outreach team met and where sex workers came to report and receive condoms and other materials for distribution. I learned from the program coordinator that the area's sex workers are predominantly home-based and that the program's goal was to reach six hundred sex workers in the neighboring slums.[19] With the major truck stop next door, truck drivers and maintenance workers are among the clients of local sex workers. Even though a tall wall separates the Savera office from the truck stop, while sitting in the office I could hear the starting and stopping of the engines and the chatter of the drivers and supervisors as they guided the trucks through loading and unloading.

During one of my visits to the outreach office on a summer afternoon in June 2009, I asked Shyamala (name changed), a peer educator, if I could accompany her on her regular outreach work. Shyamala was busy finishing her paperwork and asked me to wait. I knew that the slum where Savera has its operations must be close, but from the office there is no visible sign of a slum. When Shyamala was done with her paperwork, she took her outreach bag and asked me to follow her. She was slender yet very strong looking; I guessed from her looks that she might be in her mid-thirties. We started walking north of the Savera office, and within twenty feet we reached a five-foot wall. Shyamala walked through a breach in the wall, and I followed her. As soon as we got to the other side, I was surprised to find a large slum. While I was amazed at how close and yet how hidden this slum was from the outside, I saw Shyamala confidently walking through a small alleyway. I walked fast to catch up with her, and in less than five minutes we were close to a cluster of houses where Shyamala wanted to make a stop. As we walked closer, we saw two elderly women resting on a *charpoy* (bedstead made with woven ropes) under a shady tree, and there were a few children playing around the tree as well. Upon seeing Shyamala, the women called out to the children and asked them to gather their mothers and neighbors.

Within a few minutes of our arrival there were around fifteen women gathered around us. They were of different ages, but the majority seemed to be in their twenties and thirties. Shyamala gave friendly nods to some of the women there, and as she was reaching into her outreach bag, she called out to the children, ordering them to leave. However, the elderly women did not move, nor did Shyamala seem to mind them being there. Moreover, Shyamala did not address sex work specifically but pitched a general message about health. Given the nature of the space—that is, the difficulty of segregating women from their home environments and the lack of privacy, making it impossible to talk to women alone—women generally did not openly admit that they performed sex work. Shyamala told me that it was therefore important to camouflage her message as a general note about health and STIs so as not to appear to be targeting one specific group of women in the slum. What fascinated me was the way she navigated both the space of the slum, where women's sexuality is not discussed explicitly, and the space of her NGO, where medicalized notions of sexuality circulate as health discourse and notions of "risk" pitch sexuality in terms of "danger" and "disease."

Shyamala made a short speech about Savera's work and why she was there. She then took a condom out of her bag and asked the women who had gathered around if they knew how to test whether a condom was good or expired. Her question elicited some giggles; in a chiding voice, Shyamala told them to be serious and not to laugh. Her question elicited a satisfactory answer from one of the younger women, who showed the audience how to test a condom. As the young woman was finishing, Shyamala reached into her bag again and took out a wooden dildo—an educational tool often used by peer educators—and demonstrated for the group how to put on a condom. As she was demonstrating, she noticed a group of young men gathered around twenty feet from where we were. Shyamala seemed a bit uncomfortable with the close proximity of the young men, yet they didn't deter her from her task at hand.

She finished her demonstration and reached into her bag a third time, this time removing an STI manual in Hindi. She passed it on to the woman next to her, without any introduction or discussion. I could see that the atmosphere suddenly transformed from playful to serious, and it seemed that Shyamala was herself uncomfortable. I could see disgust but not much shock as the women quickly paged through the manual and passed it around. It did not take much time for the manual to come back to Shyamala, at which point she reached into her bag a final time and took out a handful of condoms, telling the women they could take them if they needed them. The public way in which the condoms were offered made me wonder if anyone would feel comfortable drawing attention to themselves by reaching for them. The crowd started thinning and the women started leaving without taking condoms; eventually only five women were left, and a slender figure reached out and took few condoms from the pile. Shyamala later told me that this was not the only way condoms were distributed by her organization. Condoms are available to women through easy access points in the slum, and they can also visit the office to receive them. As she was explaining to me how condoms were distributed in the slum, we stopped at a small hut and called for a woman in the house.

When she came out, Shyamala made friendly inquiries and left several handfuls of condoms with her. As we were walking back to the office, Shyamala stopped briefly at a public tap where a small group of women were waiting to fill their water containers. Her chat with the woman was mostly about vaccinations for infants and the health of pregnant women. I was amazed by the ease and comfort with which she answered questions concerning pregnancy and maternal health. Shyamala later told me that prior to her association with Savera she had experience working as a midwife and had earned her credibility among women residents.

Shyamala's other responsibilities include talking to individual sex workers about their condom use and recording the number of encounters with clients per week as well as their visits to the clinic operated by her NGO for STI testing. In the early days of the program, Shyamala said they were distributing condoms for free but were not checking whether or not they were actually being used. However, now they make a point to ask and record information about how many condoms each individual woman used and how many sexual encounters they had that week. When I asked Shyamala if the women wanted to use condoms, she said, "Previously it was difficult to convince them about the usefulness of condoms, but they take them now as they take *rasgullas* (sweets)."

In this particular slum, outreach workers such as Shyamala are able to identify fellow sex workers in ways outsiders may not be able to and bridge the knowledge gap between the HIV/AIDS prevention programs and their target population. Outreach workers maintain detailed weekly diaries, keeping track of the sexual behavior—down to the smallest details possible—of individual sex workers. Their records allow them to generate monthly reports linking condom use, STI testing, and the prevalence of HIV infection, which in turn become important data in developing evidence-based knowledge for state and transnational projects.

Constructing this relation of friendship between sex workers and state biopower projects better facilitates sexual health, brings new technologies and regimes of power to previously marginalized groups, transforms stigma into risk, and defines risk management as a shared value of the state and sex workers. Therefore, these strategies and tactics not only disperse state power but also make individuals like Shyamala responsible for regulating and monitoring sexual risk and behavior.

Intensifying Behavior Change and Surveillance: Partners of State

As mentioned earlier, HIV/AIDS programs are designed by NACO in consultation with other national and transnational donors and NGOs. These groups often collaborate with the state, and even when they work separately they develop technologies of governance (identification, dissemination, surveillance, and others) that are shared among various agencies. These technologies are tested and disseminated and best practices are promoted and emulated among various agencies. In this sense, even if these programs have different goals there is a common agenda of improving the tactics and technologies of biopower.

An important shift for the Indian HIV/AIDS programs came when the Bill & Melinda Gates Foundation decided to fund a major initiative in India called the Avahan India AIDS Initiative. Avahan was launched in 2003 and became one of the largest initiatives outside NACO in India. Avahan was implemented in the six Indian states that were reported to account for 82 percent of HIV/AIDS infections in 2002, and around $258 million were provided for the initiative.[20] While the architects of the Avahan program believed that the NACP II's approach to high-risk groups was sound, they felt that the coverage was low and uneven. Avahan's main goal was to slow HIV/AIDS transmission by "raising prevention coverage of high-risk and bridge groups to scale by achieving saturation levels (over 80 percent) across large geographic areas."[21] To scale up HIV/AIDS intervention, the Avahan program relied on peer-to-peer interventions as well as incorporated community mobilization as their goal.

The two most at-risk populations addressed in the five years of the Avahan program (2003–2008) were sex workers and MSM, with a goal of reaching 217,000 sex workers and 80,000 MSM.[22] The Avahan program worked with state governments as well as local NGOs to implement the project. It was reported that within five years 67 percent of sex workers contacted had used STI treatment services at least once, and 75 percent of MSM had received the comprehensive package of services focused on drop-in centers, condom distribution, and peer educators. More importantly, Avahan promoted community engagement as important for the success of these programs. According to their 2008 report,

In Avahan's experience, involving high-risk communities in the program helped align program services with their needs and drove the rapid uptake of services. Initially Avahan engaged with the community in discrete activities such as community mapping but then began developing processes and systems to involve them more directly in the services. Working with the communities also helped the program understand and address their underlying vulnerabilities, paving the way for them to adopt safe sex behaviors. Increasing program ownership by communities bodes well for the development of an active, aware, and articulate set of customers for HIV prevention services, which is a key consideration for the long term.[23]

Furthermore, the program also emphasized data monitoring and evidence-based research that relied on the everyday work of peer educators. Detailed accounts of individual sexual behavior, number of encounters with sexual partners, areas of operation, and condom use were recorded by peer educators. The information collected was used to evaluate and monitor these programs as well as transmit best practices across various organizations. Avahan further strengthened the idea that it is not enough to provide services to communities; there must be a focus on changing the behaviors of high-risk groups, which can be done only by involving communities as partners in these programs.

Because the Avahan program was originally funded for only five years, its design from the beginning took into account the need for an eventual transition to the Indian government. Avahan's key discoveries were incorporated into the third national policy, NACP III (2007–2012).[24] In particular, Avahan's emphasis on scaling up interventions among high-risk groups, community mobilization, and behavior change were incorporated into NACP III.

NACP III is considered one of the most important AIDS programs in India because it showed significant commitment from the government of India toward AIDS prevention. The main focus of NACP III was increasing the coverage and reach of its programs to at least 80 percent of high-risk groups as well as integrating these programs with care and service. The Indian government also increased its HIV/AIDS budget by 400 percent between the second and third phases of its national programs, from $500 million to $2.5 billion, and 70 percent of the budget in this period was allotted for prevention programs.[25] Another substantial shift in the program was its emphasis on community mobilization and community ownership. According to NACO, "When the community defines HIV Prevention as part of its own agenda, uptake of services and commodities is higher than when services are imposed on them."[26]

Through NACP III, NACO also included MSM and transgender/hijra groups among the core groups for whom intensified HIV prevention and care programs were implemented. Before then, the initiatives that addressed the needs of MSM were supported by community organizations such as the NAZ Foundation International, Naz Foundation India, and Humsafar Trust and by international donors such as Avahan, Oxfam, and International HIV/AIDS Alliance. But since NACP III, most of this funding has come directly through NACO, which implements its programs with the help of local NGOs and CBOs. This move to widen the coverage among MSM in the national policy indicates that the Indian state is finally serious about providing services to these groups, hence acknowledging its responsibility toward previously stigmatized groups.

It is estimated that 2.35 million MSM live in the country, and service provision to them was dismal before 2007. According to a 2011 UNDP report, HIV prevalence among MSM populations was 7.14 percent, versus the overall adult HIV prevalence of 0.36 percent. In NACP III, concerted efforts were made that resulted in a reach of 274,000 MSM through 155 exclusive intervention programs called targeted intervention. This represented a sevenfold increase from NACP II and is expected to increase through MSM CBOs and efforts toward community strengthening.

Until 2007, hijras/transgender people (especially transwomen) were included under the category of MSM in HIV/AIDS programs. Since 2001 there has been an increased emphasis on including transgender people and hijras in HIV/AIDS prevention programs; the state of Tamil Nadu in southern India pioneered this effort. There, separate HIV/AIDS programs were created for transgender people and hijras as early as 2001. It took another six years for this to be translated into national policy. This focus on the trans community is necessary since recent studies among hijras/transgender women have indicated a very high HIV prevalence (17.5 percent to 41 percent), whereas HIV/AIDS prevalence among female sex workers is only 2.67 percent.[27] The fourth and current phase of NACO promises to intensify and consolidate prevention services for high-risk groups and to scale up coverage.

Peer educators form the core of NACO programs, illustrating the importance given to educators from high-risk groups. They are valued not only for their acceptability and credibility in the peer community but also as the state's best means for generating accurate information, usable data, and programmatic evidence. This role is contingent not on their existing level of health awareness but on the access they have to local communities; reaching out to these communities is understood as the most difficult and risky aspect of HIV/AIDS work. Because the inclusion of "true peers" is the gold standard of effectiveness, it is in the pragmatic interest of the state to include high-risk groups in these programs.

These epidemiologically driven transnational health developments emphasize both community monitoring and the generation of bodies of knowledge about patterns of sexual behavior, behavior change, condom use, STIs, and HIV status. High-risk groups are identifying other members in the community, mapping patterns of sexual behavior, working out strategies to reach out to other peers, creating strategies for the regular monitoring of condom use, and ensuring regular checkups at STI clinics. This work requires the in-depth and detailed management of bodies, which can happen only with the willing involvement of high-risk groups themselves. Because of the state's biopower concerns, which were reflected in the state's engagement in these complex projects of surveillance and changing behavior, high-risk groups became more integral to the state's own success and thus became subjects of and extensions of biopower programs. Therefore, these strategies and tactics not only disperse state power but also make individuals responsible for regulating and monitoring sexual risk and behavior.

It is thus remarkable that the recognition of previously marginalized groups as capable of negotiating life and well-being with the state is happening precisely at the moment when their bodies are under intense surveillance. High-risk groups are needed to generate knowledge of the community and thus become the "domain and object of knowledge." Their involvement in this program is important not only for building knowledge but also for transmitting behavioral change and self-regulation. In this sense these biopower projects are successful when the communities and individuals regulate their own sexual behavior without external pressure as well as take ownership of these programs. Since HIV/AIDS projects require the micromanagement of bodies and their sexual behavior, they are deemed successful only when there is effective participation among the community. As a result, language describing these groups has shifted from criminal registers to economic ones, discussing them as consumers of services: "Community-led initiatives allow members of the community to enable high-risk groups to play the role of a pressure group as consumers to maintain and reinforce the quality of services, leading to sustained demand for high-quality services."[28] The terms "community," "pressure group," and "consumers" are notable in this excerpt because they indicate how epidemiologically driven health programs articulate these new forms of governance. The introduced mechanisms of discipline and regulation are not directly repressive, but they facilitate new modes of accountability and enumeration through technologies of data collection and legitimate risk reduction. Drawing high-risk groups into these programs as pressure groups and consumers enables these programs to bridge the moral distinction between the state and its agents. And the everyday role of peer educators like Shyamala is very important for mobilizing the community. The promoters of these HIV projects thus mobilize the high-risk groups as agents of these programs by reimagining them as communities with the right not only to be served but also to be heard. The goals of NACP III in scaling up prevention among high-risk groups and community ownership were further incorporated into the design of NACP IV (2012–2017), indicating that these are still important goals for furthering the state's biopower concerns.

Strengthening Community Ownership

NACO's emphasis on community ownership of HIV/AIDS programs since NACP III is further strengthened through the Pehchan (translated as "identity") project of the Global Fund. The project itself is a result of prominent members of the MSM and LGBT community coming together as a core group to strengthen community ownership of the HIV/AIDS program. The group organized around the idea that MSM and transgender communities must be equal partners in the national HIV response. This group has worked collectively to increase funding and expand programming for MSM and transgender communities. The core group, together with other key leaders working with sexual minorities in India, became the driving force behind the successful Pehchan proposal, which has become the Global Fund's largest single-country grant to date focused on HIV response for vulnerable sexual minorities.

Pehchan was initiated in 2010 as a five-year program to strengthen CBOs that undertake TI programs funded by NACO.[29] The Pehchan project overlaps with both NACP III and NACP IV. Pehchan is implemented through a consortium of organizations that work closely with NACO's TI programs.[30] In particular, the Pehchan project is currently implementing a program in seventeen Indian states that strengthens the abilities of two hundred CBOs to provide effective, inclusive, and sustainable HIV/AIDS prevention. The program also aims to increase access to legal services and health through community-based and peer-led social support systems. One of the key goals of Pehchan is to provide organizational development as well as technical and capacity-building support to new and existing CBOs that work with MSM and transgender communities, and hence Pehchan is described as a community systems-strengthening program. The program claims to use a rights-based approach to develop CBOs who serve as implementing partners with NACO. Through its goal of building strong CBOs, Pehchan addresses issues that often prevent communities from receiving government funding. During my interview in 2015 with Abhina Aher, a program officer from Pehchan, she explained the goal of the program to me:

> The Pehchan program was envisaged to support NACO's objective to halt and reverse the epidemic. The objective of the program is to get in sync with the government program. However, the approach of the program has been a little bit different. Now, why am I saying that the approach is little bit different? It is because the government, when they talk about HIV/AIDS interventions, they are mostly focused on service delivery and health referrals. However, Pehchan does something different. We focus on strengthening the community, and a lot of energy and time are spent in creating civil society organizations and CBOs with MSM, transgender groups, and hijras. Because its ultimate byproduct is visibility, it gives them empowerment, but the most important thing is that it puts the key communities in the *driver's seat rather than just beneficiaries.* So that is one of the major pillars of the program.

Despite the fact that NACO's programmatic agenda since NACP III has focused on community management and ownership of the programs as a path to empowerment, the language of empowerment is often subsumed under that of TIs. One of the critiques of TI is that it is numbers-driven and puts unnecessary pressure on communities to reach programmatic goals of the maximum number of high-risk groups. This emphasis on numbers, as many HIV/AIDS advocates argue, often contradicts NACO's agendas of community ownership and empowerment. Programs such as Pehchan intend to rectify this by shifting the focus from the targeted approach to community ownership. Moreover, the intended goal of community ownership of these programs cannot be achieved unless significant attention goes into training members of the community so that they can have real ownership of the programs. Members of MSM and transgender communities may not have experience running an organization or even finding proper channels for registering an organization because their lack of a civil identity prevents them from registering an organization in their name. Pehchan's goal is to fill this gap by providing training and strengthening community initiatives. Putting communities in the driver's seat also means increasing their bargaining power with the state; ironically this is happening at a time when their sexuality is under state surveillance.

Conclusion

The Indian state's relationship with sexually marginalized groups has shifted from merely seeing them as transmitters of infections to making them partners and even extensions of these programs. Whereas during the initial phases of the HIV/AIDS epidemic the state focused on suppressing the epidemic by forcefully confining in prison people who contracted AIDS, it yielded to national and international pressure and subsequently developed policies that focus on prevention of the epidemic. Since NACP III, the focus has been on including high-risk groups as owners of these programs. These policies emphasizing behavior change, surveillance, and condom use include sexual minorities as peer educators (like Shyamala from Savera) as well as draw them into these programs to map and identify previously marginalized communities. These groups who were earlier deemed unimportant by the state are now deemed important for maintaining the health of the nation.

As public health programs have moved from denial to simple condom distribution and information dissemination to behavior change, behavior surveillance, and behavior monitoring, the role of high-risk groups in these programs has also shifted from mere objects of the programs to agents and implementers of them. Since NACP III, the Indian state has officially acknowledged that it needs to work "with communities" and create an environment for empowerment to successfully prevent the spread of HIV as well as to draw these communities into programs as enthusiastic participants. This work with communities not only makes them partners but also extends the state's biopower projects as community partners perform duties of the state such as enumeration, identification, and outreach. State projects thus transform HIV/AIDS programs into active extensions of transnational health projects; these individuals then become agents of governmentality and of the state. Currently, the state sees its goal as forming communities that are asked to internalize this responsibility and carry on the task of prevention and management of the disease. NGOs are not just providing services to high-risk groups but also training them to administrate and monitor health services. NACO's current goal is to directly fund CBOs that are led and run by members of high-risk groups themselves, to successfully manage and implement the state's HIV programs.

Constructing this relation of friendship between "high-risk" groups and state biopower projects better facilitates sexual health, brings new technologies and regimes of disciplinary power to sexuality, transforms stigma into risk, and defines risk management as a shared value of the state and marginalized groups. Therefore, these strategies and tactics not only disperse state power but also make individuals responsible for regulating and monitoring sexual risk and behavior. Drawing marginalized groups into these programs bridges the moral distinction between the state and its agents. Since governmentality projects aim to optimize life, an optimal high-risk individual for these governmentality projects is also one who understands prevention, can negotiate safe sex, and exerts active agency in their social environments. As a result, the promoters of these HIV governmentality projects mobilize high-risk groups as agents of governance by reimagining them as a community with the right not only to be served but also to be heard. In the routine, mundane, and seemingly banal practices of targeting marginalized groups, these biopower projects produce discourses and subjects capable of greater political agency.

While serving as a stark reminder of the past social marginalization and invisibility of sexually marginalized groups, the statement "HIV is our friend" also points to the effects of the state's new focus on previously marginalized groups as a result of the HIV epidemic. New friends who appear in this articulation are NGOs, public health experts, and health activists who otherwise would have been absent from this space. And this need for engagement is by no means unilateral. It was not only marginalized groups who needed friends as they sought visibility, but also NGOs, the state, and public health experts, which soon realized that it would not be possible to work on HIV/AIDS without actively involving the communities that are affected. While some marginalized groups refer to this as friendship, the relationship between the state and marginalized groups is also formalized through the language of partnership. The partnership these biopower projects offered not only made affected communities beneficiaries of state actions but also offered opportunities to reform the ways state authorities related to them. Nonetheless, communities still needed protection from violence, and getting the state to recognize that would be its own struggle.

2

Challenging "Bare Life"

Since the mid-1990s, the Indian state's interest in sexual minorities has shifted as it has taken on the mandate of promoting life in the context of HIV/AIDS. By the later part of the decade, groups dedicated to HIV/AIDS were responding to India's AIDS crisis but found they couldn't perform the required outreach work because of pervasive police violence against impacted communities. The police violence included illegally detaining peer educators, seizing and destroying condoms and educational materials, and subjecting sexual minorities to physical and verbal abuse. And the tension between police and peer educators remains very palpable. When I asked Bobby, a peer educator from the Naz Foundation India (hereafter Naz), about challenges faced by peer educators like him in their HIV/AIDS prevention work, he responded,

> In the public cruising places where there are public toilets and bushes, this is where real trouble happens. Most of the kothis have sex in wild bushes and behind trees. That is the only place where they can have sex. Cops arrest kothis and extort money, or have forceful sex with them. Along with the cops there are local thugs, they engage services of kothis with a promise that they will pay, but they don't pay. So, when these thugs take kothis into bushes, they beat them up, threaten them with knifes and weapons, and snatch the money or possessions from them. The cops also stop kothis on the pretext of arresting them, take them behind bushes, have forceful sex with them, and also snatch their possessions. Cops behave the *same way* as thugs.

Sexually marginalized groups are exposed to juridical power of the state and are subject to extreme forms of state violence, and this was the primary way they encountered the state before the HIV/AIDS epidemic. Human rights groups that documented violence against sexually marginalized groups in India have also referred to the violence they are subjected to as "unthinkable."[1] This is life that is exposed to violence by the state's refusal to treat them as worthy citizens and extend them equal legal protections. It is exposure to the "raw power" of the state, where the exception (of lawlessness and denial of life) becomes the norm, "where life is defied and death like conditions are wished on subjects by the state."[2] This is what Giorgio Agamben refers to as "bare life," life that is unprotected, exposed to violence, and brought close to death, such that death is always threatened and within immediate reach. Furthermore, once condemned to the status of the "to be killed," a life is no longer protected from anyone or anything.

Unlike in the contexts of concentration camps (used by Agamben to formulate his theory) where law was completely suspended and became the basis for the suspension of life, the Indian police are armed with the law to carry on their violence and abuse. Laws such as Section 377 (anti-sodomy law) and ITPA, which criminalize consensual adult same-sex sex and soliciting for paid sex in public, respectively, as well as public nuisance laws are arbitrarily deployed by the police to justify coercion and force. These criminal legal frameworks thus produce an "under-class of permanently targeted people who at any time are liable to be assaulted in public, merely because they happen to be there, taken away to the police station, wrongfully confined and restrained there, subjected to humiliating treatment, their earnings taken away."[3] By creating an underclass or a class of "unapprehended felons," criminal frameworks equip law enforcement agencies with the de facto power to carry on physical and verbal abuse, extortion, and violence with impunity. While these encounters with state violence are not unique to sexually margin-alized groups alone and are on par with the experiences of other mar-ginalized groups in India, the one major difference is that unlike other minority groups, sexually marginalized groups are criminalized.[4]

This criminalization and arbitrary state violence are exposed in the context of HIV/AIDS prevention work. Bobby's comments above re-veal that HIV/AIDS outreach work brings two different modes of state power vis-à-vis sexually marginalized groups into explicit tension with each other: the juridical mode of exclusion through violence and the biopower mode of inclusion through governance, where they are simul-taneously criminalized and asked to be responsible for their sexual prac-tices as partners in these programs. Peer educators like Bobby are placed on the cusp of this competing state power as they undertake HIV/AIDS prevention work. Are such peer educators able to fight arbitrary state violence using the imperative of biopolitics? How do these competing modes of state power shape the political assertions of marginalized groups? These are the questions that animate this chapter.

The chapter begins with an ethnographic insight from my field research in Rajahmundry, South India, where I witnessed firsthand the threat of violence faced by a group of sex workers. I use this vignette to elaborate on how sex workers and LGBQK and transgender/hijra individuals face the raw power of the state, where violence and extreme neglect have been the story. The second section focuses on how the violence and abuses faced by sexual minorities are brought to light in the HIV/AIDS prevention work undertaken by peer educators belonging to these communities. Peer educators from all three groups report rampant violence and abuse at the hands of the police when they undertake outreach activities such as condom distribution and spreading safe sex messages. The experiences of peer educators showcase the contradictions within the state regulatory regimes (juridical vs. biopower) as well as how peer educators are caught in between these contradictions. The final section focuses on collective efforts of sexual minority groups that challenge the everyday violence, stigma, and criminalization they face. Theoretically this chapter argues that biopower projects can potentially transform the formal structures of the state itself, as the Indian state shares power with communities to combat HIV/AIDS, where the state is pushed toward more accountable forms of governance as well as compelled to take a stand against the arbitrary use of force and violence.

Bare Life and Sexual Minorities

In the winter of 2007 I had the opportunity to accompany Vijaya, a member of the Godavari Mahila Samakya (GMS) sex worker collective based in the city of Rajahmundry, on the coast in the southeastern state of Andhra Pradesh, to visit highway sex workers. The highway-based sex workers meet their clients at rest stops or in wooded areas along major motorways. GMS had just begun to work with highway sex workers, motivating them to join in the activities of their collective. The HIV/AIDS program associated with GMS had just managed to find a few motivated peer educators who could bring condoms and messages around safe sex practices to the highway-based sex workers. In order to get a better sense of the needs of sex workers in the area, some members of the collective were visiting the highways to have conversations with their peers about their working conditions. Vijaya, an outgoing and energetic member of GMS, invited me to accompany her that day. She prefaced her invitation by saying that the area we were visiting was closer to the city limits and thus not as precarious as other areas. I was aware from my previous conversations with sex workers that highway-based sex work is the most exploitative and dangerous because working locations are remote and isolated and clients are transient. Because of the remoteness, it is hard for sex workers to find help when confronted with violent clients or abusive cops. In fact, highway sex workers function as a cautionary tale: the worst conditions and the lowest pay. Even sex workers who are adept at navigating dangerous public spaces dread visiting the highways, and some who solicit in those areas try not to be there alone and especially not during the night.

We made arrangements to reach the highway around one o'clock in the afternoon and had a trusted auto rickshaw driver who would take us there. Vijaya had also been in touch with Gouri, a peer educator and point person on that particular highway. The auto rickshaw ride took around forty-five minutes from the GMS office, and during the drive the landscape changed from concrete buildings to lush tree cover. We got dropped off on the shoulder of the highway, and from there it took us just a few minutes to enter the wooded area where sex workers would be hanging out. While the clients are predominantly transient—truck drivers or motorists—the nearby village (a mile away) also brings clientele. Most recently the sex workers have also gained unexpected clients; a newly opened engineering school changed the socioeconomic profile of the clients, bringing younger and "refined" clientele as well. Vijaya told me that while parents think that their sons might be attending college, some of them wander into the woods looking for sex.

As we made our way into the wooded area, we saw three women sitting in the shade of a tree. Vijaya recognized one of them as Gouri, and she introduced us to Laxmi and Satya, the other two there. Gouri was lean and tall and looked like she was in her mid-thirties, whereas Laxmi and Satya might have been in their early twenties. After the introductions, Gouri led us into a nearby area with denser tree coverage for privacy, so that we would not be easily interrupted by foot traffic or clients. Despite the fact that we were only a few meters away from where we first met Gouri, the place she chose was more secluded. Yet it was not cut off from the surroundings, and Gouri and her friends could easily keep an eye on the area. Since it was still early in the afternoon, the client traffic was thin, and as a result Gouri and her friends had some free time to chat with us. However, we also told them that they should not hesitate to take their leave if they had clients.

We found random rocks for seats. Gouri pointed to a plastic bag, hung from a branch, that served as a condom box—provided free to her peers. But protection means more than just condoms. Gouri mentioned that it was dangerous for women to come there alone to conduct their business. As a result, they try to come in groups of at least two or three to ensure their safety. This way they can watch over each other and signal to each other about other threats including cops. Even though sex workers demand that clients pay up front, clients often end up not paying and sometimes even rob them of the cash they have from previous engagements. This cooperation does not mean that there is no competition among them for clients, but camaraderie is critical for their own individual safety, as that is the only way they can ensure some protection for themselves.

It was Gouri, the most senior and most experienced among the three, who was doing most of the talking. Whereas Laxmi had a few years' experience working on the highway, Satya was new to sex work as well as the highway. As we were engrossed in the stories Gouri was telling us, we suddenly heard a male voice yelling and screaming, which disrupted the previously calm and relaxed atmosphere. Even though the voice was coming from a few meters away, we could sense the rage and anger in the voice. Laxmi walked in the direction of the voice to see what was happening. She came back and reported that the angry person had been there since before Gouri had arrived. Because he was very drunk, neither Satya nor Laxmi agreed to offer their services to him. Their refusal outraged him, and he kept hurling profanities at them, saying that they could not refuse to have sex with him because they were whores and whores cannot refuse a man sex. His verbal threats did not change their decision. Realizing that his threats did not work, the man retreated toward the village. But now he had returned and seemed even more drunk. Moreover, he held a machete. We stopped our conversation and remained silent for a few minutes to see if the man would retreat on his own. But the profanities became louder and his rage grew. The situation was tense, and what seemed like a verbal threat started to feel like a real danger, as the man started saying that he would kill the "whores who insulted him." Gouri sensed that the man might be coming toward us, as the yelling was growing louder and closer, and she was afraid that the verbal threats might actually turn into physical violence. Moreover, the man seemed drunk and out of control. Gouri stood up and signaled that she would face him and try to deescalate the situation. Before she left she instructed us—especially Laxmi and Satya—to stay where we were and not follow her.

While I couldn't see Gouri from where I was sitting, I could faintly hear her voice. She told the angry man that there was no one around except her and that the women he was looking for had just left, but her answer didn't seem to satisfy him. He continued to hurl profanities. Gouri started apologizing to him on behalf of her colleagues and told him that they were new to the line of work and hence needed to be taught to respect the clients. But her apologies did not seem to matter much; the man would not stop. I feared for Gouri's safety as she was tackling an irrational and armed man on her own. If he attacked and injured her, there would be no way for us to stop him before harm was done, as we were a few meters away. The yelling and heated conversation went on for a few more minutes, but something suddenly shifted and the man seemed to calm down a bit. I could hear Gouri continuing her apologies. After making sure that the man left and would not come back, Gouri returned to where we were. She mildly chided Laxmi and Satya for not using tact with clients. When asked how she deescalated the situation, she told us that she had no choice but to fall on the man's feet and apologize. Reason would not have worked since he was out of control and armed. Falling on the feet is an act of complete surrender and subordination, and by doing so she was able to temporarily appease the outraged client and take control of the situation.

Once things calmed down a bit I asked Gouri, "Were you not afraid to face him alone?" Gouri said that she was a little nervous but was not afraid as she had faced dangerous situations alone before. She had faced worse, she said, and she started recollecting an incident from a few years prior. The day of the incident she had come to the highway alone. As it was a festival day, she could not find a fellow sex worker to accompany her. But she needed cash, so she decided to work for a few hours and then return before it got dark. Since she was in a hurry to get there, she forgot to remove her gold earrings—her only valuable possession. Noticing that she was alone, local thugs robbed her, but they did not stop there. They stabbed her and almost buried her alive. It was a miracle that someone came there and rescued her, as otherwise she would have been dead. After sharing that incident, she said in a nonchalant tone, "I have faced every possible violence you can imagine and even came close to death. How much more harm can anyone inflict on a person who faced so much suffering? I don't think anything worse can happen to me."

I share this ethnographic encounter not to construct extreme vulnerability or to romanticize the agency of sex workers. It is also not my intention to construct the highway only as a dangerous space for sex workers. In fact, Gouri's tact and courage in the face of risk and danger that day are a great reminder of the resilience of sex workers despite the extreme violence and precarity they face. Rather, I use this anecdote to point out how sex workers are exposed to bare life where they face deathlike conditions and are left to their own devices by the state. Had the situation with the drunken client escalated and become violent, Gouri might have faced serious harm. Reporting to the police is not an option in such a situation, as officers likely would not even arrive on time. Furthermore, even if the sex workers reported the incident to the police, they would not record the incident, as violence is seen as justified by the women's solicitation of "illicit" sex. Even the time when Gouri was rescued from the near-death situation, it was a passerby who found and rescued her. She never registered a complaint against the thugs who caused her grievous harm and since she knew that the police would never consider it an assault. Moreover, the potential for further abuse by police also prevents sex workers from even approaching them with incidents such as this. A pan-India survey conducted with sex workers found that 37 percent have been physically abused by the police; 51 percent stated that they had faced verbal abuse from law enforcement officers, and 22 percent had been forced to pay bribes to the police.[5] Sex worker groups in India and elsewhere have argued that it is criminal laws that breed exploitative work conditions such as these rather than sex work per se being exploitative (an argument often launched at them by anti-prostitution groups).

LGBTQKHI groups also report experiencing state violence both directly and indirectly. During my trip to a cruising site in New Delhi for gay men and MSM, I heard several stories about police abuse and violence, but Krishna's stood out for me. Krishna had migrated to New Delhi from the southern state of Tamil Nadu and identifies as a kothi. During one of his visits to the cruising site, a (cisgender male) cop stopped Krishna and forced him to have sex with him. Krishna said he had no choice since it was the cop who was asking him, and Krishna did not want to face any physical violence or risk detention. So he complied. However, after forcing Krishna to have sex with him, the cop started thrashing him with his *lathi* (stick) and hurling abuses at him. The cop's behavior totally confused Krishna, as he had already complied with the officer's demands. He wasn't sure why the cop resorted to beating as soon as he had finished the sex act. In a perplexing tone, he said, "I don't know why the cop fucked me in the first place and [then] also beat me!" Krishna's account is not unique. In fact, there are many accounts such as these where cops not only rape but also beat and humiliate the "victim" of their crime. The officer's supposedly "irrational" behavior indicates internalized homophobia in his brutalization of Krishna. Sexual minorities may comply with demands from cops for money and sex in order to avoid arrests and/or long and financially arduous legal battles they rarely have the resources to fight. Moreover, the social stigma and vulnerability of sexual minorities (especially kothis) also breed arbitrary police violence.[6] Because of the stigma around nonnormative sex and gender, sexual minorities are often secretive with their families about their sexual preferences and/or gender identity, and an arrest would bring them shame. Thus, police detention could also lead to further hardship, such as family condemnation, violence, and abandonment.

Violence and humiliation by cops is not rare but mundane and pervasive. The People's Union for Civil Liberties Karnataka (PUCL-K), a human rights group based in the southern city of Bengaluru, documented violence against sexual minorities, and police violence and entrapment figured prominently in the accounts of those sexual minorities they interviewed in the city. A vignette from their 2003 report captures the disturbing level of violence that police inflict on these communities. Aishwarya, a hijra sex worker, was waiting at a bus station when the police, having just arrived, started extorting money from kothi and hijra sex workers in the area. When they demanded money from Aishwarya,

> I told them that I only have money to go back home. When I said this, they just snatched away the wig I was wearing and threw me into the police van. They were all laughing at me, they asked me what was there in my blouse, whether they were real breasts or artificial ones, then they started pressing them and feeling them even after I told them that they were not real. They demanded that I should pay the money or else I would be booked under a theft case. I fell at their feet and said that I am poor, I do sex work for food, but their ears were deaf. Finally, I was taken to the police station and kept there for three days.[7]

Touching the breast and snatching away the wig are ways of discrediting gender identity and extreme acts of dehumanization. Aishwarya had to endure not only this level of dehumanization but also further threats and violations by being detained at the police station for three days. Such violence is incessant, widespread, and an ever-present reality in the lives of sexually marginalized groups. This does not mean that cops are always violent toward sexual minorities nor that the interactions always place them in a vulnerable position. During my field work I have also encountered sex workers, MSM/kothis, and hijra/transwomen having romantic ties and relationships with police officers. There are also cops who show benevolence and restraint. But much of this ends up as personal benevolence, and systemic violence continues as the legal and social stigma attached to nonnormative sex and gender continues to give institutional power to the police.

In this climate where cops constantly behave as if sexual minorities are "unapprehended felons," there is little recourse left for them to bring a complaint to the police about violence faced by other cops. As some of my interviewees mentioned, "How do we report about violence of cops to other cops?" Even when sexual minorities approach the police to file complaints against their violators (who are not cops), instead of registering complaints the police humiliate and illegally detain the victims. Orinam, a human rights group, reported that Kokila, a twenty-one-year-old hijra from Bengaluru, was raped by several men in June 2004. When Kokila attempted to seek redress from the police, she was arrested, abused, tortured, and forced to remain naked for several hours in the police station. Instead of taking her violations seriously, the police arrested her under Section 377.

While sex workers, MSM, hijras, and kothis are subject to everyday scrutiny from the police, privileged gay men are not above this scrutiny. In August 2004, Pushkin Chandra, a son of a top-ranking bureaucrat, was found murdered in his plush South Delhi home along with his partner. The police who investigated this case sensationalized the murder as a result of a "reckless gay lifestyle," including picking up unknown men from public places, as the cause of the crime. The attention in this case completely shifted from the crime itself to a "gay lifestyle" that was represented as rife with recklessness and crime.[8]

These accounts of violence reveal that until the HIV/AIDS epidemic, this was predominantly how sexual minorities experienced the state—as "unapprehended felons" and subjects whose rights can be disregarded at any time. Since the mid-1990s, the Indian state has been compelled to have a different relationship with sexual minorities because of the fear of the spread of the HIV/AIDS epidemic. As high-risk groups, they are recruited into HIV/AIDS prevention programs as peer educators as well as outreach workers by NGOs who work alongside the state to effectively tackle HIV/AIDS among these communities. The HIV/AIDS biopower produces a different relationship between sexual minorities and the state, one where they are for the first time considered not just as criminals but also as partners for these biopower projects. They encounter state power in a productive and decentralized manner.

"Epidemic of Abuse"

The juridical and biopower projects of the state come into direct contact and explicit collision with each other, especially during the early stages of the HIV/AIDS epidemic. Peer educators and outreach workers report police violence as a major obstacle to their HIV/AIDS prevention work. In many instances, carrying condoms for outreach work is itself seen as evidence of criminal activity (either sodomy or prostitution) by the cops. There are reports of condoms being seized and destroyed by the cops, and carrying condoms itself is perceived as an intention to have "illicit" and "unlicensed sex." This attitude should also be situated within the overall social context, where there is very little awareness of condoms. Even though since 1952 the Indian state has been undertaking one of the world's largest population control programs and promoting birth control practices, awareness around condoms remains minimal, and condom promotion by the state is rare when compared to other forms of birth control, such as sterilization and intrauterine devices.[9] Moreover, the population control programs targeted women (primarily through sterilization) with an assumption that men will not be willing to use condoms.[10] A survey conducted in the early 1990s showed that only 5 percent of couples who use family planning methods used condoms.[11] Moreover, a lack of privacy also prevents working-class people—especially women—from accessing condoms. The 1991 release of the Kamasutra brand of condoms in India marked the first time that condoms had been marketed to the middle classes. The brand started to promote an idea of pleasure-based use of condoms in contrast to the state's condoms (*nirodh*), whose name itself invoked prevention. Even though the Kamasutra brand had used the opportunity of HIV/AIDS to market its products, it also refrained from talking about AIDS, as it was mostly associated with promiscuity and commercial sex.[12]

It is ironic that while condoms symbolize safety in the HIV/AIDS community, the very icon of safety can further subject peer educators to violence, as having condoms indicates to cops the intention of having illicit sex. Moreover, for the police the distribution of condoms and spreading awareness about safe sex practices are seen as promoting homosexuality and prostitution, and peer educators are often accused of spreading "vice" and "disease." Furthermore, the "moral panic" around homosexuality and prostitution is often used by cops to justify their behavior toward peer educators. Imran from Bharosa Trust, an HIV/AIDS prevention organization working with MSM and kothis in the city of Lucknow, shared with me during an interview in 2007 that in this repressive climate peer educators cannot demonstrate condom use, as carrying materials for doing so would be misconstrued by the police as an act of public indecency. Hence groups like Bharosa rely mostly on leaflets and printed materials for HIV/AIDS awareness, but this limits their message, as there is a large percentage of MSM, kothis, and hijras who are not literate. In addition to seizing condoms and detaining peer educators for carrying them, police also refuse to believe that peer educators can play an educational role in their communities.[13] There are also reports of cops threatening to arrest peer educators if they take on such a role.[14] The fact that HIV/AIDS outreach workers can contribute to the social good is unpalatable to the cops, who often ridicule them and say that they are not worthy enough to contribute any good to society. Since education and educators are held in high regard in India, the police sneering at outreach workers who aspire to be teachers of safe sex is rooted in the idea that these communities are unworthy of such regard. Moreover, education also means knowing one's legal rights, and cops might fear that this would amount to a loss of their power to extort and seek bribes. One way some of the HIV/AIDS organizations try to protect their peer educators is by issuing official identity cards and instructing them to not to go to outreach areas without identification. While this may offer some protection to peer educators, sometimes police completely disregard the identity cards worn by peer educators and treat them as criminals soliciting sex.[15]

The violence against HIV/AIDS outreach workers has been so widespread that Human Rights Watch referred to it as an "epidemic of abuse." In addition to seizing educational materials and condoms, cops also threaten to use criminal laws against peer educators if they carry on HIV/AIDS work. While the threat of the law is often used to justify the abuse of HIV/AIDS workers, police rarely bring up formal charges. Peer educators from Lucknow and New Delhi, whom I interviewed in 2007, also confirmed this behavior and mentioned that they have been detained and mistreated at police stations numerous times. Even though formal charges were not filed against them, these detentions served as a cautionary tale and a threat to both the peer educators and the organizations that are undertaking HIV/AIDS prevention work. While these conflicts seem like the result of tension between police, who have authority, and peer educators, who have little, they also reveal a symbolic struggle between juridical and biopower modes of state engagement with sexually marginalized groups.

However, there are instances where formal criminal charges, including Section 377, *are* used to harass HIV/AIDS workers. The infamous 2001 Lucknow incident for the first time brought the repression faced by NGOs working on HIV/AIDS prevention into the national and international limelight. In July 2001, the staff members of Bharosa Trust and Naz Foundation International (NFI; not to be confused with Naz Foundation India), both groups based in Lucknow, were arrested by the police on the pretext that they were having public sex and spreading homosexuality. The previous day, in a park frequented by MSM and kothis, the police had arrested ten people, including a staff member from Bharosa, on the allegation that they were having public sex. The police then raided the offices of NFI and Bharosa, seized educational materials on safe sex, and arrested three other staff members including NFI's executive director. The four staff members were charged formally under several sections of the IPC, including Section 377, the national security act, and other criminal statutes.[16] Section 377 defines "unnatural" sexual acts as crime regardless of whether consent is involved or not. Even though there was no sexual act that took place, this case reveals the arbitrary ways in which the law is often used. In their official report, the police claimed that the four arrested staff members were picked up from a park while having public sex, but the NFI reported that their staff members were arrested at their office and that safe sex educational materials, including televisions and videocassettes, were confiscated during the police raid.

The arrested individuals were denied bail several times and were detained for forty-seven days. The police presented the seized HIV/AIDS educational materials as evidence of the spread of pornographic literature. The case diary of the arrests describes everyone in the office at the time of the raid as carrying something "objectionable" in their hands. The police were also believed to have represented to the trial court that the accused had been arrested for watching videos showing men indulging in "unnatural sex" with each other and running a gay "sex racket."[17] One newspaper reported, "On investigation by the police it was clear that in its advertisement material the organization claimed to control AIDS, but from all angles stated homosexuality as natural and worked extensively to promote it."[18] These opinions were not limited to the media but also reflected in the attitudes of the judges who heard the bail applications of the NGO staff arrested in Lucknow. A newspaper quoted the judge who denied bail as follows: "They were a group of persons indulging in these activities and are polluting the entire society by encouraging young persons and abetting them to commit the offense of sodomy; *that the offenses are being committed in an organized manner.*"[19] The judges expressed such attitudes despite the fact that the defense attorney acknowledged before the court that there was, in fact, no case against the arrested under Section 377.[20] The incident revealed not only the blatant way in which the police misused Section 377 but also the generally repressive environment that surrounded the conversation around HIV/AIDS and its prevention at the time. Media outlets represented NFI and Bharosa Trust as organizations responsible for running gay bars and promoting pornographic literature, as well as perverse individuals spreading "unnatural" sex.

The general paranoia was that in the name of HIV/AIDS these organizations were promoting homosexuality itself, which was seen as foreign and a Western import. Moreover, the work of these organizations was seen as an "international conspiracy" by Western nations to contaminate Indian culture, which was represented as free of homosexuality. Ironically, in the name of protecting Indian culture from a "Western" onslaught, officials take recourse to a colonial law to establish homosexuality as "un-Indian." The contradictions in using colonial laws to fight "Western" ideas and diseases become clearly evident in these articulations. Moreover, the "political homophobia" and the depiction of homosexuality as "Western," "un-Indian," and "antinational" is not unique to the Indian context but also true of other postcolonial contexts where the state and nationalist discourses deploy these arguments to police and discipline nonnormative gender and sexual subjects and establish heteropatriarchy as the legitimate form of state practice.[21] Homosexuality itself was depicted as reckless and criminal behavior at the same time that working for the health of sexual minorities was construed as a threat to "national security." While the Indian state was committed to preventing HIV/AIDS, it was mostly targeting heterosexual sex (and commercial sex) and often denied the existence of homosexuality. Much of the work with MSM, kothi, and gay men was undertaken by NGOs through funding from international donor agencies, and it was not until 2007 that NACO included MSM in their national programmatic agenda. Despite the fact that NFI had been providing technical support to HIV/AIDS NGOs funded by the state, these organizations are branded as foreign with unaccountable money flowing into them to spread a reckless gay lifestyle. By framing it as a national security issue, the police and the judiciary justified their behavior of stripping the arrested individuals of their rights. Local media outlets published the pictures, names, and addresses of the arrested individuals as a way to publicly shame them. In 2007, six years after the incident happened, I had the opportunity to visit Lucknow and interview Arif Jafar, the executive director of NFI and one of the arrestees. He described the 2001 arrest and the terror as follows:

> The judge who heard our bail petition remarked that these people are a curse on the society and that they should not be let out to roam free. You see, that particular statement has nothing to do with the law; the court should decide based on the evidence. If they had looked at the evidence, they would have granted us bail in the first place. We had to languish in jail for forty-seven days. When we appealed in the high court, it questioned the lower court for not challenging the cops for implicating us under Section 377! But their argument [the lower court's] was that they were charging us with promoting homosexuality and conspiracy to promote homosexuality.

As Arif stated, there is no law in India against promotion of homosexuality, but the police used the clause in the criminal law that can bring charges against a person who abets the commission of a crime to implicate these individuals. The experience of the imprisoned Lucknow NGO members demonstrates the ability of the police and the judiciary to abuse the law to promote fear and terror when popular morality is against homosexuality. Public opinion, protests, and national and transnational lobbying on the issue (since NFI is based in the United Kingdom, letters were sent by UK MPs to the Indian state) led to the release on bail of the four staff members after forty-seven days, even though the harassment continued in other forms. Arif also shared with me that although the police eventually had to drop the charge related to Section 377, the fear and terror caused by the arrest and the public visibility (as the issue was extensively reported in local and national media and sensationalized in the media) had ramifications for the members even after their release on bail. While Arif was open with his family about his sexual preference as a gay man even before the arrests, other colleagues who were arrested along with him were not. This had dire consequences for them as their names and pictures were published.

The arrests had implications not only for the individuals but also for the organizations' essential outreach work with the MSM and kothi communities. Under these hostile conditions, Arif shared in the same interview, "NFI and Bharosa offices were sealed after the arrest and remained closed for three months, but it took us eight months to resume our services." Imran mentioned that the terror was so palpable that kothis feared attending Bharosa drop-in center activities because the organizations were in the police spotlight. It took Bharosa several months to regain the trust of the community and for the drop-in center activities to resume.

In 2006, Lucknow police arrested four men under Section 377 for allegedly having sex in a public park. Newspapers again sensationalized the story and published the pictures, names, and addresses of all four men. While the police stated in their records that those arrested were taken from a public park while having "unnatural sex," an independent investigation by human rights lawyers and groups found that the police actually entrapped one of the arrested men in an internet chat room and coerced him to give up other homosexual men in the city.[22] Even though the arrested were not affiliated with NFI or Bharosa Trust, Imran mentioned that there was a looming threat of police raiding their office again when this incident happened. The staff had to relive the fear and terror they experienced in 2001 when the 2006 arrests took place.

While the fear of homosexuality and the stigma of same-sex intercourse created a repressive climate for NGOs working with HIV/AIDS prevention among MSM and gay men, sex worker groups also faced police violence and repression. In 2002 SANGRAM/VAMP, a sex worker collective, had to suspend its anti-AIDS operations when local thugs drove its members out of the home they had purchased in order to provide care services for HIV-positive sex workers in Nippani, Karnataka. The thugs conducted this operation with the complicity of a local police official. Before this disruption, SANGRAM/VAMP built up a program that delivered 350,000 condoms per month.[23] Even though after the raid it managed to reestablish most of this work, the harassment by the police remained a concern for many NGOs working with sex workers to fight back against AIDS. In Kolkata, the sex worker organization DMSC faced similar abuse and intimidation during its attempts to organize sex workers. When DMSC filed a complaint with police about the beating of one of its members, local thugs publicly assaulted the president of the organization in the presence of the police who had been called for help. It was only when sex workers organized a mass demonstration that the police arrested two of the perpetrators.[24] As the police often collude with local power structures, they also aid in perpetuating violence against HIV/AIDS groups when powerful individuals raise objections. Sangama, a group working with sexual minorities in the city of Bengaluru, received various threats to close their office if they worked with hijras. The neighbors in the area where the Sangama office was located complained to the local police, and the police threatened to close down their office unless hijras stopped showing up. With the intervention of human rights groups Sangama was able to stop the police threats.[25] The sex workers' protests and the lobbying Sangama had to do marked a success for biopower projects, as they were able to make police at least temporarily accountable for their behavior.

The violence directed at peer educators and NGOs reveals the tension between juridical and biopower projects—and contradictory state actions toward gender and sexual dissidents. While the Indian state was compelled to take up HIV/AIDS intervention programs due to pressure from national and international groups, it was not completely committed to protecting the organizations that were implementing these programs on their behalf. The Lucknow incident is an illustrative example: even though Bharosa Trust was working with state agencies closely, they did not issue any statement supporting the activities of the group when the arrests happened. Often NACO, the national body responsible for funding and designing AIDS policy in India, has been reported as saying that this violence is more sporadic than systemic.[26] Furthermore, NACO put forth a public image that suggested it was interested only in preventing HIV/AIDS—not in promoting the rights of groups that it was working with. As a result, much of the burden of handling this violence fell on NGOs and individual peer educators who had to protect themselves. Furthermore, they had to force the state to be accountable for the violence faced by sexual minorities as well as to take ownership of policies and programs that it had promised to implement.

Biopolitics and State Violence

In addition to having to address violence against their own workers, these biopower projects soon realized that it was not possible to carry on HIV/AIDS work without addressing criminalization and juridical exclusion by the communities they worked with. As early as the 1990s, HIV/AIDS groups realized the importance of working with the community on violence and other pressing issues, and sex workers pioneered these efforts. This sentiment is captured in the words of Dr. Jana, a public health expert who helped establish one of the biggest interventions with sex workers in the city of Kolkata: "We started recognizing that [sex workers'] priority issue is neither HIV [nor] health; their priority issues that came up through interaction with them were police violence and violence they face from local hooligans. We felt that we had to address those so that *they can feel that we are their true friends. Frankly speaking, it was clear that HIV is our agenda, not their agenda, so it was very clear, how to make our agenda theirs.* And it cannot be done until and unless we accept their agenda." While HIV/AIDS is a concern for these biopower projects, it was not an immediate concern for already stigmatized and marginalized communities. The social and biological death that HIV/AIDS brings seems abstract and far away when compared to the everyday death they experience in the hands of cops and hoodlums. It is thus unsurprising that criminalization and police violence, not HIV/AIDS, is the most immediate problem faced by these communities. In order for HIV/AIDS to become the agenda of these communities, these programs are forced to also address state violence. And this becomes a condition for recruiting members into the program.

The Sonagachi project—named after the largest red-light district in Kolkata where the program started and headed by Dr. Jana—not only included sex workers as peer educators but also saw collective mobilization as a way to increase the sex workers' bargaining power with police, clients, and brothel owners. Originating in these interventions, "respect, recognition, and rights" became both a way to approach stigmatized and criminalized groups and a popular demand the groups raised in turn. A booklet published by the DMSC spells out the connection in a way that is more politicized than Dr. Jana's explanation: "Because the practice of safer sex, we felt, cannot be dealt with in isolation, we adopted the strategy of understanding the *power structure,* and combining empowerment with the enhancement of negotiating skills *of the sex workers, for the sex workers, and by the sex workers.*[27] Understanding the power structures that impacted safer sex practices meant acknowledging the systemic violence faced by sex workers and, as a result, articulating criminalization as one form of systemic violence rather than the sporadic violence of a few corrupt cops.

During an interview with members of a sex worker collective from South India in 2007, workers described how their relationship with the police and other state agencies had started to change since they began forming collectives. As Kumari, a sex worker, explained to me, "Previously, when we used to go to the police station, we used to be very scared and would stand meekly in a corner and cover our faces because of shame. Now it is not like that. We go with our head high, and they ask us to take a seat. If we go to the collector's office, they are asking us to sit. MLA is asking us to sit, a municipal councilor is asking us to sit." A collector, an MLA (member of the legislative assembly), and a municipal councilor refer to the county-level bureaucrats and political representatives that sex worker collectives' approach when they find local police unresponsive to incidents of violence, face arbitrary arrests, or want access to state-sponsored welfare programs. Kumari's comment does not indicate that police violence against individual sex workers has ended or that harassment and threats from other entities have gone away. Instead, the quote indicates that sex workers' consciousness as community organizers has enabled them to access political spaces as valued participants in biopower projects. While this access may be limited to the sites in which sex workers are collectively mobilized, I found evidence of a more general shift in sex workers' relationships with the police. Sex workers in South Delhi, who collectivized in the same way as Kumari's group, also shared with me that they had stopped paying bribes to the police due to the strength of their participation in the NGO.

Members of sex worker collectives in West Bengal articulated similar experiences with the police. Bharati Dey, who rose from the ranks of peer educator to executive director of DMSC, one of the largest HIV/ AIDS intervention programs run by sex workers, shared similar shifts in sex worker–police relations in an interview in 2009: "Because we are sex workers, when we used to the go to the police station with any complaints they didn't give us any respect. Now they give us respect, they say, come have a seat." When I asked her why this shift happened, she responded, "If a peer educator is going to the police station, she is not going as an individual. She is going as a member of a collective. She is doing health work. Since the collective is doing good work, they see that these women are also doing good work." In the words of both Kumari and Dey, police asking them to sit indicates respect, especially because of the history of extreme levels of mistreatment, dehumaniza- tion, and humiliation previously experienced at the hands of the police. Sitting also represents dialogue and partnership instead of the force and humiliation they previously faced when they "hanged their heads in shame." As Dey succinctly put it, this was possible only because of their mobilization in numbers, their collective power, and the good they are contributing to society. HIV/AIDS workers in India also wear the new identities and political subjectivities formed through these programs as a "badge of pride."[28]

I have also witnessed how the collective strength was mobilized to advocate against police violence and arbitrary arrests. In Rajahmundry, I witnessed the swift actions GMS took to get one of their peers who was detained by the cops out of jail. The access they have now with political leaders, bureaucrats, and other local power brokers helps them to fur- ther advocate for themselves. Before their collectivization, individual sex workers had to fend for themselves, but now there is a sense that they have the collective behind them. This does not mean that collectives are always egalitarian, but the fact that they were able to tilt the power toward themselves and make these institutions, which were otherwise unresponsive, receptive is a huge achievement.

By the time I interviewed Bharati Dey, there were approximately two dozen sex worker collectives in India, all organized under the aegis of HIV prevention projects. Some of these collectives are large. For ex- ample, DMSC has a membership of around sixty-five thousand. Some collectives were recently formed, like the previously mentioned GMS in Rajahmundry. The National Network of Sex Workers, a national body that brings together sex worker groups from all over the country to have a national voice, has a membership of approximately two hundred thou- sand sex workers. In contexts where sex worker collectives are strong, these groups have managed to work for their rights on multiple levels, including creating cooperative banks that can provide credit at an accessible rate, securing civil identity and voter registration for their members, maintaining schools for their children, and forming self-regulatory committees that regulate trafficking and the entry of minor girls into the industry. Thus, these groups establish their credibility as organizations that are instituting changes in their communities. Moreover, sex worker collectives such as DMSC are also seen as models for the collective organization of women, not just sex workers.

Since sex workers were the first group to mobilize under HIV/AIDS despite the violence they faced, they were able to form strong collectives and a national network. For gay men, MSM, and kothis (hijras were included in the umbrella category of MSM at this point), such mobilizations had not yet happened. This may be due to the heavy repression they have faced or the hidden and secretive nature of their community. But individual organizations have tried to address police violence against this community, and I have also noticed that peer educators from MSM and kothi communities feel more emboldened to discuss and challenge police violence. Soon after the Lucknow incident in 2001, Naz decided to file a petition in the Delhi High Court appealing for decriminalization of adult same-sex intercourse, bringing the questions of criminalization and police violence into the national spotlight and forcing the state to take a position regarding legal reform.

Conclusion

While sexual minorities are subject to juridical power and reduced to bare life where they have experienced the state in a top-down and centralized manner, in the HIV/AIDS era they are also inscribed in what Foucault calls the "arts of government," as governance of bodies (in contrast to juridical violence and exclusion) seems more urgent and necessary for effectively tackling the epidemic. "In this sense then contemporary biopolitics is a political economy of life that is neither reducible to state agencies nor to the form of law."[29] This brings a wide array of actors into the biopower projects and disperses state power as national and international donors, medical and legal experts, NGOs (which primarily implement these programs), peer educators, and individuals also share the state's concerns.

These two distinct modes of power do not always reside easily with each other. The interactions between police and peer educators reveal the split between juridical and biopower projects when peer educators are confronted with disruptive police behavior. In places where sexually marginalized groups had a strong collective presence, they were able to force law enforcement agencies to change their behavior. While violence against sexual minorities has not stopped, the biopower projects have been able to bring attention to this violence and, in the process, also offer new "moral frameworks" for communities to use to fight violence. As the peer educators I quoted above said, "They are doing good to the society," indicating new politics of visibility and legitimacy with which they are engaged. This discussion around violence and biopower also has analytical implications for understanding biopower in a Third World context like India. While queer and feminist scholars often tend to conceive of subjectivities produced through biopolitical projects as docile and compliant subjects, the Indian context highlights that these projects can also produce political subjectivities in an unexpected and unanticipated way. The interactions between the police and sexual minorities help us to understand how the imperatives of biopolitical projects are used by marginalized groups to fight violence, demand dignity and respect, as well as make the state accountable to its promises of right to life, equal treatment, and the rule of law.

While Agamben's bare life helped me understand the raw power sexual minorities are subjected to, I depart from his main thesis about the connection between juridical power and biopower. For Agamben, biopower is a condition for sovereign power—the state gives life to only take it away whenever it desires. In this sense, as Foucault scholars such as Thomas Lemke have noted, Agamben still centers a formal notion of state, which is top-down and centralized. While the Indian state still has the power to take life away and continues to be centralized in some areas, it is also important to pay attention to the processes through which state power is decentralized and dispersed. The analytics of biopolitics help parse out those aspects of the state that are harmful and those that are amenable to the demands of marginalized groups. It is through disaggregating the state that we can understand the politics of the governed and their struggles to fight violence and arbitrary state power.

Biopower projects are not only external to the state, if by that we mean that they are directed only at individual bodies. Rather, they can also potentially transform the formal structures of the state itself, as the state is obviously diffused. They can also push the state toward more accountable forms of governance that redirect state attention toward the rights of marginalized groups as well as compel the state to take a stand against the arbitrary use of sovereign power. These biopower projects have to confront not only those state agencies that are directly responsible for life-affirming projects but also other state institutions—especially legal ones—in order to bring more sustained and lasting changes to protect the rights of individuals and communities.

3

Empowered Criminals

In 2005, the Indian Women and Child Development Ministry (WCD) proposed "progressive" reforms to the Immoral Traffic Prevention Act (ITPA). The WCD reasoned that these reforms, if passed, would criminalize clients' purchase of sex and hence reduce demand for prostitution. This was in response to increasing pressure on the Indian state to curtail sex trafficking and represented the first time that Indian legal attention had focused on criminalizing clients. Yet Indian sex workers protested the amendment as detrimental to their rights and livelihoods, ultimately preventing the vote that would have allowed the amendment to pass in parliament.

Eight years later, in 2013, in a major blow to sexual minorities, the Indian Supreme Court upheld India's anti-sodomy law (Section 377), reversing a progressive 2009 judgment by the Delhi High Court that decriminalized adult consensual same-sex intercourse. The regressive 2013 judgment was rendered despite a strong national and transnational campaign to reform Section 377. When compared to the outcome around Section 377, the outcome for sex workers was positive since they were able to stop the ITPA amendment from passing in parliament. Despite these differences, there are many significant parallels between these two campaigns. Both are focused on decriminalization and reducing state intervention in sexual commerce and sexual privacy. The legal campaigns have also benefited from the HIV/AIDS prevention platform since it provided a ground for mobilizing sex worker and MSM groups and supported their demands for decriminalization.

These legal campaigns raise important questions: What specific opportunities do sex workers and MSM groups have to challenge criminalization? How do state agencies respond to these appeals against criminalization? What are the implications of these struggles and state responses for understanding the changed nature of the Indian state vis-à-vis marginalized groups in the era of HIV/AIDS? These questions drive the comparative analysis in this chapter and support its main goal: an analysis of how previously marginalized groups utilize the state and their roles in HIV/AIDS prevention programs to claim political citizenship. The change in the Indian state's stance toward marginalized groups indicates that, in the context of biopower, the state is compelled to share power and therefore is open to claims from marginalized groups. Sexually marginalized groups have also used the imperatives of biopower to speak back to the state in its own language: improving life and longevity and contributing to collective good. Hence, I ask, can marginalized groups use biopower in their own favor?

The ITPA: Legal Occupations, Illegal Acts

The legislative and legal framework for the regulation of prostitution in India is contained in ITPA of 1986. The Indian statutory approach claims to balance the views that sex work is immoral, that the sex trade is exploitative, and that sex workers need to be rescued and rehabilitated. The law does not prohibit prostitution per se but criminalizes a third party benefiting from prostitution (such as procuring women for brothels), punishes adults over eighteen for living off the income of a prostitute, and punishes any person who solicits or seduces for the purpose of prostitution or engages in prostitution in a public place. The act also established correctional institutions in which female offenders are to be detained and reformed, and special police officers used to enforce these provisions. Existing research on the ITPA indicates that police rarely use the law against brothel keepers, traffickers, and customers and that sex workers are punished disproportionately under the law.[1] Before the 1990s, individual and collective efforts to challenge the law met with little or no success. A critique of the law from the standpoint of sex workers themselves did not emerge in the public sphere until the late 1990s. With the emergence of HIV/AIDS as a public health issue, sex workers began to organize and make demands to decriminalize sex work.[2] But their voices against ITPA are often unheard or muffled because there is a powerful anti-trafficking discourse that tends to conflate sex work and trafficking and/or that promotes the Nordic model—where the focus of penal laws shifts from the sale of sex to the purchase of sex and the punishment to Johns who seek sex for money—of criminalizing clients as the ultimate feminist response to the exploitation of women in the sex industry.

Indeed, in 2005 the WCD introduced a bill in Indian parliament recommending amending the existing trafficking and prostitution laws in accordance with the Nordic model. While it is unclear how much of this bill reflects pressure from the global anti-trafficking lobby, it embodies some of the concerns expressed by this camp. This bill was the first in India to introduce Section 5C, which criminalizes clients who visit brothels for the purpose of exploitation. In addition, the bill enhances penalties for managing brothels and adds a new Section 5A to the penal code to criminalize human trafficking for the purposes of sex work. This section takes its language from the UN Protocol to Prevent, Suppress and Punish Trafficking in Persons Especially Women and Children, which is a supplement to the UN Convention Against Transnational Organized Crime. Yet while the international instrument also covers human trafficking for non-sex-work situations, Section 5A is restricted to trafficking for prostitution only, thus conflating sex work and trafficking.

Along with these proposals, the WCD minister also recommended decriminalizing the solicitation of sex work through repealing Section 5C of ITPA, a change that sex workers had been demanding since the mid-1990s. These amendments to ITPA were proposed as progressive gender reforms that would remove the sexual double standard of punishing sex workers rather than clients and thus fit the feminist agendas of enforcing gendered and sexual rights through a criminal justice approach. I interviewed the former WCD minister Renuka Chowdhury, architect of these amendments, in 2009. I asked her what had motivated her to propose the amendments; she replied, "You have to target the demand side, if you only target the supply side nothing is going to happen. Because the supply side is going on for centuries and as long as there is demand there is going to be supply." Ms. Chowdhury's remarks clearly reflect growing transnational attention toward punishing clients who purchase sex. Sympathetic lawyers alerted sex worker groups about the bill, which was poised to pass with little fuss. Once sex workers found out about the bill, they launched a scathing critique of the amendments and protested against it. Despite the fact that these amendments were pushed as positive and progressive, sex workers rejected them as an affront to their livelihoods.

As a show of protest, in March 2006, four thousand sex workers from sixteen states in India marched to Indian parliament to show their disagreement with these amendments. This protest was a huge success for sex workers since it was the first time they were able to mobilize and show their strength in front of parliament, an icon of Indian democracy. They argued that the amendments were introduced without consulting them and stated that the legal reform pertaining to sex work should be undertaken only with proper consultation and involvement of the community. In their critique of the amendment they indicated that the bill would significantly damage their ability to make a living and drive prostitution further underground, increasing their risks of human rights abuses and HIV/AIDS transmission. While these reforms were presented as progressive and positive by the WCD ministry, sex workers challenged them as regressive. In the words of one sex worker, "Previously they used to stab us in our stomach now they are stabbing us in our back." This sex worker's powerful distinction between the "stomach" and "back" indicates the way that both approaches (criminalizing sex workers or clients) are simply different ways of disenfranchising sex workers. Through their protests and petitions they appealed to the Indian state:

> The entire attempt in the process of amending the ITPA seems to us to be a backdoor method of abolishing prostitution. We wish you to understand that sex workers have become more visible, more aware of HIV and its prevention modes and have taken the responsibility to arrest the transmission rates of the virus. If such amendments are allowed to be passed as a law, it will only help push the entire industry underground, bringing untold miseries to *women who have become empowered and have started owning up to their responsibilities* through a process of breaking all structural barriers. *The proposed amendments will reverse the entire process and make us invisible once again.*[3]

These protests clearly articulated sex work as a means of securing one's livelihood and sex workers as an important group responsible for HIV prevention. Sex workers showcased their role as change agents in HIV/AIDS prevention by declaring that they are indispensable for the success of these programs, thus adopting the very language that is used by governmentality agencies to make them partners in the biopower projects. In doing so, sex workers are not merely voicing the sexual health discourses and needs presented to them by the state and transnational HIV projects. More importantly, they and their supporters have crucially transformed the discourse by demanding rights and recognition for themselves and their work and by redefining themselves as more than merely vectors of disease transmission to be managed. Unlike the process of co-optation, in advocating for their own rights, sex workers deployed the claims of the state and redeployed the language of biopower as counterclaims against state regulations.

Sex workers' protests and their lobbying led the government to appoint the Parliamentary Standing Committee on Human Resources in May 2006 whose role was to gather broad opinions around the bill. This was a big success as sex workers were able to temporarily stall the legislative process. Sex worker groups from all over India approached the committee, presented their arguments, and submitted petitions. After several months of deliberations, the committee submitted its report in November 2006. One of its major recommendations was to remove the clause on criminalization of clients, aligned with sex workers' demands. Despite this positive development, there was concern among sex worker groups that the WCD would proceed with its original bill and discount the recommendations of the committee.

I witnessed the uncertainty sex workers felt about this legislative process when I attended the All India Sex Worker Conference in February 2007. The conference was hosted and organized by one of the largest sex worker collectives in India, DMSC, in the city of Kolkata a few months after the parliamentary committee came out with its report. As part of the conference, a team of lawyers from the Lawyers Collective (LC), a human rights organization based in New Delhi (the same organization that had originally alerted sex workers to the impending bill), organized a workshop with sex workers to discuss the parliamentary committee's recommendations and to strategize in case the WCD went ahead with its proposal. While DMSC has an advocacy group based in New Delhi to lobby lawyers and parliamentarians about the bill, this workshop was organized specifically to have a conversation with sex workers at their own conference. The workshop was scheduled at the end of a long, packed day, and other parallel events were taking place at the same time. Still, the makeshift tent used to house the workshop was packed with around a hundred people—including sex worker representatives from five different states and adult children of some of the DMSC members who are also active in the organization. The workshop showcased not only the enthusiasm of the sex workers toward defeating the bill but also the lead role sex workers took in the political process. As Mr. Anand Grover, the senior lawyer from LC, said, it was sex workers who educated their organization on the implications of the bill. Until sex workers articulated their critique of the bill, even very empathetic lawyers' groups such as theirs could not completely comprehend the adverse effect of the bill on sex workers, indicating that sex workers are not just advocates of their cause but also educators to human rights groups such as LC.

The discussion that ensued was charged as participants talked about the conflation of sex work and trafficking (which is the major issue sex workers had with the bill) and strategies for approaching political parties to lobby against the bill. Some members voiced the opinion that whereas trafficking is a crime sex work is work, and that conflating them as the bill intended to do is very harmful. At this point in the conversation, one of the lawyers pondered whether they would find it less objectionable if Section 5C was more clearly worded and stated that only clients who went to underage sex workers would be punished, so as to make sure that traffickers would not go unpunished. This elicited a strong response from the group, who felt that such wording may lead only to confusion as it is often hard to tell a sex worker's age and also because this approach often focuses on the intent of the client (as it is hard to know if the client is a trafficker or a consumer). Moreover, they argued that any ambiguous wording in the law would impact them adversely as it would put them at the mercy of law enforcement agencies.

At one point, Mr. Grover asked how they as a group could counter one of the main points that WCD and anti-trafficking groups make about sex work: that it can never be voluntary. To this question, Kamala, a sex worker who seemed to be in her thirties and who at first glance looked like any ordinary working-class Indian woman, responded in a charged tone, sharing a powerful story about her own journey as a sex worker. Kamala shared that she came from a poor family; although she was married she had to leave her husband because he was abusive. Since her family doesn't have the resources for her remarriage, she is compelled to remain single. Kamala stated that even though her family is poor, she became a sex worker not just because of economic compulsions but also for *sharir kaa bhookh*—body hunger. By talking about body hunger (i.e., her sexual needs), Kamala challenges the dominant understanding that economic compulsions push women like her into the sex industry. Her story and her candid comments elicited not surprise but cheers. At platforms like this, I saw sex workers openly talk about their own desire, refusing to be viewed only as the victims of male lust. Such articulations complicate the idea that sex workers, especially from a "Third World" country like India, are always compelled into sex work because of their economic circumstances. Rather it can also be a space where women can experience sexual desire outside the constraints of patriarchy. Somewhat differently, a sex worker from South India, Nalini Jameela, powerfully frames sex work as service work and even as therapeutic work in her book *Autobiography of a Sex Worker*. The book counters the idea that sexual service to clients is always objectifying and degrading to women. In her book she states, "Ask any sex worker, and you're sure to find out that not all clients approach us for physical sex. Most clients come for advice or to talk. It is those who have fled society who come for physical sex."[4]

I heard such articulations of sex work as a form of service work all through the weeklong conference as attendees dialogued with feminist groups, local politicians, and international and national NGOs. In fact, the 2007 conference planners had invited several civil societal groups to participate as allies and partners to broaden the dialogue around sex work. DMSC named that year's conference "the entertainment workers' forum," inviting communities from all over India that are tied to dance and entertainment.[5] In this way, DMSC experimented with the idea of "entertainment" as a broader platform inclusive of multiple kinds of work to test if sex workers could find common ground and form alliances with other groups. While I am not certain about how successful this forum was in forming long-standing alliances—many of the communities associated with dancing did not want to be associated with sex work—it nonetheless indicated a need to reframe the debate around sexual labor as well as to broaden the dialogue about what constitutes sexual labor itself.

Sex workers' arguments against the conflation of sex work and trafficking and against WCD's amendments were not confined to just sex worker platforms. They also made concerted efforts to involve HIV/AIDS groups whose support they sought to defeat the bill.

Contradictions in the State's Position on ITPA

Less than a year after the Kolkata conference, in November 2007 I had a chance to attend a daylong consultation on "HIV and law" sponsored by NACO, the state agency that is primarily responsible for implementing HIV/AIDS programs and that was organized by LC in New Delhi. Up to that point most of the consultations organized on the bill focused on mobilizing sex workers, such as the one in February 2007 as part of the Kolkata conference with sex worker groups and collectives. This meeting was different in that it brought together organizations and donors working on HIV prevention to take a stand on the bill. Participants at this workshop included representatives of sex worker collectives from various regions of India, HIV/AIDS donor agencies, national and international NGOs, and supporters of sex worker rights—including feminist groups, NACO representatives, and a few supportive political leaders.

While sex worker groups have been clearly articulating their stands against anti-trafficking agendas and fighting against criminalization, this was the first time that HIV/AIDS groups took a more explicit stand on the bill and hence toward sex workers rights. Until then much of the response toward sexual workers' rights had been ad hoc. Through my conversations with sex workers, I gathered that the march to parliament they undertook in 2006 was made possible because of an all-India meeting on HIV/AIDS in New Delhi a few days prior. Sex worker groups were able to take advantage of the travel to and accommodation in New Delhi and organize their protest after this official meeting. But this support was not overt, and HIV/AIDS programs did not want to take an overtly political position by supporting sex work as work or by opposing the changes to ITPA. But the sex worker collectives formed alongside these programs functioned autonomously and thus were able to strongly articulate their political agenda and influence the HIV/AIDS NGOs to take a stand against anti-trafficking discourses that reduce sex work to trafficking. Hence having these groups support sex workers' stand against the amendments was a major achievement for the sex workers.

At the same New Delhi consultation in 2007, the then-director of NACO Ms. Sujata Rao expressed concern about the impact of the proposed bill on HIV prevention work. She advised HIV/AIDS groups to devise careful strategies and language to communicate with WCD, as the amendments they proposed conflated sex work and trafficking. The WCD's approach, Ms. Rao argued, would force sex work underground and make it impossible for safe sex messages to reach the community; in turn this would undo all the gains made within the sex worker community, especially in reducing the prevalence of HIV/AIDS. Her stand on ITPA was motivated by the fact that the bill would have adverse effects on the biopower projects her organization undertook, especially the identification of and outreach to sex workers. While the conversation that day was specifically focused on the bill, the discussion during the meeting also touched broadly on ITPA itself and its function in suppressing sex work. Sex worker collectives not only critiqued the bill but also asserted that ITPA does not protect sex workers and only reinforces mainstream morals and establishes that sex work is morally wrong. They called for a complete repeal of ITPA, arguing that there are already many provisions in the IPC that can be deployed to curb trafficking in all sectors where it occurs, not just sex work (such as sections regulating underage trafficking and kidnapping).

While extremely powerful, these critiques of the law and efforts to challenge these laws don't often gain visibility because sex worker organizations are weighed down by the effort to articulate the separation between sex work and trafficking. Sex workers' immediate critique of the amendments to ITPA found a place in the HIV/AIDS agenda during the workshop. The memorandum developed during this consultation stated,

> The recent attempts at sex work law reform have been informed by concerns arising out of trafficking alone and are unmindful of public health considerations. While the existing legislative framework has done little to inhibit trafficking, community-led, targeted interventions are proving effective in containing and even reducing STIs and HIV. That this has happened despite an unfavorable legal environment is due largely to strategies that are *pragmatic, non-judgmental and respect the rights of sex workers*. On the contrary, anti-trafficking measures have been knee-jerk, moralistic and antithetical to rights, and shown ineffective over a long term.[6]

Here a pragmatic, nonjudgmental attitude is justified as coming from "objective" and scientific approaches to epidemiology and presented as better than anti-trafficking measures, which are seen as "knee-jerk, moralistic and antithetical to rights." The statement reveals the contradictions in the state: one part focused on health and another on penal laws. By noting the "unfavorable legislative environment," the statement accepts and validates sex workers' critiques of the law. In fact, the fear that this legislation would impede HIV/AIDS prevention led many HIV/AIDS organizations and donors who had never before taken a public stand on sex work to endorse sex workers' position on the bill.

NACO's and the WCD's position on ITPA divided the state to a point where considerable disagreement around the amendments surfaced between these two agencies and they could not come to an agreement. The conflict reached a point where the federal cabinet had to intervene by setting up a committee to resolve the two ministries' differences regarding the bill. This conflict indicates both a crisis of legitimacy for each of the state agencies and that in the context of biopower the state can be further divided. These different voices within the state indicate that the state is dysfunctional, which creates great pressure on state agencies to resolve these differences.

In 2007, after the disagreement between the ministries erupted, I had the opportunity to meet with the joint secretary of the WCD (a high-level bureaucrat), who was busy preparing a brief on behalf of the WCD ministry to the committee charged with resolving the impasse. In the brief time we met, she explained that the WCD was trying to take an approach that advocated for the rights of clients' wives, pursuing the angle that gender rights were being ignored in this debate. While I cannot vouch for how much of this opinion was expressed in the official meeting (which happened behind closed doors), even the conversation about the rights of wives versus the rights of sex workers perpetuated stereotypes about many oppositional categories. Here sexuality is primarily defined as male pleasure and gender is defined as women's vulnerability; these conceptualizations are constantly present in the official arguments presented by the WCD.

The sharp difference between WCD and NACO was further revealed to me in an interview in 2009 with Ms. Renuka Chowdhary. After two months of trying to get an appointment for an interview with her, I finally met her at her New Delhi residence. Between the time she had proposed the amendments and the time I met her in 2009, Ms. Chowdhary had lost in the 2009 parliamentary elections. She had stepped down as the WCD minister, but the party she represented still held power at the federal level and she was still hopeful that her successor would push her amendment. She was still residing in her government-provided residence, a white bungalow with a large lawn iconic of legislative and bureaucratic power, in a plush central Delhi neighborhood. During our brief interview (which was frequently interrupted by phone calls), Ms. Chowdhary expressed her dissatisfaction with the health ministries and blamed internal politics within the ruling party at that time as a cause for the defeat of her ITPA amendments. She was very emphatic that the criminalization of clients was the best path toward gender equality because it transfers the crime to the clients instead of sex workers.

But she rarely discussed sex workers' march to the parliament or their resistance to her amendments. When I brought up the issue of the protests, she brushed it away as instigation by HIV/AIDS agencies and donors: "My biggest opponent was NACO. They have so much money and no accountability. They argued that sex work will be driven underground and that the amendment would affect HIV prevention. Which is a false claim." Ms. Chowdhury's argument was that her interest was in protecting women and minors who are trafficked and not women who willingly choose sex work (a dichotomy that is often used to discredit sex workers' rights). She attributed the disagreement on the bill to a political conflict between herself—a woman minister upholding women's rights—and her male colleagues in the health ministry upholding patriarchal attitudes by supporting sex work. NACO and the health ministry's support for sex work as work is upholding patriarchal ideas of women's sexuality as expendable and consumable in her eyes.

When I tried to bring the conversation back to sex workers' opposition to the amendments, she acknowledged that sex worker groups approached her with petitions against the amendment, but she presented them as poor, victimized women. Through this interview and others, it became clear to me that sex workers' stalling of the amendments was seen by the WCD minister not so much as an act of empowered women speaking on their own behalf but as women controlled by and speaking for the interests of men and brothel owners. Anti-sex-worker groups that claim that these are organizations of brothel owners often discredit sex workers' collective efforts. In Ms. Chowdhury's view, sex workers are capable of neither helping themselves nor making political claims. While she acknowledged that sex workers who came to petition her spoke about their general vulnerability and the exploitation they face (especially unwanted sexual advances, such as sexual harassment in other informal jobs such as domestic work and construction work) and that sex work actually gave them control over their bodies, she didn't seem to understand their critique of the underlying patriarchal assumptions about sex work as trafficking. While sex workers challenged the idea that sex work is the only sector where women face exploitation, Ms. Chowdhary interpreted sex workers' experiences as exemplifying their general vulnerability as well as the limited opportunities for sex workers to pursue livelihoods. She strongly believed that her amendment would uphold the rights of poor and marginalized women as it could eventually provide a path to abolish sex work.

The state's internal disagreement, the large and visible political protests of the sex workers, and the 2009 parliamentary elections delayed the presentation of the bill to parliament, which subsequently lapsed. This lapse meant that if the bill was to be discussed, it had to be reintroduced in parliament and go through the entire process again. The sex workers' ability to stall the amendment represented a huge success to them. Had they not protested and forced the government to set up a parliamentary committee, the bill would have been passed without controversy. Moreover, their protests and their success in stalling the bill indicate that sex workers were able to find legitimacy for their demands from NACO (and by extension the Health Ministry), an important agency of the state that is responsible for implementing biopower projects. This legitimacy was offered to them on the basis of shared responsibility with the state in the HIV/AIDS biopower projects.

HIV/AIDS as Opportunity to Challenge Section 377

Whereas sex workers' collectives were able to successfully leverage their role in preventing the spread of HIV/AIDS to stop the ITPA amendments, MSM/gay groups had difficulty convincing the state of this shared responsibility. Their struggle was to make the state more accountable for the promises it had implicitly made to the community to improve health and livability. They found their opportunity to hold the state accountable by challenging the anti-sodomy law that they viewed as central to the repression faced by MSM/gay groups.

The British colonial state had introduced an anti-sodomy law in India in 1860 under Section 377 of the IPC. The law defines "unnatural" sexual acts (carnal intercourse "against the order of nature" with any man, woman, or animal) as punishable by life imprisonment.[7] By designating punishments for consensual, non-procreative sexual acts, the law established such acts as abnormal and deviant. Interestingly, the law targets both homosexual and heterosexual acts that are deemed against the "order of nature." In India, the number of recorded cases prosecuted under Section 377, especially consensual sexual acts, is miniscule. Rather, in its long history, the law has often been used to bridge the lacunae in rape laws.[8] Section 377 is often used to supplement rape laws since until 2012 rape was defined strictly as penovaginal penetration.[9] Despite the fact that very few cases of consensual adult homosexual acts are prosecuted, MSM and gay groups have argued that the implications of the criminalization are far-reaching for their communities. They moved the legal conversation away from formal prosecution (in courts) to informal persecution (police and law enforcement agencies).

Explicit challenges to Section 377 did not surface until the mid-1990s. The Delhi-based human rights group ABVA (AIDS Bhedbhav Virodhi Andolan, or Struggle against AIDS Discrimination) filed the first legal petition challenging Section 377 in 1994. ABVA was one of the first groups in India to take up issues of discrimination against HIV-positive communities, including truck drivers, professional blood donors, sex workers, and gay men. ABVA's decision to file the legal petition came in the wake of a report from a medical team that visited a Central Prison in New Delhi and reported a high incidence of homosexual activity in the male wards. The team recommended providing condoms to prisoners as the WHO guidelines suggested, as there was a risk of HIV infection being transmitted among inmates. But prison authorities refused to distribute condoms, claiming that doing so would encourage male homosexual behavior in the prisons and would serve as a tacit admission that homosexual behavior exists in prisons.[10] Following this response from prison officials, ABVA petitioned the High Court, challenging the constitutional validity of Section 377 and pleading with the state to restrain officers from segregating or isolating prisoners with homosexual orientations or those suffering from

HIV/AIDS. Even though the status of the petition is unknown because ABVA dissolved soon after filing the petition, its challenge to the law remains the first in legal history.

Challenging Competing State Agendas: The Naz Petition

In contrast to sex workers, who were reacting against legal changes that were imposed on them, MSM and gay groups were proactively seeking changes to laws that they saw as repressive. Legal momentum around Section 377 picked up in 2001 when NGO representatives in the city of Lucknow were arrested. The Lucknow case became iconic because it showed that organizations of national and international repute were not above state repression. Soon after this incident, the Naz Foundation India (Naz) decided to file a petition in the Delhi High Court challenging the constitutional validity of Section 377. Anjali Gopalan started Naz as an initiative offering support to MSM and people living with HIV/AIDS in 1994. In an interview with Gopalan at her South Delhi residence in December 2007, she shared with me the roots of her organizational goals:

> I had come from the US to start Naz Foundation in 1994. In the US I was working with the gay community on HIV/AIDS, at that time. In the US HIV/AIDS was already linked to the gay community. Since I had a lot of gay friends in India it made a lot of sense when I was talking to them, I said look this information should go to the community and I said you guys [educated gay men] have this information but what about those guys in the parks, what about those who cruise in the park? That is how I got to work with the community, which is now identified as kothi. Initially, obviously, for me it was a huge learning experience.

Since then Naz had grown into one of the most important MSM and gay groups in India.[11] In the same interview Ms. Gopalan expressed that her organization decided to file the petition because she and her staff were tired of going to police stations to get outreach workers and peer educators out of detention: "It was really getting difficult to continue doing the work we were doing." Ms. Gopalan's words echo research showing that since 2001 Naz has reported increased police abuse and violence against its outreach workers.[12] Moreover, the Lucknow incident also heightened awareness among NGOs like Naz that under a repressive climate even NGOs of international stature and repute were not safe from repression.

In contrast to sex worker groups, which took to the streets, MSM and gay groups took to the courts to challenge criminalization. While sex worker groups were organized under the HIV/AIDS platform in large numbers, direct repression by the state of MSM and gay groups made impossible any large-scale organizing during the initial stages of the contestation. Moreover, when Naz decided to file the petition in the Delhi High Court, there were only a handful of MSM and gay groups openly fighting for their rights in India. Hence the Naz petition was not a result of a deliberative process that involved sexual minority groups all over India but was a strategic decision that a few groups made to approach the court to stop the repression of HIV/AIDS organizations. In order to do this, Naz took the route of public interest litigation and approached LC (the same group that worked with sex workers on stalling the ITPA amendments) to be the legal counsel in these cases.[13] Mr. Anand Grover, the senior lawyer from LC who played a key role in the Naz petition, expressed why they chose to challenge Section 377 in an interview in 2009: "There was already international legal precedence [for] the repeal of anti-sodomy law," including *Lawrence v. Texas*, wherein the US Supreme Court struck down sodomy laws in Texas and thirteen other states and declared same-sex sexual acts legal, and UN human rights treaties. With increased public awareness of police harassment and violence against MSM and gay men in India, this transnational legal precedent presented an opportunity to hold the state accountable for hostility and repression toward NGOs working with MSM and gay men on HIV/AIDS prevention.

The main goal of the petition was revising (not repealing) Section 377 so that it did not apply to adult consensual homosexual acts.[14] The group argued that Section 377 was being used for harassment and extortion of MSM and gay men and that the social effects of Section 377 were driving them underground, with a devastating impact on HIV/AIDS prevention efforts. It further added that once underground, MSM and gay men become extremely vulnerable to HIV/AIDS because their secretive nature makes it difficult for these individuals to negotiate safe sexual behaviors. The impediment to identification and outreach—important aspects of HIV/AIDS biopower projects—was very central to the arguments that

Naz made to reform the law: "A direct consequence of driving the activities of sexuality minorities, MSM and gay men in particular underground is that Section 377 renders it difficult to identify such groups and thus target HIV/AIDS interventions. The situation is exacerbated by the strong tendencies created within the community to deny MSM behavior itself. These tendencies arise as a result of the strong social stigma attached to same-sex sexual preference."[15] This dire social impact of Section 377, they argued, violates the fundamental right to life as guaranteed under Article 21 of the Indian Constitution: "The outdated presumptions underlying Section 377 include a blatantly prejudicial perception of same-sex relations and sexuality minorities. Thus, the presence of Section 377 has led to the *systematic harassment, intimidation, blackmail and extortion by enforcement agencies, family members and the public generally of sexuality minorities, gay men and MSM in particular.* Clearly, Section 377 created a class of vulnerable people that is continually victimized and directly affected by the provision."[16] In its wording the law targets all "unnatural" acts regardless of sexual orientation, and it is equally applicable to heterosexual acts. But, as the Naz petition argues, in practice Section 377 does not just regulate sexual behavior but also targets a certain class of the population (i.e., homosexuals). Activists consistently voice this criticism.

Moreover, the Indian state's investment in governing nonnormative sex is not lost in these legal contestations. The Naz petition highlighted the state's proclaimed duty to address the HIV/AIDS epidemic and its collaboration with international NGOs in HIV/AIDS prevention work:

> Indeed, SACS [State AIDS Control Societies] sponsor many NGOs in order to increase MSM and gay male awareness of HIV, its risk of transmission, the need for condom use and other safe sex practices. These SACS realize that it is imperative that the MSM and gay communities have the ability to be safely visible so that HIV/AIDS prevention may be successfully conducted. Clearly, the major stumbling block for the implementation of such programs is that the sexual practices of the MSM and gay community are "hidden" because they are subject to criminal sanction.[17]

As this quote reveals, the petitioner argued that the accurate identification of sex and sexual behavior for the purposes of public health initiatives were already part of the state's agenda and that the continued existence of Section 377 would hamper its public health interest. The Naz petition further argued that Section 377 not only imposed criminal sanctions on MSM and gay men but also exacerbated social stigma and discrimination against sexual minorities, making an effective response to the epidemic difficult. Put another way, the Naz petition attempted to hold the Indian state accountable for its promise to promote health and life among stigmatized groups. This awareness of the state's interest in sexual minorities was more explicitly articulated to me in an interview I had in Mumbai with Pallav Patankar from the Mumbai-based Humsafar Trust in 2015: "A large part of the argument against Section 377 was using the HIV route. And that has helped us to kind of address the issue, because the government is as interested in reducing the incidence of HIV/AIDS as we are. Government is not interested to give us marriage rights!!! That is what I want! So, it is a meeting point for the two of us. *Let's admit it otherwise they were not even interested in talking to us [LGBT groups]*." Pallav's comment succinctly captures not only the pragmatic approach of activist groups in their approach to the state but also the opportunity that HIV/AIDS epidemic provided for groups like Naz to find a common ground with the state. Even if this might be an afterthought by Pallav, these insights indicate the way in which activist groups approached the state not as an adversary but as a potential partner who could help them make legal reform successful.

Fragmentation: State Agencies' Responses to Section 377

The Naz petition highlighted the fact that NACO, a state agency, works with the MSM community and has done so since the Indian Health Ministry and NACO committed to approaching the HIV/AIDS epidemic as a public health issue in the 1990s. The state couldn't refute the argument that they had a shared responsibility in promoting public health. As part of its commitment, Indian state representatives participated in various transnational forums and declarations. As early as 1995, Indian state agencies acknowledged the need for a global response to effectively tackle the epidemic and to reduce stigma and discrimination against "high-risk" groups.[18] And in 2006, the Indian federal minister for health at the International HIV/AIDS Conference in Toronto assured the international community that Section 377 was to be amended as part of the government's measures to prevent HIV/AIDS. In 2014 I interviewed lawyer and activist Aditya Bandopadhyay, who shared with me the interaction that led to this assurance:

> I was attending to the Toronto AIDS conference that Dr. Anbumani Ramdoss [then federal minister for health] was also attending. I stood up there and I said okay, enough beating around the bush. You tell us [Indian activists] what is your position on the law. Are you for or against Section 377? Don't beat around the bush! You are here and I am asking you for a response. You are an intelligent person and a doctor yourself, you tell us what your position is! That was my question to him. And he blinked twice and said, I don't know about the government of India, but the health minister is for decriminalization of homosexuality. Within four hours of his admissions it became news across all of India.

Since the 2001 Lucknow incident, NGOs, the media, and other human rights groups have compelled NACO to take positions on violence toward and criminalization of MSM and gay men. In an interview conducted by Human Rights Watch in 2002, then-NACO director Mr. Prasada Rao took the following stand on the anti-sodomy law: "We will say we cannot criminalize this behavior; it is better to recognize it as a social aberration and deal with it. I can't say whether decriminalization comes from repeal or amendment [or another strategy], but we have to protect minors—this is the main thing."[19] This quote suggests that NACO is tiptoeing around the issue; as an HIV/AIDS prevention agency, it supports decriminalization but still considers homosexual acts a "social aberration." In some instances, NACO representatives have mentioned that the violence reported by HIV/AIDS outreach workers is sporadic and localized, thus minimizing the violence and harassment faced by the MSM and gay communities. Due to consistent advocacy with NACO, in 2006 the organization took an unequivocal position on Section 377. The NACO petition in the Delhi High Court stated,

> It is submitted that the enforcement of section 377 of IPC can adversely contribute to pushing the infection underground, make risky sexual practices go unnoticed and unaddressed. The fear of harassment by law en-

forcement agencies leads to sex being hurried, leaving partners without the option to consider or negotiate safer sex practices. As MSM groups lack [a] "safe place" and utilize public places such as railway stations, they become vulnerable to harassment and abuse by the police. The hidden nature of MSM groups further leads to poor access to condoms, health-care services and safe sex information. This constantly inhibits/impedes interventions under the National AIDS Control Program aimed at pre-venting [the] spread of HIV/AIDS by promoting safe sexual practices by using condoms or abstaining from multi-partner sex, etc.[20]

By echoing some of the same concerns expressed in the Naz petition (such as lack of access to safe sex education and condoms and driv-ing the community underground), NACO's response gave legitimacy to the claim that this is a matter of public health. NACO's submission further stated that it is essential that there be an enabling environment where people involved in "risky behavior" may be encouraged not to conceal information so that they are provided total access to the services of the National AIDS Control Program.[21] This enabling environment includes changing the legal context in which HIV/AIDS policies are implemented. NACO's stated goal of 100 percent outreach to high-risk groups could be achieved only if the affected communities are able to take ownership of prevention work. NACO argued that this wouldn't be possible if the state continued to penalize consensual adult homosexual acts. NACO's response highlights not only the shared responsibility between the state and MSM/gay groups and individuals in the light of HIV/AIDS but also the tension between juridical and biopower projects and the need to change these juridical frameworks in order to effectively tackle HIV/AIDS among MSM and gay groups.

While NACO's affidavit and position on reforming Section 377 were critical for activists who were fighting Section 377, it was not the only position of the Indian state. Since 2005 the federal Home Ministry (the ministry responsible for law and order) had been arguing that homosexu-ality was foreign and alien to India and that an amendment to Section 377 would open the floodgates of delinquency and be misconstrued as "unfet-tered license for homosexuality": "Section 377 has been applied to cases of assault where bodily harm is intended and/or caused and deletion of the said section can well *open floodgates of delinquent behavior* and be misconstrued as providing unbridled license for the same."[22] The Home Ministry further denied that Section 377 has any impact on MSM and gay groups and argued that the law does not impact public health interventions and argued that there are very few recorded cases of prosecution of consensual adult homosexual acts: "Section 377 I.P.C. shows that it has only been applied on the complaint of a victim and there are no instances of its being used arbitrarily or being applied to situations its terms do not naturally extend to."[23] Discrediting the argument by Naz that the law targets a specific group of people but saying that it is used mostly in cases of child sexual abuse to protect children and women whose bodily violations are not covered by the provisions of rape law in India, the Home Ministry's argument was that Section 377 is important in controlling perverse heterosexual acts (as there is a lacuna in the rape laws) and that it was not applied to homosexuals and does not criminalize their behavior: "If indeed homosexual acts make a person 'extremely vulnerable' to HIV/AIDS and other diseases as the petitioner argues, then Section 377 of IPC actually helps prevent the spread of such diseases by discouraging rampant homosexuality."[24] That the law acts as a deterrent for people and that it can actually prevent the spread of HIV is an argument that is presented consistently in these contestations by people who oppose reform of Section 377.

In addition to arguing that Section 377 does not apply to homosexuals as a class, the Home Ministry also argued that Indian society is not ready for homosexuality and that any changes to the law should be attuned to prevailing social attitudes about the issue. To make its case, the Home Ministry relied on an outdated report of the Indian law commission that stated that homosexuality is generally unacceptable in India. "The issue whether or not to retain Section 377 IPC was considered by the Law Commission of India in its 42nd Report and it observed that Indian society by and large disapproves of homosexuality and disapproval was strong enough to justify it being treated as a criminal offence even where the adults indulge in it in private."[25] This argument was put forward despite the fact that the 172nd law commission in 2000 recommended the repeal of Section 377.[26]

These responses reveal contradictions in the state's position, wherein different branches of the Indian state took varying positions on the law, with NACO supporting reform and the Home Ministry opposing it. These debates took the form of "public morality" versus "public health," with the Home Ministry upholding the public morality argument and NACO taking up the public health position. These differences between different state agencies did not go unnoticed. Importantly, the judges of the Delhi High Court's bench, who were hearing final arguments and noted that it is one of the peculiar features of the case, noted the dissonance in the state's response: "There are two arguments that you [the state] have put forward. One is on public morality and the other is on public health and safety. All of the literature including the NACO affidavit points to the contrary of what you [Home Ministry] are suggesting in terms of the second argument [public health]. NACO is telling us that continued criminalization will result in the denial of the right to health of this group." Indeed, the Indian state's need to govern and manage homosexuality in light of the HIV/AIDS epidemic was not lost in this legal battle. In delivering their judgment in 2009, the Delhi High Court justices urged the Indian state to follow global trends in its approach to the epidemic by decriminalizing adult same-sex sex so as to better identify and reach out to afflicted populations: "[That] Section 377 IPC has generally been used in cases of sexual abuse or child abuse, and conversely that it has hardly ever been used in cases of consenting adults, shows that the criminalization of adult same-sex conduct does not serve any public interest. The compelling state interest instead demands that public health measures should be strengthened by decriminalization of such activity, so that they [MSM] can be identified and better focused upon."[27] By declaring that the compelling state interest resides in effectively identifying and working with MSM groups, the judges gave legitimacy to the state's biopower. In addition to supporting NACO's position, the Delhi High Court justices' emphatic statements about the need to protect minorities and its focus on constitutional morality have shifted the state's tone regarding Section 377. Soon after the Naz judgment the Congress Party (then in power at the federal level) indicated that it would support the Delhi High Court's decision and abide by it. This was in contrast to the ITPA amendment struggle, where the state agencies could not come up with a unified stance on the issue. The resounding victory and worldwide attention forced the Indian state to take a stand supporting the reform of Section 377.

The state's positive stand toward the Naz judgment did not stop religious groups from challenging the Delhi High Court decision. Soon after, religious groups filed a petition in Indian Supreme Court challenging the Naz judgment. After four years of deliberations, in 2013 the Supreme Court issued its decision. The two-judge SC bench felt that the Delhi High Court was hasty in declaring Section 377 unconstitutional and argued that there was no substantive evidence to show that it persecuted homosexuals as a class.[28] This judgment was a major blow to activists who celebrated the Naz judgment as a landmark victory; activist groups responded by appealing to the Supreme Court to reexamine its decision by filing a review petition. Although review petitions are rarely admitted, the SC admitted it in this instance, itself is a huge success for activists. At the time of writing, this petition remains pending and is due to be reviewed by an SC constitutional bench.

Surprisingly, the Congress government's position to support Section 377 reform found its way into the 2014 parliamentary elections campaigns: Congress leader Rahul Gandhi supported the rights of sexual minorities in calling for reform of Section 377. But the party's loss in 2014 to the Bharatiya Janata Party (BJP) has led to the formation of a government at the federal level that is sexually conservative and right-wing, Hindu-leaning.

When the BJP came to power MSM and gay groups expressed widespread fear that they would face backlash from Hindu right-wing groups. That the newly formed government at that time was silent on Section 377 did not assuage their fears. While the official position of the present government was not clear at this point, occasional news reports suggested that the current home minister unambiguously endorses Section 377 because he considers homosexuality a crime. But a more liberal position was taken by Mr. Arun Jaitley (another influential minister in the current cabinet) that India should follow the global trend of state-recognized homosexuality. While this indicates a split in the BJP's position on Section 377, it remains unclear whether this is just a disagreement or if this will turn into a political battle between the two ministries. But the official position of the current government on Section 377 was not available until 2018. Despite the fact that activists and NGOs did not gain the legal outcome they sought, they were successful in garnering state legitimacy for their demands, even if it was disrupted by a change in political power.

Biopolitics and the State: A Comparative Analysis

These two instances of attempted legal reform have many important parallels. First, both sex workers and LGBTKQHI groups mobilized resources and discourses available to them through their participation in the HIV/AIDS biopower projects to gain legitimacy for their demands for the decriminalization of homosexuality and sex work. While sex workers used their role in the HIV/AIDS programs as a way to demand their inclusion in the legal process, MSM groups used HIV/AIDS as an opportunity to challenge Section 377. In both these campaigns, they argued that criminal laws adversely affect their participation in biopower projects and drive sexual minorities further underground. The state is then unable to identify and work with their peers to effectively tackle the HIV/AIDS epidemic. This inversion of power provided marginalized groups with new spaces and possibilities for different forms of resistance—visible protests, lobbying, networking, legal petitions—and new moral discourses around health, life, and longevity as a basis for political negotiations with the state. These legal campaigns thus highlight the transformative effects of biopower for marginalized groups. The reconfiguration of power between the state and marginalized groups initiated by responses to the HIV/AIDS crisis enabled sex worker and MSM groups to speak back to the state in its own language, that is, bettering the health of the population and promoting the greater good of society. In this sense, they used the same logic of biopower and transformed the language to seek legal reform.

Second, both sex worker and MSM groups were able to gain support from NACO (and hence the health ministry), critical for furthering their demands. NACO representatives took an unequivocal position against criminalization and argued that stalling the reform to ITPA and reforming Section 377 would be important for more robust HIV/AIDS prevention. NACO's position was important not only because it endorsed the fact that criminal frameworks repressed MSM/gay and sex worker groups but also because it gave legitimacy to these groups based on the shared responsibility they had with the state in biopower projects. This legitimacy from NACO further emboldened MSM and sex workers to negotiate with the state agencies that do not directly work with them but nevertheless have significant impact on their lives, such as WCD and the Home Ministry.

Third, state agencies were divided in their positions around legal reform in both of these instances, with NACO taking a favorable position and WCD and Home Ministry taking adversarial positions. In the case of ITPA, NACO's position differed significantly from the WCD position, and the differences resulted in a stalemate; a federal cabinet had to set up a committee to resolve them. The split in the state further delayed the discussion on the amendment in the parliament and eventually caused the bill to lapse. This was a huge success for sex workers, who essentially were able to defeat a bill that could have adversely impacted their livelihoods and their contributions to biopower projects as partners with the state. Similarly, in the case of Section 377, state agencies were divided in their positions. NACO's position supported activist demands that the law in the current form would adversely impact HIV/AIDS prevention among MSM and gay groups, whereas the Home Ministry argued that the law would be a deterrent to the spread of HIV/AIDS and homosexuality. The Delhi High Court judges not only noted this disagreement among various state agencies regarding Section 377, but also commented that this disagreement made this case very unique. They also directed the state to come up with a uniform position vis-à-vis the law, despite the fact that the 2009 Delhi High Court Judgment forced the state to put forth a more uniform position that favored the reform of Section 377. The divisions within the state illustrate the tension between the old approach (exclusion and disciplining) and the new approach (inclusion through governance and shared power) vis-à-vis sexually marginalized groups. While these tensions are not necessarily irreconcilable, they are also not insignificant. In both these cases state agencies were asked to come up with a uniform decision, indicating that these legal struggles also generated a crisis of legitimacy for the state. The tension reveals that when the state agreed to share control of marginalized communities for the HIV/AIDS epidemic, it also opened itself up to demands for greater political power like those over ITPA and Section 377. In this process, the state itself had to internally reconcile the pressures created by demands from these groups.

Last, sex worker and MSM/gay groups have been able to gain legitimacy from the state for their demands and have been empowered to claim rights on the basis of sharing the state's responsibility for public health. This is a changed status compared to the previous eras, when their voices were not recognized or even heard. Yet this legitimacy does not guarantee protection from criminal laws. Despite the fact that the ITPA amendments were defeated, sex workers remain in an occupation that is defined primarily as criminal. While MSM and gay groups were able to achieve temporary gains in the courts, they did not gain the outcome they wanted, and Section 377 remains on the books. These developments position sex worker and MSM/gay groups in a contradictory manner vis-à-vis the state: empowered to claim legitimacy based on the shared responsibility of tackling the HIV/AIDS epidemic, yet criminal because sex acts and sexual labor continue to be criminalized.

Conclusion

I began this chapter by asking whether marginalized groups can use biopower for their own benefit. These two legal campaigns indicate that marginalized groups utilized the imperatives of biopower to demand greater responsibility from the state for their welfare. The shift in power provided sexual minorities with new spaces and possibilities for different forms of resistance (visible protests, lobbying, networking, legal petitions) and new moral discourses around health, life, and longevity as bases for political negotiations with the state.

These campaigns around law and legal change show that, as Foucault has observed, power and resistance go hand in hand. Sexually marginalized groups' displays of resistance were not always leveled against the state, nor did these displays place them outside the realm of state power. In fact, their participation in the biopower projects enabled this resistance, and by being within the realm of state power they were able to resist and negotiate state power (asking for better services, making the state accountable for its promises, demanding legal reform). In this sense, then, resistance is not always about being outside state power but can include negotiating power from within, indicating that governance in the context of HIV/AIDS is not set in stone but rather available for contestation, appropriation, and even reversal of power. These empirical struggles also remind us that focusing on governmental technologies from the perspective of the "governors" alone misses the point that subjection is neither complete nor smooth but characterized by contestations, conflict, and instability.

4

Tolerable Identities, Intolerable Sex Acts

> Section 377 does not criminalize a particular people or identity or orientation. It merely identifies certain acts which if committed would constitute an offence. Such a prohibition regulates sexual conduct regardless of gender identity and orientation.
>
> —Koushal Judgment, 2013[1]

> Right to choose one's gender identity is integral to the right to lead a life with dignity, which is undoubtedly guaranteed by the constitution of India.
>
> —NALSA Judgment, 2014[2]

These remarks from two different decisions of the Supreme Court of India indicate the complexity sexual minorities faced vis-à-vis their rights until 2018 (when the Supreme Court finally declared Section 377 unconstitutional, reversing its earlier decision). Whereas in the Koushal judgment the SC declared anti-sodomy law legal and retained a colonial-era law, the same court in 2014 recognized transgender rights while responding to a petition filed by NALSA. For the first time in postcolonial Indian history, NALSA recognized the gender identity of transgender people and hijras and granted redistributive rights (including affirmative action in employment and education). By framing gender nonconformity as a matter of rights, NALSA also marked a break from a paternalistic approach of the Indian state toward these groups and extended to them the constitutional right to equality and equal protection before the law. Despite the fact that the Koushal judgment was overruled in September 2018, it is important to comparatively examine the Koushal and NALSA judgments as they stand as two important legal decisions on sexual minorities in India and sufficiently generated social movement attention. A comparative analysis of these contradictory legal outcomes indicates that biopower operates in heterogeneous fields with heterogeneous outcomes.

Unlike the Koushal judgment, which reversed legal gains and brought negative attention to the state's intolerance toward homosexuality, the NALSA judgment put India on the global map for the advancement of transgender rights. While these two judgments seem contradictory on the surface, they have the same effect—tolerance toward identities and intolerance toward sex acts. Despite the fact that transgender groups gained significant legal rights, their sex acts remained criminal (until the most recent decision on the SC of India in September 2018 when it declared Section 377 unconstitutional). Whereas Section 377 is often perceived as a law that prohibits homosexual acts, the gender and sexual nonconformity of transgender people (especially hijras) puts them at higher risk of violence by the police and law enforcement agencies when compared to homosexual men.[3] As a result, even though NALSA grants them the right to gender identity, the continued presence of Section 377 means that hijra and transgender people still face the threat of persecution under criminal law. These legal developments raise important questions: How does a law that regulates sex acts become important for rallying sexual rights and identities in India? Why are nonnormative identities more widely tolerable than nonnormative sex acts? These questions not only get at the heart of the contradictions for legal rights of sexual minorities but also reveal the uneven impact of biopower on rights claims of marginalized groups.

While HIV/AIDS biopolitical projects provide the political opportunity to challenge and seek legal rights for both homosexual and transgender groups, these legal struggles go beyond health projects and also galvanize groups that are not included in them (for example, lesbians and queer women, transmen). Furthermore, these rights-based struggles go beyond extending life to groups previously condemned and excluded by the state into questions of what constitutes a good and worthy life. In addition to the right to life and health, the right to privacy, the right against discrimination, and the right to identity and orientation are also debated in the legal arena. The law is thus a critical site where questions of both the appropriateness of the state's intervention in sexuality as well as the human rights of marginalized groups are debated and worked out in contemporary India.[4]

There is a general skepticism around rights discourses and rights-based claims among critical feminist and queer scholars, who often see rights discourse as a liberal move and an endorsement of state power.[5] In this understanding, rights discourses are nothing but an entrenched form of the state's disciplinary power. As a result, rights discourses have the capacity to resubjugate marginalized groups to state power, the very power that these groups try to challenge in the process of claiming rights. While this skepticism is important, rights discourses are often an important means for previously excluded groups to demand inclusion from the state as well as a means to put forward alternative social and political visions to the state. Drawing on the interpretations of Foucault's later work by the political philosopher Ben Golder, I move beyond thinking of rights discourses as *only* regulatory (that is, as regulating identities and subjects) and consider them also as tactics and strategies that can be deployed by marginalized groups to widen their political goals and agendas.[6] Rights projects are an "open ended and never-ending process of contestation," as well as political tools used in the service of constructing and reconstructing different social and political visions.[7] Hence, I understand rights-based struggles as simultaneously emancipatory and regulatory, producing unexpected political outcomes.

From a Legal Petition to a Social Movement: Section 377 Struggles

An important turn for Section 377 struggles came about when Voices Against 377 (Voices) was formed in New Delhi in 2004. Voices is a broad-based coalition of LGBTQ, women's rights, and human rights groups that was formed in response to the federal Home Ministries remark in the Delhi High Court that reforming Section 377 would lead to the opening of the floodgates of delinquency.[8] From the time it was formed, one of the goals of Voices Against 377 was to expand the discussion on Section 377 beyond the courtrooms by taking up public campaigns against the law as well as to generate broader awareness of the impact of the law on sexual minorities. Voices' approach to law was rooted in the perspective (offered by the feminist struggles in India) that positive social change would not be possible unless legal battles were accompanied by social movement struggles that focused on raising an awareness not only on the role Section 377 played in the persecution of sexual minorities but also on sexuality and rights in general. It is with this understanding that Voices started off as a group that would amplify civil societal voices against Section 377. In this sense, then, groups like Voices see the fight against anti-sodomy law not as an end in itself but rather as a means for broadening political debate around the marginalization of sexual minorities.

Public awareness campaigns, dialogues with other social movements, protests, and generating public campaign materials are some of the forms that Voices' activism took. As part of social movement building, Voices had organized the Million Voices Campaign to collect signatures against Section 377 in December 2004. Through this campaign, they hoped to bring together diverse opinions on and experiences of sexuality as well as to counter myths and taboos around nonnormative sex, as a response to Section 377. In addition to the public campaigns, Voices also brought out a report that was used to broadly circulate the coalition's understanding of Section 377. The report, "Rights for All: Ending Discrimination Against Queer Desire under Section 377," succinctly articulates Voices' position on Section 377: "Section 377, as it exists today, violates equal access to the rights of life, health and choice. This is a law that affects all of us, regardless of our sexual orientation and goes against the fundamental beliefs of this nation—democracy, equality, a belief in human rights, dignity and freedom from violence for all. DISCRIMINATION OF ALL KINDS UNDER SECTION 377 MUST END NOW!"[9] While Voices' position is that Section 377 stands as a law that orders "normal" and deviant sex acts regardless of whether they are homosexual or heterosexual, it balances this by also articulating the particular ways in which sexual minorities are impacted due to the presence of the criminal law. For example, in the same report Voices articulates the impact of Section 377 on lesbians and queer women: "In India, lesbians and bisexual women are organizing and demanding visibility and social recognition of their relationships, demanding an end to harassment and violence. Ironically, the current marginalization in law is also seen by some to be advantageous, since female-female sex is not specifically criminalized. Section 377 has nevertheless been used to harass lesbian women and compel them into heterosexual marriages."[10] Because of the law's focus on penetrative sex, women's same-sex desire is often seen as falling outside the purview of Section 377. While this might seem as an advantage by some, the flip side is that queer women's desire is completely erased from state and legal discourses. Despite the absence of women's same-sex desire in law, as the statement above indicates, women still face actual threats and criminalization.

In India, lesbians and other queer women have argued that Section 377 is used to police their sexuality by families and communities (with the complicity of the police) and as a way to subject them to forced heterosexual marriages. Even though this conversation about the impact of Section 377 on queer women's desire didn't make it into the legal petitions at this point of the legal contestation, the legal process offered a space for lesbian and queer women to challenge the centrality that male homosexuality found in these debates.[11] Thus, the anti-sodomy law is seen not only as targeting male same-sex desire but also as performing a broader symbolic function of state intervention in the "privacy" of the individual. Indian social movements, in light of legal campaigns, have transformed the discussion on Section 377 from a campaign that challenged the harassment of gay, MSM, and hijra groups to a campaign that includes a broad spectrum of nonnormative sexualities and identities.

Even though Voices' initial goal was to make a significant impact outside the courtroom by generating awareness of Section 377's impact on sexual minorities, in 2006 the group decided to join the formal legal fight as copetitioners with Naz in Delhi High Court.[12] Voices joining the petition not only helped to expand the debate around Section 377 (as the petition focused on discrimination and stigma faced by sexual minorities—not just MSM and gay men) but also brought activist voices from outside the courtroom into the legal debate. As one of the members of Voices put it to me in an interview in 2007: "I think that ironically the government has really helped by their reply that if we are thinking about the court case, it will never be enough. And I think that Voices came at the perfect time to make that claim, and Voices was able to make that to the LGBT people and to non-LGBT people in a very respectful way [by] saying it matters what you think about sexuality, it matters what your position is about rights. It expanded the space of the court." In this way, social movements in India actively engaged with the legal process. This interest in the legal process by a broad spectrum of sexual minorities was also articulated by Chayanika, founder of LABIA, a queer women's collective based in Mumbai, during my interview with her in Mumbai in 2015: "Once it became a wider petition and addressed the issue of rights and spoke from angles from other than health, everyone joined. So, 377 has been something that we could all come together [on] because it has been a core point that connects everybody [sexuality rights groups] that we have all been with the campaign and raised our concerns from time to time." This does not mean that there were no disagreements among various groups about the role of Section 377 in the lives of sexual minorities, nor that they always agree about the arguments and tactics employed in the courtrooms. Yet 377 became a flash point for sexual minority groups in India to come together and fight for a common cause.

March in New Delhi and Positive Legal Outcome

I witnessed the broadening of the debate around Section 377 at various meetings and events held by Voices and other groups as well as at various other forums such as the Queer Pride March during my time in New Delhi. On June 28, 2009, when I attended the second Queer Pride March, I saw the enthusiasm of hundreds of people who marched through the streets of New Delhi. Activists from all spectrums of sexual minority organization and their allies (feminist groups and social justice groups) attended this march, and I witnessed the energy and enthusiasm of the marchers. The streets of central Delhi were flooded with rainbow flags, as several thousand activists took to the streets, some wearing colorful masks to hide their identity and some marching without masks.

In addition to the marchers, I could not miss the cameras and satellite dishes around the march's path. There was a huge media presence, as this was one of the biggest marches in New Delhi undertaken by sexual minorities. It did not take much to notice how central 377 was to the march, as slogans and signs reading "repeal Section 377," "queer *azadi*" (queer freedom), and "377 quit India" (implying the foreignness of the law, as the law was introduced by the British colonial state) spread throughout the crowd. In this way, the marchers explicitly linked the reform of Section 377 to the freedom of sexual minorities. The marchers showed not only strength in numbers (as a counter to the argument made in the court that they are a miniscule minority) but also their resistance to Section 377. The next day, the front pages of major newspapers were filled with pictures of the march and the celebration of the marchers. The sense of solidarity and gaiety despite the marginalization of the community pervaded the pictures and media coverage.

It was not a coincidence that the march happened a few days before the Delhi High Court was going to deliver its judgment. Even during the march, I heard from the organizers that they were anticipating the judgment, and as a result, the march became even more important as it showcased the strength of the community. Significant numbers of sexual minorities attended the court on July 2 as a show of strength and support for the Naz petition. Their enthusiasm indicates sexual minorities' pervasive interest in the legal process and in the final hearing, as they showcased their support for legal reform to the judges who were to deliver the judgment.

This enthusiasm was further amplified by the positive approach of the Delhi High Court justices. They declared Section 377 unconstitutional, arguing that it violated the rights of sexual minorities. The 2009 Naz judgment was a landmark victory and one that gave activist groups such as Voices an affirmative nod regarding their struggles. In addition to the judges' positive approach to the reform of Section 377, the strong voice of social justice and the need to protect minorities in the country caught the attention of not only sexual minority groups. The judges proclaimed, "If there is one constitutional tenet that can be said to be underlying theme of the Indian Constitution, it is that of 'inclusiveness.' This Court believes that Indian constitution reflects this value deeply ingrained in Indian society, nurtured over several generations. The inclusiveness that Indian society traditionally displayed, literally in every aspect of life, is manifest in recognizing a role in society for everyone. Those perceived by the majority as 'deviants' or 'different' are not on that score excluded or ostracized."[13] I witnessed on television and through friends' accounts the exhilaration and tears of joy that were shed in court. To celebrate this major victory, sexual minority groups organized events across the country. The resoundingly positive judgment energized activist groups, which displayed enthusiasm about moving forward with their fight for social justice and human rights now that the demise of Section 377 had decriminalized adult consensual same-sex sex. In a 2015 interview, Gowthaman from the Alternative Law Forum (ALF) shared with me the importance of this victory: "It was like a higher victory for the simple reason that the judgment's potential was not just limited to LGBTQ groups. It spoke about minorities per se and not just LGBTQ or sexuality minorities. In fact, we were so thrilled by the judgment that we were like totally dreaming. We were thinking that we won the way forward." Gowthaman's comments indicate that the Naz victory was a victory not only for *sexual* minorities but for all minorities in general, and this was the sense that was also expressed by many commentators who wrote opinion pieces on the Naz judgment.[14] The reverberating and resounding victory not only helped activist groups dream of the further possibilities (such as fights against employment discrimination, marriage rights, etc.), but also emboldened individuals to openly discuss their sexuality and sexual orientation with their families and communities. There was a sense that the courts conferred legitimacy on their sexuality. As a result, a law that was meant to criminalize nonnormative sex acts became central to rallying sexual rights and identities, as slogans like "the court made us legal" were widespread during these celebrations. Even though the court had not expressed any opinion about identities, the idea that legislative acts are used to police identities was established in the Naz petition.

Legal Setback: The Koushal Judgment

The positive and overwhelming response nationally and globally toward the Naz verdict also came with resistance. Soon after the Naz verdict was delivered, religious groups banded together and filed the Koushal petition in the Supreme Court. In addition to the arguments that Section 377 guards Indian culture and tradition, the petitioners argued that the High Court did not have the constitutional power to deliver its ruling and that it was ultimately Indian parliament that should decide whether there can be a reform to the law. The SC not only entertained the petition but just four years after the Naz verdict, on December 13, 2013, in *Koushal v. Naz* (Koushal hereafter), a major blow to sexuality rights, reversed the gains made in the Naz verdict. The two-judge bench of the Indian Supreme Court concluded that the Delhi High Court was hasty in declaring Section 377 unconstitutional and argued that there was no substantial evidence to prove that Section 377 affected the rights of sexual minorities nor that the law was used to prosecute them: "Respondent No.1 [Naz Foundation] attacked Section 377 on the ground that the same has been used to perpetrate harassment, blackmail and torture on certain persons, especially those belonging to the LGBT community. In our opinion, this treatment is neither mandated by the section nor condoned by it and the mere fact that the section is misused by police authorities and others is not a reflection of the vires of the section."[15] The judges further stated that in its hundred fifty years of existence, only two hundred people had been prosecuted under the law, which was not a sound basis for its repeal. Moreover, they also remarked that sexual minorities constitute only a miniscule fraction of the population as a justification of their decision. By focusing only on the formal application of Section 377, the judges not only upheld this archaic law but also delegitimized the argument (advanced by both Naz and Voices) that any discussion of Section 377 should focus not just on formal prosecution but also on the informal persecution of sexual minorities due to the presence of the law.

Sexual minority groups in India responded to the Koushal judgment by organizing a global day of rage and protests throughout the country and globally as well as filing a curative petition appealing to the Supreme Court to reexamine its decision.[16] This time, in addition to organizations like the Naz Foundation and Voices, several other groups joined the petition, including parents of LGBT children. This coalition attested to the broadening of the struggles around Section 377 since Naz filed its petition in 2001. Despite the fact that curative petitions are very rarely admitted in the SC, the court accepted the petition, giving some hope to activist groups about continuing the fight against Section 377. As of this writing, the curative petition remains pending in the SC, and most recently the court appointed a constitutional bench to investigate the matter.[17] However, even this stark and negative judgment has provided some positive outcomes.

"No Going Back": Continuing Fight Against 377

While sexual minorities were galvanized before 2009, after the major victory in the Naz judgment much of this energy and momentum fizzled out. I was told that the Koushal verdict unwittingly brought sexual minority groups together and reenergized their fight against Section 377. Gowthaman expressed this sentiment to me in the same interview in 2015. "It is also important to say that when the 'no-going back campaign' happened there were thousands of people on the street. January 15th, 2013, we had a protest in Bangalore and it was phenomenal. The only good thing that happened because of this travesty is that it reignited the people to fight. And within a few days the pride march has happened, the Bangalore queer festival has happened. Nothing stopped." In fact, as Gowthaman stated, nothing has stopped. There have been many queer pride marches across the country, and groups have been galvanized to fight for reform.

I witnessed some of the activism against Koushal during my research in 2015. In July 2015, despite the Supreme Court's unfavorable decision, the Delhi Queer Pride Committee decided to use the occasion to organize a gathering to mark the Delhi High Court's July 2, 2009, decision as a day of victory for sexual minorities. The decision also coincided with the BJP's (right-wing political party with a conservative sexual politics) political ascendancy at the national level, and LGBTKQHI activists were uncertain as to how the new government would respond to Section 377. During the planning meeting that I attended a few days before the event organized by the Delhi Queer Pride Committee, activists were apprehensive about the political climate as there was no real way for them to gauge the newly formed government's position on Section 377 because it has been silent on the issue. They also feared violence, and individuals didn't want to draw attention to themselves in what was seen as a repressive political climate for sexual minorities. The fear seemed palpable to me, as the turnout at the planning meeting was sparse. Despite this, the New Delhi Queer Pride Committee members present decided not to be silenced by their recent setbacks in the SC and in political developments nationally; they decided to go ahead with organizing the annual event despite their fears of a low turnout. While the organizers wanted the event to mark their protest to the Koushal verdict, they also did not want to lose sight of their 2009 victory.

A few days after the preparatory meeting, on a hot and sultry July 2 afternoon, around seventy-five people gathered under the banner of the Delhi Queer Pride Committee at Jantar Mantar, the area in central Delhi officially designated to hold public gatherings and protests. Even though the attendance here was much less when compared to the huge draw of people for the 2009 march, for me the gathering that day symbolized the space created by the legal struggles against Section 377 by the sexual minority groups in India.

The atmosphere was informal and lively despite the sense of fear and apprehension expressed during the preparatory meeting. Short speeches (from activists, lawyers, community members, and feminist activists), protest songs, and passages read from the Naz judgment marked the event. The organizers strategically chose to read the New Delhi judges' remarks on the Indian constitutional value of diversity and respect; in this way, despite the Koushal verdict, the Naz judgment became a manifesto for sexual rights advocacy. It was a high point that could not be taken away—not even by an apex court like the SC. One of the speakers at the meeting articulated the empowerment felt by sexual minorities despite the unfavorable legal climate: "The [Supreme Court] judges who thought that they are going to put us down by reinstituting such regressive law, that we would shut up, but the good thing is that our voices have grown louder. We have learned to speak against the state, and we have learned to speak against all those institutions that control our bodies and our sexualities, institutions that control who we sleep with, who we want to love, and what dresses we wear, and where we go." This sentiment was also reflected in the voice of another speaker at the same protest: "July 2nd [when the Naz judgment was delivered in 2009] gives us hope that the gain will not be for the nationalist and patriarchal forces but for the hijras, kothis, lesbian and bisexual women, and for the gay people. The victory is not going to be for them [conservatives], but it is going to be our victory!" What comes out powerfully in these articulations is a sense that the legal struggles have mobilized a broad spectrum of sexual minority groups even though the desired legal outcome hasn't been achieved.

Reflecting on more than fifteen years of legal struggle, in a 2015 interview Ms. Gopalan shared with me that when Naz decided to file the petition in the Delhi High Court in 2001, there were only a handful of LGBTKQHI groups in the country and very few groups had voiced their opposition to the law. However, in the decade and a half of the legal battle, these numbers had increased tremendously, and today these groups are not scared of fighting the law openly. This shift is the landscape of sexual minority politics was also evident to me in the comments by Aditya Bandhopadhya, a lawyer and activist who shared this insight with me during an interview in New Delhi in 2014:

From 2001 onwards, since the Lucknow incident, which I represented, at that point of time the tone [in the media] was completely like "you are running sex brothels for boys" and stuff like that. From that to a nuanced understanding of sexuality focused on rights is a very big change. I think that the change was also in a way catalyzed by the visibility of the community. Earlier in the 1990s, if you wanted to talk to a gay man, you had five gay men in India. Literally, you count them on your fingers. And they were dispersed across India. But now you go to any website, you go to any Facebook page, or, for that matter, anywhere—we are there. You just call for a meeting, you have a small film screening, and fifty people turn up, and they don't have any problem identifying as belonging to the LGBTQ community.

Even though in this comment Mr. Bandhopadhya did not directly mention Section 377 as the cause of this expansion of sexual minority politics, it was evident to me from the rest of the interview that Section 377 struggles played a very key role in mobilizing sexual minorities. A similar sentiment was expressed to me by Chayanika from LABIA in the same interview in Mumbai: "The fact is that even if it [377] was a single-issue campaign, the media was responding to it, other movement groups were responding to it. Other groups were responding to it; it has also mattered for a lot of people. In the last fifteen years, you see, it is something you can talk about. It is something that you can raise at any point. So, in that sense, they have been victories. They have been gains, and the fact that everybody came together and made noise—that does help." Despite the uneven legal outcomes, the fight against 377 is not lost. It helped generate social movement around sexuality and rights, and it brought to the national attention many issues related to marginalized sexualities that were previously absent.[18]

Recognizing Gender Identity: The NALSA Judgment

In a sharp contrast to the 2014 Koushal judgment, less than a year later the same court delivered a judgment favoring transgender rights. Responding to a petition filed by NALSA, the court declared transgender identities legal and extended constitutional guarantees of equality, freedom, and liberty to transgender groups. NALSA was hailed in the national and international media as a monumental judgment, propelling India to the lead in the global arena with regard to transgender rights. This victory for transgender groups came in contrast to the Section 377 struggles that had seen a huge setback in the same court.

NALSA's petition was the culmination of the work of organizations such as UNDP that had, as part of the HIV/AIDS agenda, been supporting the collective mobilization of transgender and hijra groups in India since 2007. There had been concerted efforts by NACO, UNDP, and other groups to form CBOs with transgender groups (mostly transwomen) and hijras to address the risk of HIV/AIDS in these communities. During my interview with Earnest Noronha, a UNDP representative and transgender activist, they explained the role HIV/AIDS in mobilizing hijra and transgender communities as follows:

> We started our engagement with hijra and trans groups around 2007–2008, trying to understand hijra community and their issues with HIV/AIDS. UNDP provided the leadership under the umbrella of HIV and development. Since UNDP is a development agency looking at overall human development, it could afford the luxury of talking about other constraining issues, not just HIV/AIDS. And that is when we started a national dialogue around what are the most crucial interventions for men who have sex with men and transgender communities in 2008. When we started this meeting, we realized that the needs of the community are beyond HIV/AIDS. We had to look at it in the broadest way possible. At that point of time, the transgender community said that we need to have a separate conversation and also said that they don't want to be clubbed with MSM and that their needs are different and our needs of collectivization are different.

Noronha's remarks indicate the shift in association between male homosexuality and feminization that was widespread in the HIV/AIDS arena.[19] This separation means that transgender people are marked as a gender category and MSM and kothis are marked as sexual categories in these biopower projects. I witnessed this move to divide often-overlapping categories such as hijra and kothi into separate categories in some of the UNDP workshops I attended in 2007 and 2009.

While the transgender category became more common with the globalization of transgender rights, the inspiration for these national policies comes from the southern state of Tamil Nadu, where since 2001 there have been significant strides made with regard to transgender rights. In this state, senior *aravani* (a regional term for male-to-female transgender people) community leaders initiated the formation of CBOs and succeeded in getting resources for implementing HIV interventions. Additionally, the first transgender CBO received government funding in 2001.

In addition to being the first state to implement the HIV/AIDS programs with transgender and hijra groups, Tamil Nadu also had the distinction of being the first state to create institutions to secure social and economic rights for transgender groups and hijras. In 2008, the state government set up a welfare board that serves as a nodal body to protect the social rights—including housing, education, income/employment, and healthcare needs—of transgender people/hijras. The welfare board addressed the social protection needs of transgender people by introducing transgender-specific schemes of its own and facilitating them to access the existing government schemes implemented by other government bodies. The Tamil Nadu welfare board has also been lauded in the HIV/AIDS and development circles for its involvement of aravanis representatives as equal partners in decision making. In addition, the welfare board also has issued identity cards to transgender people and hijras, who can use them to avail themselves of state services such as old age pensions and housing for the poor. Additionally, transgender groups in Tamil Nadu have also made legal strides; when they approached the state High Court, and the court granted them the right to vote as male or female.

The decision to file the NALSA legal petition in the Supreme Court of India came after significant legwork with the judiciary and collaboration among various groups. In the same meeting I had with Noronha, we discussed the background for the NALSA case as well as their organization's efforts with the judiciary:

> In 2009, we started off with six national consultations trying to understand how [to] define what is transgender and what is *hijra*. We wanted to highlight communities' own understanding of their own issues and hence we brought out a social brief called "HIV Human Rights and Social Exclusion by Transgender and Hijra Communities in India." So, that is the time when we invited other stake holders, people from judiciary,

people from the government and we also had the Member Secretary from NALSA who was also present at these meetings.[20] The NALSA representatives were very interested in taking this discussion forward, especially in the rights context. And in partnership with NALSA in 2011, a national seminar on "transgender and law" was conducted. It was a large-scale event we had almost five hundred judicial officers, policemen, judges present. It was hosted by NALSA in partnership with UNDP. There were chief justices [from high courts] who were present too.

Later that year UNDP also organized a public hearing on transgender issues in twelve states in India. The public hearings not only gave visibility to transgender human rights but also sensitized the judges to transgender issues. As Laxmi Narayan Tripathi (a prominent hijra activist and one of the copetitioners in NALSA) shared on a television interview about her experience, "I was sitting next to a judge at one of these public hearings. I did not know that the person sitting next to me was a chief justice of a high court. I was chatting and talking to him about everything, including sexual harassment and bullying I faced." Laxmi's candor and her openness to discuss issues might seem exceptional, but what this quote indicates to me is the opportunity to bring community leaders like Laxmi and high-level judges together within the same platform. In these meetings UNDP sensed that the judiciary was sensitive to transgender rights.

UNDP decided to take advantage of the judicial support and not lose the momentum that it generated during these public hearings. Based on my interview with Noronha and others, I gathered that UNDP sent an official letter to NALSA suggesting the need for a legal intervention. NALSA, as a state-run agency responsible for providing legal aid to marginalized communities, had also been filing social-action petitions in the courts to secure rights for marginalized groups.[21] NALSA responded positively to UNDP's request to file a petition in the Supreme Court but went ahead and filed the petition in October 2012 without involving UNDP or other community organizations. To add a community voice to the petition, three petitioners, including Earnest Noronha and Laxmi Narayan Tripathi, joined the NALSA petition.

It was not only the judiciary that became sensitive the transgender community's needs. By 2013, the Ministry of Social Justice and Empowerment took significant interest in transgender issues and constituted an Expert Committee to look into the status and problems of the transgender community. Representatives of the Federal Ministries of Law & Justice and External Affairs and the Department of AIDS Control, state government representatives, NGO functionaries, and transgender and hijra community members attended the Expert Committee meeting. The committee recommended various strategies, including increased awareness regarding transgender rights, access to public facilities such as bathrooms, as well as including transgender people in housing and employment programs.

The committee report also served as background material in the NALSA case and showcased the support of the Indian state toward the issue. In this way, state agencies evidenced substantial interest in transgender rights and presented opportunities for transgender groups to articulate rights-based concerns. Whereas in the Koushal judgment the Supreme Court retained an archaic law, in the case of NALSA the same court issued a positive judgment that granted rights to transgender people and hijras for the first time. These contradictory judgments, while coming from the same court, were delivered by different benches with different sets of judges presiding.[22]

According to LC (the lawyer's group that argued on behalf of the petitioners), NALSA marks a break from a paternalistic and charitable approach of the state toward the transgender and hijra community by framing their concerns as a matter of rights.[23] The right to equality and right to equal protection before law—two important fundamental rights guaranteed by the constitution of India—have been held as standards by NALSA petitioners as a way to seek state recognition. "Gender identity refers to each person's deeply felt internal and individual experience of gender, which may or may not correspond with the sex assigned at birth, including the personal sense of the body which may involve a freely chosen, modification of bodily appearance or functions by medical, surgical or other means and other expressions of gender, including dress, speech and mannerisms. Gender identity therefore, refers to an individual's self-identification as a man, woman, transgender or other identity category."[24] Underscoring the right to personal autonomy and self-determination under Article 21, the Court observed that self-identification is enough to prove that a person is transgender. NALSA recognizes the right of a person to choose the gender they identify with (that is, male, female, or third gender) irrespective of medical/surgical status. This was a huge victory for transgender and hijra groups, as they no longer needed to rely on a medical certification or psychiatric evaluation to prove their identity.

The NALSA judgment is crucial not only because it recognizes the gender identity of transgender/hijra groups but also because it combines redistributive aspects as well. The judges recommend affirmative action in education and employment for transgender people and hijras. When it comes to health and HIV/AIDS, the court recommended establishing separate HIV sentinel serosurveillance sites for transgender people and hijras (in order to understand the impact of the epidemic on these communities); it also recommended financially supporting the creation of CBOs with transgender groups. In addition, the court also recommended that state and federal governments design policies to increase access (to healthcare or bathrooms, for example) for marginalized groups, as well as integrate services for transgender people with state welfare programs from which they were previously excluded. In this sense, NALSA balances identity politics with social, political, and economic rights. Despite the fact that there is still a long road ahead in terms of implementing these rights, this is still a massive gain and one that puts Indian transgender and hijra rights on the national political landscape.

Legalizing Identities Ignoring Acts

Despite this positive development, there are some important shortcomings of NALSA to note. While the judgment also includes the category "intersex," issues particular to intersex people are not explicitly addressed. Additionally, even though hijras are folded into the "transgender" category and, as a result, have gained recognition, this came at a cost to these communities. While there is some acknowledgment of the rights to own property for transgender persons in the judgment, no specific protections are offered regarding hijra lineage and kinship practices through which property and resource distributions are organized. While NALSA does provide affirmative action in education and employment for transgender people, this would only help those hijras who are educated; the majority of hijras lack educational skills and hence rely on "traditional" livelihoods, such as seeking alms in public spaces and tholi badhai (the practice of blessing newborn children and newlywed couples). The continuation of public indecency and anti-beggary laws will continue to criminalize hijras who depend on these practices to make a living.

Another important omission (one that I will focus on in the rest of the chapter) is that NALSA does not touch upon the sexual rights of transgender communities. This is ironic because the legal petition itself came in the context of HIV/AIDS work—that is, managing sexual behavior. Yet, the discussion on sex and sexuality is nonexistent in the judgment. Moreover, there was no conversation around Section 377, which is often seen as impacting transgender groups like hijras more so than homosexual men, as even their public presence causes suspicion among police about their sexual activity. The judges, while delivering their remarks, did acknowledge this history of abuse: "Section 377 of the Indian Penal Code was misused and abused as there was a tendency in British period, to arrest and prosecute TG [transgender] persons under Section 377 merely on suspicion."[25] Even though the judges acknowledged that Section 377 was used to prosecute hijras, this issue was quickly relegated to the past.[26] Despite this nod to Section 377, the judges were not always consistent in their remarks: "A Division Bench of this Court in Suresh Kumar Koushal v. Naz Foundation has already spoken on the constitutionality of Section 377 and hence, we express no opinion on it since we are in these cases concerned with an altogether different issue pertaining to the constitutional and other legal rights of the transgender community and their gender identity and sexual orientation."[27] While the judges acknowledged the sexual orientation of transgender people, this was only a passing reference, as the rest of the judgment did not really reference sexual orientation or any rights based on sexual orientation. By merely giving a nod to sexual orientation and not elaborating on the specific rights, the judgment undermined sexual rights. This limitation became obvious to me when I interacted with transgender and hijra groups.

On a spring afternoon in 2015, a little over a year after the NALSA judgment was delivered, I visited Mitra Trust in New Delhi to meet with Rudrani, a hijra activist who also heads an HIV/AIDS intervention program in North Delhi. I spent the afternoon talking with Rudrani about NALSA and transgender and hijra rights. Even though I witnessed Rudrani's enthusiastic support of the NALSA judgment in various public forums I attended where she was a speaker, in our private conversation it was apparent to me that she was more ambivalent toward the judgment. Our conversation went on for almost two hours, and we talked about not only the limitations of the court's recommendation but also some of the challenges in taking it forward. As we were winding down the conversation, Rudrani's staff reminded her that a group of hijras were waiting for her to start their weekly gathering. Rudrani invited me to join her and mentioned that it was an informal and fun space where hijras are able to sing and dance; I could not pass up this invitation. We wrapped up the conversation, and I followed Rudrani into a room on the second floor of the building.

In contrast to Rudrani's office, which was crammed with computers and office dividers, this room was more spacious and barely furnished. When we arrived, there were around twenty-five to thirty people (mostly hijra and kothi identified) sitting on the floor in a circle or singing and dancing. The mood in the room was upbeat and playful. The songs included hit Bollywood songs as well as folk songs that were completely unfamiliar to me. The folk songs had more explicit sexual content, including references to sex acts, as opposed to the Bollywood songs, which were more about romantic love. In addition to dancing and singing, I was also party to side conversations where the participants were teasing each other about their sexual partners and making raunchy jokes. I have often witnessed during my research how seemingly sanitized spaces like this turn into zones of pleasure with explicit sexual language and uninhibited expression of desire through dancing, singing, and casual jokes. As they participated in songs that explicitly expressed their sexual choice, desire, and practices, the participants defied the myth of the asexual hijra that is widespread in mainstream society. I spent the next hour witnessing the singing and dancing, and as the event was coming to an end, I said my good-byes, thanked Rudrani and the participants there, and got ready to leave.

While I was walking out of the room I saw K and J also leaving the Mitra Trust office. The office is located in a neighborhood with small alleys, and getting to the main street to catch a bus or an auto rickshaw requires a good ten-minute walk. I was going to catch an auto rickshaw to my South Delhi residence, and K and J were planning to take a bus.

As we were walking together, we were mutually admiring each other's jewelry and making small talk. As we were approaching our respective destinations, J asked me what brought me to Mitra Trust. I told her about my interest in understanding NALSA and the hijra community's reaction of to the judgment. J said that she heard of NALSA but wasn't sure if the court gave them the right to marry! She asked me if I knew anything about the right to marry in NALSA. Even before I could answer, J went on to say "if it doesn't, then it doesn't mean anything to me." I wanted to talk more about the issue of marriage, but by then we had gotten close to the main street. As I did not want to cause K and J to miss their bus, we parted ways. I did not get a chance to talk to them again, but our brief conversation stayed with me. While J specifically referred to marriage and not sex in her comments, I interpret this conversation as pointing to the lack of discussion of sexuality rights in NALSA as well as the inherent contradiction of recognizing gender identity while ignoring sexual rights. This contradiction is further reveled in the remarks of Laxmi Tripathi: "Over here the ministry is saying that I have a right to choose my own bathroom. But tomorrow if I choose to go to the men's bathroom will I be safe there? And if I get raped there, does the rape law cover me? Today, [if] I am in a live-in relationship or I am having an affair, if the police walk into my bedroom and puts me under Section 377, does that verdict [NALSA] save my dignity?"[28] Despite the fact that there are no reported cases of police intervening and arresting hijras in the privacy of their bedroom, Laxmi's comment suggests that Section 377 stands as a symbol of state-sanctioned homophobia and the continued oppression of marginalized groups like hijras. This connection between Section 377 and NALSA was also expressed in other articulations. For example, Dr. Akkai Padamsai, a hijra and trans activist from South India, also critiqued NALSA in the same vein: "If you read the NALSA and Koushal judgment together, it essentially says that trans people are excellent people; they will have all their rights including right to identity, right to livelihood, education everything, but they cannot have sex. Because any sex they have will be categorized under Section 377. So, you don't look at us as sexual beings essentially. That is quite shocking." It is clear from this articulation that Section 377 is seen as an important fight to be fought by the members of the transgender and hijra communities. And there is already a broader articulation of sexuality and rights connected to Section 377. Challenging this bifurcation of rights, in 2015 Dr. Padamsai along with two other transgender activists filed a petition in the Supreme Court asking the court to reconsider the Koushal judgment in light of NALSA. In her petition, Dr. Padamsai states,

> The Hon'ble Court has held that one's gender identity is not limited to one's sex. Hence if transgender persons were to have intercourse with their partners, the same would fall foul of the section [377] and would amount to a criminal offence. Section 377 would thus not give them equal protection of the law, as transgender persons would be particularly vulnerable to being criminalized under Section 377. Further, if they were to express their gender identity through dress or actions as guaranteed under Article 19 (1) (1) (a) [freedom of speech and expression], they would be immediately identified as a transgender person, making them further vulnerable to Section 377.[29]

The contention here is about how the sex acts of transgender persons can be viewed as "unnatural" as a result of their gender identity not always matching their assigned biological sex. Moreover, this petition also brings the court's attention to the fact that it is often those who are perceived as "habitual sodomites" who are policed and criminalized under Section 377, and clothing and gender expression have often been important for this perception by law enforcement agencies. The freedom that NALSA grants transgender people to express their gender identity will be of no avail if law enforcement agencies continue to police gender expression as a way to regulate nonnormative sex acts. In this way, the petition challenges the dichotomy between acts and identities expressed in the Koushal judgment. Will the Supreme Court reexamine its decision in light of NALSA? Will Section 377 be reformed so as to enable the full expression of gender identity of transgender people? It is still a matter of speculation at this point.

Politics of Rights: Comparative Analysis

Despite different outcomes, these two legal developments have at least three important parallels. First, law became a very important site where rights claims were made for both homosexual and transgender groups.

Whereas in the case of Section 377 Naz approached the Delhi High Court seeking reform to an archaic and colonial-era criminal law, in the case of NALSA it was about extending civil and constitutional right to equality and freedom to previously marginalized groups. While these legal claims started as a petition in the courtroom, they also transformed into social movements that brought questions about the state's role in sexual governance and the human rights of sexual marginalized groups into national debate.

Furthermore, the struggle against the law provided the space for marginalized identities to emerge and consolidate. Even though these petitions were filed not because of mass mobilization but rather because a select few organizations initiated the process, engaging with law is dynamic. Groups like Voices not only brought concerns from outside the courtroom into the courts but also used the discussions in the courtrooms to further their struggles on the streets. For example, after the Koushal judgment, LGBTKQHI groups in India decided to thoroughly document the harassment faced by sexual minorities due to the presence of anti-sodomy law, a move made in response to the judges' remarks that Section 377 is not used to prosecute identities. A group named 207 Against 377, a coalition of 207 organizations implementing rights-based HIV/AIDS intervention under the platform of Pehchan (an initiative by global health to bring a rights-based approach to HIV/AIDS work), was formed to undertake advocacy against the Koushal judgment at the grassroots level. Other organizations such as ALF in Bengaluru have started to meticulously document the everyday impact of Section 377 on sexual minorities. This shows the dynamic process in which law and social movements work.

In the case of NALSA, transgender and hijra groups secured legal rights without having to put up much fight. The legal activism by groups like UNDP and NALSA before the filing of the petition in 2012 was strategic and helped them to gain a positive judgment. The positive legal outcome does not mean that engagement with law has ended. They have to work with officials at the state and federal levels to make the rights they gained in NALSA a reality, as there are still many hurdles in the implementation of the law, including the current federal government's attempts to undermine some of the gains made through NALSA by proposing a bill in parliament in 2016.[30] Transgender and hijra groups across the country protested, demanding that the state include them in the legislative process as well as implement NALSA recommendations. In this way, law and social movements have been working concurrently with each other.

Second, both Koushal and NALSA indicate a connection between biopolitics and law. The biopolitical project of HIV/AIDS initially drew marginalized groups into contestations over legal claims, making part of the demand to adjust the needs of sexual governance with older juridical laws. Because of the existence of criminal laws, such as Section 377, that affect a broad spectrum of sexual minorities, this became an important target for activist groups after 2001. Despite the fact that the HIV/AIDS biopower projects rallied for these legal changes, these struggles are not limited to groups that are included in these programs. A broad spectrum of sex and gender minorities are drawn into these legal struggles and, as a result, expand the rights-based claims made on the state. In fact, queer women were also able to use the legal field to demand visibility.

Additionally, these projects move beyond rights-based health claims into other realms and afford an opportunity for activist groups to also demand protections against discrimination and violence, as well as demand equality before law. Whereas in the case of NALSA groups such as UNDP used the context of HIV/AIDS to sensitize the judiciary and lay the background work for a positive legal outcome, in the case of Section 377 HIV/AIDS became an important argument in the initial contestations in the courtrooms. Even if HIV/AIDS is the background or the foreground of these debates over sexual governance, identities that are part of modern governance (and hence biopower) are unleashed in this process.

Third, despite different legal outcomes, a close reading of both Koushal and NALSA indicates that there is tolerance toward identities and intolerance toward nonnormative sex acts. The Koushal judgment upheld the anti-sodomy law and argued that Section 377 does not violate constitutional rights to liberty and dignity. Furthermore, the judges remarked that the sodomy law does not discriminate against sexual minorities as it regulates acts, not identities. By doing so, the apex court constructed acts in opposition to identities. As Janet Halley points out, "The duality of sodomy status [as] sometimes an index of identity, sometimes an index of acts—is a rhetorical mechanism in the subordination of homosexual identity and superordination of heterosexual identity."[31] In declaring that identities are not prosecuted, Koushal denied the fact that identities are policed through acts. Furthermore, acts are used as alibis to deny recognition of identities. This legal instability also gave activist groups the opportunity to periodically challenge the dichotomy between acts and identities. While homosexuality should not be reduced to sodomy, in the process of rallying against anti-sodomy law, activist groups made connections between identities and acts, and they continue to fight for the state to recognize their oppression due to the presence of the anti-sodomy law.

This debate around acts and identity is further complicated in the case of NALSA, and it indicates a discrepancy in the legal investment in identities. While NALSA recognizes transgender and other gender-variant identification as a fundamental right guaranteed by the Indian Constitution, by remaining silent about sex acts, the court has also bifurcated acts and identities. Because of the history of policing of hijras and transgender people in India, Section 377 gains prominence not only as an anti-sodomy law but also as a law that regulates the personhood of gender-variant persons. In the case of transgender people, their personhood and gender expression are used to police acts, and yet this is completely ignored in NALSA. As a result, the implications of Section 377 on the routine and everyday policing of gender-variant bodies are denied. Once again, there is an opposition that is constructed between acts and identities in the legal arena. Recognized identities are hollowed out, with sex acts playing a major role.

Conclusion

These developments indicate that these rights projects produce complicity, ambivalence, and entanglement with the state for marginalized groups. This is evident in the fact that despite the efforts of minority groups to articulate rights in a broader framework, the courts granted them only rights that are very narrow in their focus. This does not mean that rights projects have to be completely rejected. Section 377 struggles showcase how rights debates in the courtroom also generated a social movement that broadened the understanding of sexual rights and other issues faced by sexual/gender minorities in India. Despite disagreement among activist groups about the centrality placed on Section 377 to further LGBTKQHI rights, the law generated productive conversations around sexuality and rights. The struggles in the courtrooms also served as a means to broaden the politics of sexual minorities.

In contrast to long legal battle against Section 377, in the case of NALSA, within two years of filing petitions in the Supreme Court there was a positive outcome. This was because strategic voices in the judiciary were successfully mobilized by governmentality groups to gain legal recognition in the courts. Moreover, in contrast to Section 377 legal struggles that encountered opposition from conservative religious forces, NALSA did not generate any such opposition. The focus on civil rights in the petition and the demand to extend constitutional guarantees of freedom and dignity to previously marginalized groups were favorably received by the judiciary. Similarly, in the case of NALSA, while transgender and hijra groups received positive recognition, this does not mean that it will easily materialize into substantive rights unless these groups actively monitor the state. Sealing oneself off from processes of government that permeate all of society may not be an option; rather, it may be more useful for activists to assume tactical positions within the regimes of governance themselves. Governmentality projects can also produce active political subjects.

The comparative study of Koushal and NALSA illuminates how biopower strategies can produce different outcomes for different groups, indicating the unpredictable impact of these projects on differently marginalized groups. Despite the fact that LGBKQ and transgender/hijra groups have been part of the same HIV/AIDS biopower projects and their political subjectivities mobilized in and through these projects, the legal outcomes are different. This might be because despite the stigma and marginalization of gender nonconformity, transgender/hijra subjects are not perceived as foreign and un-Indian. The hypervisibility of hijras in the Indian public sphere would make such a denial impossible. In contrast, the argument that homosexuality is un-Indian is widely used by groups that oppose reform to Section 377. But the temporary defeat of Section 377 does not mean that biopower projects have been totally defeated nor that governmental strategies are completely ineffective in challenging juridical state power. Rather, it indicates the messiness and unpredictability of the governance processes as well as the continuing tension and conflict between shifting modes of power. But the messiness and unpredictability are not debilitating per se. The contradictory legal outcomes in NALSA and Koushal offered yet another strategic opportunity for activist groups to fight juridical power. Activist groups used the NALSA judgment to poignantly highlight the contradictions of recognizing identities but criminalizing sex acts. When the SC admitted a review petition to reconsider the Koushal judgment in 2016, LGBTQKHI groups were armed with the newfound rights that they gained from NALSA and tactically used this to challenge Section 377. More particularly, transgender/hijra groups made particular submissions to the court highlighting the contradictory ways in which the court had granted them rights. These developments further help us to understand how biopolitical projects can also (in)directly contribute to the need and awareness for critical collaboration among the governed.

5

Interconnected Rights

I have nothing but happiness that 24 years after the first AIDS *Bhedbhav Virodhi Andolan* petition against Section 377 in 1994, queer people will have won the right to breathe and to dream. Yet, we have never been alone in not having the right to be who we are. If there is one measure of the injustice and inequalities that define us today as a society, it is how many of us live at some distance from the dignities our Constitution imagined—the dignity of a home and a wage, of a life without fear and violence, of a right to choose to live, of a right to express ourselves, of a right to believe in the possibility of justice at all.
—Gautam Bhan, 2018

On September 6, 2018, a nine-member constitutional bench of the Indian Supreme Court declared the criminalization of private, consensual, adult same-sex sex unconstitutional. This decision came after nearly two and a half decades of legal battles and social movement struggles outside the courts. The judgment was received nationally and internationally as a long-awaited and positive development. It has been welcomed as a decision that recognizes discrimination based on sexual orientation and restores fundamental rights to queer people. It has also been described by some as an important step toward building a more liberal and tolerant Indian society.[1] The court's decision also brought an overwhelming and triumphant sense that sexual minorities are finally living in a free India. The court's decision settles the matter for consenting adults in the private sphere and opens up the possibility of LGBTKQHI communities fighting for full citizenship—including marriage, adoption, and inheritance rights.

However, despite this legal victory, activists will also have to face numerous social and cultural barriers for nonnormative sex to be accepted and recognized. Even though some of the religious groups who earlier fought to uphold Section 377 changed their stance during the final hearing of the case, this should not be taken as a total defeat of conservative and anti-gay positions. Despite the fact that conservative groups did not maintain their legal fight, they continue to argue that homosexuality is "unnatural" and, by extension, unacceptable. Moreover, even though Section 377 has been reformed, this does not guarantee that everyday violence against sexual minorities will end, as the anti-sodomy law is not the only statute that regulates nonnormative gender identities and sex acts. ITPA, public nuisance laws, public indecency laws, and beggary laws will continue to be in effect. However, the awareness generated by the anti-Section 377 social movements, in addition to the gains made in the courts, might help to challenge arbitrary police violence and criminalization more broadly. Sexual minorities' success also indicates that gender identity, sexual orientation, and sexual rights now have legal precedence in India. These successes and the vision of social justice (as expressed in the quote above) that was expressed in the process of this fight indicate that rights claims and social transformation are not contradictory processes. In fighting discriminatory laws and policies, sexual minorities not only challenged violence, stigma, and discrimination but also offered new, transformative visions that would further help democratize Indian politics.

Biopolitics Three Ways

The SC's recent decision and the gains sexual minorities made in the past two decades perfectly illustrate this book's main contention that in order to be effective, biopolitical projects need the engagement of the governed. In turn, the governed can also make demands on the state. As gay men, transgender women, and sex workers were incorporated into the state's biopolitical projects, these projects did not just produce "docile" subjects; they also produced politically active subjects who used these biopolitical spaces to demand full citizenship. In this sense, then, the story of biopolitics in India is incomplete if we don't consider negotiation, resistance, and social movement mobilization. The political subjectivities that are expressed in this process showcase the resilience of sexual minorities in negotiating, resisting, and reworking these discourses in their own favor. This is succinctly captured in the words of Abhina Ahar, a transgender activist and a representative of Pehchan project, which aims to improve health services for sexual minorities through community involvement and advocating for rights. When I asked her what impact the HIV/AIDS epidemic has had on the rights of sexual minorities, she responded,

> Thanks to HIV/AIDS, MSM and transgender individuals are much more out and open. The entire movement of sexual minorities has been fueled because of HIV money. It has definitely contributed over the period of two decades to build rights-based struggles, as they have used the money and resources that were given for HIV to advocate for their rights. And today, if the communities are coming forward to talk about their issues, it is because of this. Maybe you wouldn't see the scenario you see right now if HIV was not an issue. The fortunate part is that they have used this money very wisely to organize a social movement.

While Abhina focuses on resources and how social movements have strategically used them to bargain with the state, I interpret this also as a kind of shorthand meant to describe the tactical nature of politics as well as the state's receptiveness to being challenged when it agrees to share power with marginalized groups.

However, sharing power with the state does not always lead to the desired outcomes, and the story of biopower is not always one of success. The demands of sex workers for the recognition of sexual labor as a legitimate form of work is still under assault. Additionally, the gains sex workers made in mobilizing themselves as a political community come undone whenever there is a new proposal to tighten or reform trafficking laws, as their energies are expended in fighting these agendas. Even so, in 2007 sex workers were able to successfully fight an amendment to the ITPA that conflated sex work and trafficking. They faced a similar threat when the Indian government appointed the Verma Committee to examine possible reform of sexual assault laws in light of the gruesome murder and rape of a young woman in New Delhi in 2012.[2] Although primarily concerned with targeting rape and sexual assault, the committee's proposed bill incorporated a range of other offenses dealing with violence against women. By proposing to bring consensual sex work under the ambit of sexual exploitation, the criminal law bill of 2012 conflated definitions of trafficking with consensual sex work. These proposals were put forward despite the fact that sex worker groups appealed before the committee to include violence against sex workers, which often goes unnoticed by law enforcement, in the bill.[3] However, they found not only that their appeal was not taken seriously but also that consensual sex work was being included in the definition of sexual exploitation. Sex worker groups contested these amendments, arguing that the inclusion of voluntary and consenting sex workers in any legal definition of exploitation set back the national struggle for sex workers' dignity. The National Network of Sex Workers appealed to the president of India to reject the criminal law ordinance.[4] Due to their sustained protests and appeals, sex workers' groups successfully blocked the proposed legislation.

Most recently, in 2016 the federal Ministry of Women and Child Development (MWCD) tabled in parliament a new Trafficking of Persons (Prevention, Protection and Rehabilitation) Bill, legislation that was approved by the lower house in 2018. Even though the MWCD presented the bill as an attempt to provide a comprehensive response to trafficking by broadening the definition of trafficking (the current law addresses only trafficking related to sex work), sex worker groups feel that it is yet another attack on their rights, as it conflates forced and coercive labor with consenting sex work. Some critiques of the bill are that it increases the power of state institutions to rescue and rehabilitate victims of trafficking, a strategy that has already been proven ineffective. In addition to replicating a failed model of rescue and rehabilitation, the bill also has been critiqued for a lack of clarity in how it interacts with existing laws related to trafficking and forced labor.[5] Critics of the bill fear that because Indian policy makers have often viewed trafficking purely through the lens of *sex* trafficking, the bill will adversely impact sex workers. If the anti-trafficking bill passes the upper house of parliament and becomes law, it will represent a huge setback for sex workers who, through collective mobilization, have attempted to combat the stereotype of the sex worker victim in need of rescue and rehabilitation. Rather, they have showcased their strength and agency through their political organizing.

Biopolitical discourses and anti-trafficking discourses are crosscutting; sometimes they produce contradictory and uneven outcomes for sex workers. Biopolitical projects have empowered sex workers to articulate their economic and political marginality as well as to demand rights and recognition for their sexual labor. Yet in anti-trafficking discourses, sex workers are effectively reduced to gendered victims and face opposition from anti-trafficking groups, who define sex work as fundamentally oppressive. Furthermore, because of transnational pressure on the Indian state to reform its trafficking laws and straighten its record, anti-trafficking agendas continue to undermine sex workers' mobilization for the recognition of sex work as labor.[6] In this sense, sex workers have to overcome not only national legal hurdles but also transnational carceral agendas that erase their agency and deny them their right to self-determination. It is still to be seen whether they will be able to sustain this fight in the future by relying on health projects alone.

In contrast, HIV/AIDS biopolitics and transnational human rights advocacy came together to lend more strength to gay rights than sex workers received. They have also mobilized sexual minorities to fight back against archaic and repressive laws and helped build a national social campaign that pressured the Indian state to reform its laws. In the fight against Section 377, transnational norms and legal precedents aligned well with social movement demands for reform and recognition. Even though the Section 377 struggles suffered a temporary setback in 2013, the alignment of biopolitical interests, transnational human rights, and social movement goals ultimately led to the resounding victory that activists had sought. This was a win for marginalized groups' use of biopolitics—a win that cast India in a positive light on the global stage and set legal precedent that might inspire former British colonies, many of which have exactly the same legislation in place, to reform their own penal codes.[7] Furthermore, social movement struggles around Section 377 also strengthened the gay rights movement in India. The fact that there is a robust LGBTKQHI movement in India today is attributable to the Section 377 struggles. Still, despite the fact that these struggles started as a fight against both general violence related to sexual acts (not necessarily sexual orientation alone) as well as police violence, as the movement widened this emphasis on public violence shifted to an emphasis on the recognition of identities and the protection of privacy. Identity-based and privacy-based rights are very important, and the extended way in which privacy is articulated in the jurisprudence not just as "spatial privacy" but also as a "decisional privacy" may help the wider LGBTKQIH community—not just middle-class gay men. Yet the focus on identities has relegated sexuality into an essential, fixed trait. While the strategic adoption of sexual essentialism may temporarily help the LGBTKQIH community gain social and legal acceptance, it can also exclude individuals and groups for whom sexuality is neither fixed nor an identity (which is a large majority of sexual minorities in India).

In contrast to sex workers and gay groups, when it came to transgender rights, biopolitical, transnational human rights, and national interests aligned, and there was no national or transnational opposition to their rights-based claims. By successfully mobilizing the judiciary, they were able to gain significant legal rights, including the right to self-identity (as male, female, or third gender) and affirmative action in employment and education. This was a historic win, one that potentially rectifies historical wrongs.[8] But without significant political will on the part of the federal and state governments, NALSA will remain toothless (as the SC directed the federal government to design policy to make the rights a reality). Moreover, their rights came under assault when in 2016 the Ministry of Social Justice and Empowerment drafted a Transgender Persons Protection Bill, which was approved by the cabinet. The bill was heavily critiqued by the transgender and hijra communities for watering down many important provisions in NALSA. In particular, the government's new bill does not recognize the right to self-identity and instead prescribes that transgender individuals go through a bureaucratic process to establish their gender identity.[9] Furthermore, the bill does not make any mention of affirmative action in education and employment, as was recommended by the SC. In addition, the bill also introduces new clauses that would potentially recriminalize the community, including increased penalties for begging.[10] Because it has been ostracized, begging and alms seeking has been a very important source of income for the hijra community. Despite the fact that transgender groups across the country weighed in and presented their objections to the bill, the government went ahead and presented the bill retaining these problematic provisions. Moreover, the impending trafficking bill in parliament adds to the criminalization of the transgender community, who are also often reliant on sex work for their livelihood. The contradictory move of the state to superficially recognize identities and yet continue to criminalize begging and sex work will mean that transgender and hijra groups continue to face criminalization despite being recognized as rights-bearing citizens.

In this sense, then, transphobic and transprotectionist approaches (even though they seem like opposing strategies) are closely linked, and the state can often rely on a complex interplay of both approaches in order to maintain its legitimacy.[11] By recognizing gender identity, the Indian state has established itself as modern and liberal. As a result, it has gained significant legitimacy in the international arena. However, by simultaneously criminalizing begging and sex work, thereby recriminalizing transgender communities, it also reinforces the popular norms that marginalize them.

The contradictory move by the Indian state to simultaneously recognize and recriminalize marginalized groups indicates the limitations and complexity of deploying biopower strategies to gain rights and recognition. Whereas the recognition of identity will help the state to entrench its disciplinary power in the communities, by criminalizing the acts of both begging and sex work, the state reestablishes its juridical hold on these communities. Discussion of the impending bill makes clear the risk that the political efforts of marginalized communities can be subverted, appropriated, or redeployed by the state to strengthen its entrenchment in such communities. However, the complexity of this should not alone lead to sweeping statements either against or in favor of social movements' adoption of rights-based claims. As Foucault reminds us, there are no "innocent and risk-free political strategies."[12] The fight around the bill has significantly politicized transgender groups in India, expanding their political base and struggles. On December 28, 2018, hundreds of transgender individuals and their supporters marched to Indian parliament carrying signs saying "Kill the Bill," demanding that the bill not be presented to the upper house of the parliament. They also declared it a day of rage, showing their discontent with the bill. In this sense, the state provoked these communities and in the process unwittingly politicized them to fight for their rights.

This comparative analysis of three biopolitical struggles reveals that while sexual rights discourses are expanding in India, there are also simultaneous constraints placed on these rights. Carceral voices that criminalize sex work and begging (policies that criminalize the poor) are also being strengthened because of the contradictory policies pursued by the Indian state. In this sense, then, the redistributive rights for sexual minorities is still being contested.[13] This is best exemplified by the fact that the Indian state has superficially accepted LGBTQKHI identities, yet simultaneously discounted economic rights, such as affirmative action for transgender and hijra groups and the labor rights of sex workers. Recognizing identities helps the Indian state to enhance its global image as a democratic and liberal state marching its way into modernity, allowing it to gain legitimacy in the global human rights arena.

The comparative approach illustrates that in a globalizing world, sexual minorities face multiple opportunities and challenges to their rights. And these challenges are not necessarily from within the nation-state but can also come from the transnational sphere. Within the LGBTQ human rights literature there are two competing understandings of global LGBTQ human rights. The first position views these rights as universal, undermining the particularities of sexual struggles in "local" contexts (especially in the non-Western contexts). The second position uncritically celebrates a global gay movement as inclusive and progressive.[14] These two positions don't completely capture the developments in India. Sexual minorities in India are not just merely emulating global gay rights agendas, nor are they completely rejecting them. This polarized understanding of rights misses the fact that the interactions between transnational norms and domestic structures are neither uniformly negative nor uniformly positive. This is not a simple story of surrender or resistance. Moreover, such a position fails to appreciate the complexity and diversity of organizing around sexual rights in local contexts.[15] As Ara Wilson reminds us, sexual rights are shaped by "historical moments and the particular institutions, networks, and venues of organizing."[16] For example, while sex workers in India used global health and HIV/AIDS discourses to advance their social movements, they also rejected global trafficking discourses. They coined the powerful slogan "save us from the saviors" to resist global projects that didn't take into consideration local social movement demands. Similarly, in the fight against the anti-sodomy law, social movements have used global legal precedents and global gay rights frameworks to demand legal reforms, but they have also articulated this fight as a postcolonial struggle against the imposition of colonial values and laws. Finally, transgender groups in India have strategically used the support they had in certain sections of the judiciary to gain historical recognition. While doing so they also drew on transnational discourses as well as local histories of tolerance toward gender-nonnormative individuals. To shed more light on the specificities of the Indian struggles, it is also important to understand the particular relationship between the state and marginalized groups in India.

"Enchantment of the State" and Sexual Minorities

The past few decades of sexual minority struggles in India have also helped amplify the idea that the state is responsible for social justice as well as for establishing diversity and difference as important constitutional values that need to be protected. In order to understand the particular ways in which sexual minorities make the state responsible for social justice, I turn to the particular relationship marginalized groups have with the postcolonial state. To understand this relationship, we need to understand marginalized groups' "enchantment" with the Indian state.[17] The popular conception of the state in India, as political philosopher Sudipta Kaviraj points out, is different from the nation, government, police, and bureaucracy: "It was literally a poor people's version of the welfare state which had too little to provide them with normal everyday welfare, but came to their rescue in the desperate mitigation of crisis."[18] Furthermore, the state is implicitly invoked in every demand for justice, equality, dignity, and assistance—as such demands can be made only it its name. Additionally, the state is expected to meet all these demands, revealing that it plays a major role in the imagination of marginalized groups in India. This is an "enchantment of the state" that is unique to India. Jyoti Puri points to this particular enchantment with the state and the animation of the state in the imagination of activists in the context of Section 377 legal struggles. While Puri's work helps us to understand how the state is not just external but also internal to the very groups that try to challenge it, I build on her analysis and add to this understanding by teasing out the particular ways in which these imaginations are articulated in the sight of law.

According to Kaviraj, this popular idealization of the state offers a common citizenship to disadvantaged groups even though they are disillusioned with the Indian nation. "It [the state] has cut itself loose from its attachment to the conceptions of the nation," Kaviraj writes, "but has attained a strange apotheosis as the only repository, though elusively present, of people's moral aspirations."[19] This is why, according to Kaviraj, even with liberalization of the Indian economy and the reduction of the state's interference in social and economic life, this enchantment of the state is still undiminished. This image of the state as a repository of people's moral aspirations can also help us to understand the politics of sexual minorities in contemporary India. State recognition has been central to sexual minority struggles, whether demanding rights or appealing to the state to reform its criminal law. Whereas sexual minorities did not have this "moral voice" to appeal to the state before the HIV/AIDS epidemic because they were not even part of civil society, the new relationship that marginalized groups have forged with the state as well as their roles in HIV/AIDS programs enable them to demand moral accountability from the state. Whereas earlier they had been completely denied any notion of social welfare or social rights because of their "moral" unbelonging to the state, the situational pragmatism of HIV/AIDS compelled the state to take on a developmental role, whether in distributing condoms or providing health and counseling services. Thus, biopolitical projects brought this notion of the state (even if it is elusive) as responsible for the "moral aspiration" of its citizens within the reach of sexual minorities who previously encountered only the raw and repressive power of the police. These projects also afforded sexual minorities a sense of "moral" belonging to the state, as they could use health and biological claims to demand rights.

Additionally, in the process of fighting for their rights, sexual minorities further amplified this idea of the state as responsible not only for its sexual development goals but also for social justice. And they were able to successfully expand the idea of constitutional morality, which for the first time was put forward in the case of Section 377 struggles by groups like Voices. Voices demanded that the state not rely on popular morality as a basis for deciding the rights of minority groups but rather be accountable to constitutional values and fundamental rights that are guaranteed to all the citizens.[20] Hence upholding constitutional morality would mean radically reinterpreting the constitution to include previously marginalized groups.[21] Their demand found resonance in a positive judgment of the Delhi High Court in 2009, when the judges declared that constitutional morality should prevail over popular morality and unequivocally stated that those who are perceived by the majority as deviants or different cannot be excluded or ostracized.[22] The court's judgment placed diversity and difference at the heart of Indian constitutional values and as central to Indian democracy. It was also seen as a torchbearer for a more general understanding of oppression and social exclusion, as well as the meaning of freedom and dignity. As a result, it has been hailed as a milestone in the jurisprudence on pluralism and diversity in India.[23] Despite the fact that the 2009 Naz judgment was later reversed by the SC, the sentiment about protecting the most marginalized continued to resonate widely through these social movement struggles. The SC further strengthened this understanding when it ultimately declared Section 377 unconstitutional. By emphasizing Indian constitutional values and the fundamental rights guaranteed to all citizens, the court steered the discussion away from popular morality to constitutional morality. This was poignantly expressed in the remarks of one of the justices: "There is an unbridgeable divide between the moral values on which it [Section 377] is based and the values of the Constitution."[24] Apologizing to the LGBTKQHI community for the historical wrong done to them, the judges upheld constitutional morality as a touchstone of Indian democracy, as opposed to popular morality, which can stifle rights and liberties. Moreover, the court's stance on popular morality—especially in the context of Hindu right-wing forces attacking any kind of difference as antinational—is a huge triumph for minority groups.

This emphasis on constitutional morality also means thinking of the constitution as a living and breathing document that can be adapted to the changing needs of Indian society; for example, the SC justices remarked, "A democratic constitution like ours is an organic and breathing document with senses which are very much alive to its surroundings, for it has been created in such a manner that it can adapt to the needs and developments taking place in the society."[25] These remarks are in line with the vision of Dr. B. R. Ambedkar, the architect of the Indian Constitution who envisioned it as serving the needs of a modern society.[26] In highlighting the organic nature of the constitution, the judges also focus on the idea of a transformative constitutionalism that adopts a pragmatic lens with which to interpret, change, and adopt constitutional values in accordance with the demands of society. They further highlight that it is pragmatism rather than moralism that ought to steer the country and its institutions in a democratic, egalitarian direction.

The courts have expanded the concept of social justice not only by declaring constitutional morality as superseding popular morality but also by interpreting fundamental rights and directive principles of the constitution (where the right to affirmative action and economic justice are discussed) in the NALSA case:[27]

> By recognizing TGs [transgender individuals] as third gender, this Court is not only upholding the rule of law but also advancing justice to the class, so far deprived of their legitimate natural and constitutional rights. It is, therefore, the only just solution which ensures justice not only to TGs but also justice to the society as well. Social justice does not mean equality before law in papers but to translate the spirit of the constitution, enshrined in the Preamble, the Fundamental Rights and the Directive Principles of State Policy into action, whose arms are long enough to bring within its reach and embrace this right of recognition to the TGs which legitimately belongs to them.[28]

Along with NALSA and the decriminalizing of sodomy, the Indian SC has recently come up with several other socially progressive judgments around privacy and adultery that build on this idea of constitutional morality, further strengthening sexual rights and sexual autonomy.[29] In the SC's most recent decision on charges of rape by a sex worker, the court reversed an earlier judgment and declared that sex workers have a right to refuse services and seek redress when they are forced by their clients to perform sexual acts.[30]

By paying attention to the particular relationship between marginalized groups and the Indian state, we can understand that state power can also be pressed into the service of the marginalized. Furthermore, it is by invoking the state's primary responsibility to constitutional rights and social justice that minority groups have been able to expand rights-based claims. They have successfully shown this not only by approaching the courts but also through simultaneously building social movements to amplify the idea of the accountable state. In doing so, they have also strengthened the constitutional values of freedom, equality, and social justice, which are ultimately going to guarantee and protect the rights of sexual minorities.

The Interconnectedness of Rights

On a winter afternoon in 2007, I accompanied members belonging to the New Delhi–based coalition Voices to join a protest march organized by the Narmada Bachao Andolan (NBA), a people's movement that has been fighting against big dams and challenging the Indian state's neoliberal agendas.[31] Even with my limited exposure to New Delhi's queer politics, I had known that Voices' main goals were not only to expand the Section 377 debate and build a social movement outside the courtrooms but also to build alliances and solidarity with other social movements. From its inception, Voices has focused on the links between sexuality and other social inequalities (such as caste, class, and religion) and taken an intersectional approach to sexuality and rights. This intersectional approach is best captured in one of Voices' campaigns where they explicitly articulated the need to build broad-based coalitions for social justice:

> The demand to decriminalize Section 377 is an issue of social justice that everyone, irrespective of their gender or sexual orientation should be concerned about—for the struggle against control of sexuality is directly linked with our struggle for women's rights, our fight against fundamentalism, our vision of a just world, where people have the freedom to be different and yet be treated as equal. "Voices Against 377" aims to raise awareness about the violation of people's fundamental rights and specifically the marginalization and criminalization of same-sex-desiring people, including gay, lesbian, transgender and bisexual communities enabled by this law.

While most of Voices' previous efforts have been dialogues with other social movements on the issue of Section 377 and the criminalization and marginalization of sexual minorities, that day Voices members were there to show solidarity with the NBA protesters. The protest march brought thousands of people, including farmers, tribal groups, and environmental groups, to protest callous developmental programs that disregard displacement of people and the destruction of their livelihoods. This predominantly class-based struggle, where questions of sexuality are sidelined, is not where one expects Voices to build a coalition. However, the Voices members' signs had messages that indicated queer solidarity with other struggles as well as signs protesting state violence (including a sign against Section 377). As the signs were being made, there were a few informal chats with people who showed interest, but the rest of our time there we marched through central Delhi joining in chants protesting the displacement of people by big dams. Even though Voices' presence was minor and perhaps insignificant for the organizers of the march, the symbolic value of this protest cannot be understated. However, the power of such gestures to advance and deepen conversations about coalition building between and solidarity among marginalized groups seeking social justice became apparent many years after this event.

In 2016, a popular television news channel, NDTV, organized a prime-time debate titled "Time to Scrap Section 377?" on the show *The Big Fight*. The host invited both secular and religious groups to debate the issue. There were representatives from the three major religions (Hindu, Muslim, and Christian) as well as activists, activist lawyers, and a federal minister representing the government's position. The choice of participants indicates that the host was expecting a polarized and emotional debate for and against decriminalization. But the debate took an unexpected turn when even conservative voices on the debate took critical stances on the law. Their stance was that though homosexuality is "unnatural," they disagreed with the criminalization of the queer community. This came as a surprise to the host, who even remarked, "If no one here seems to support criminalization, then who is fighting in the courts?" While this shift in the conservative position was perhaps an early indication of the legal victory that would later come, what stood out to me was a comment made by one of the activist lawyers. Toward the end of the conversation when the host solicited final comments from the participants, Danish Sheikh, an activist lawyer from the Bengaluru-based ALF, turned to one of his fellow participants, a representative from the Muslim Personal Law Board, who until then was arguing that homosexuality was "unnatural." Addressing him, Sheikh said,

> You are basing your arguments in religion and that Islam does not permit homosexuality; I am also a Muslim. By siding with the majority voice in this issue, you have done a great disservice to not only queer Muslims like me, but also to the entire Muslim community in this country. The

Delhi High Court did not just grant rights to sexual minorities alone, but it spoke for rights of all minorities. And the court has granted horizontal rights not just vertical rights. Who do you think suffers most from discrimination in housing in this country? Muslims! By going against queer groups, you have also betrayed the Muslim community, the Naz judgment would have also helped Muslims fight discrimination.

Even though this critical point was lost in the hurried debate wrap-up, for me Sheikh's comments underlined the way that Section 377 debates have progressed in the past two decades. By articulating that the injustice of Section 377 ought to be a concern to all other minorities, Sheikh argued that all marginalized people can benefit by participating in movements that uphold diversity and difference as a value. In this sense, then, Sheik's position articulates sexual diversity not as a separate value that benefits only a minority of the population but as a value that promotes diversity in general.

This need to articulate rights as being interconnected also becomes strikingly evident in another recent decision of the SC that declared privacy a fundamental right. This privacy judgment (*Justice K. Puttaswamy v. Union of India*) came from a completely unlikely place: not from sexual minority struggles but through a legal petition that challenged the Indian state's intrusion into its citizens' privacy in the name of biometrics and unique national identity (*Aadhaar*). Despite the fact that this judgment was not about sexual rights, the judges touched upon the privacy and dignity of sexual minorities, openly remarking that sexual orientation is an essential attribute of privacy. This was a huge and unexpected gain for sexual minorities, and the judges' broad articulation of privacy as a "right to be left alone" is of immense value to the communities whose dignity has historically been violated with impunity by the state. The importance of this judgment and the awareness of the interconnectedness of rights is poignantly expressed in the remark of transgender rights activist and lawyer Jayna Kothari:

While we should celebrate and savor the gains of at this far-reaching judgment [on privacy], what are the learnings? As a women's rights and transgender rights activist and lawyer, I find this judgment points out the need for the gender rights movements to align with other social movements and the interconnectedness of rights. The privacy rights battle in the context of *Aadhaar* was a battle that the LGBT movement and the women's rights movement had not engaged with. We are incredibly fortunate that we had a Court that rose unanimously in favor of declaring proudly the rights to sexual orientation and gender identity but this should only strengthen our resolve to work for the protection of rights across movements, of class, gender, caste, disability and religion if we want to strive to protect diversity and difference.[32]

Kothari's comments indicate the potential for intersectional politics to imagine new rights that are unexpected and unanticipated. In articulating the need for alliances between marginalized groups and social causes, Kothari's comments expand the idea of social justice and forge new political imaginaries. They point to the radical possibility of the law to reimagine rights in a new way, to interpret politics in a new way. It is this potential for reimagining rights themselves, rather than simply guaranteeing them for particular groups, that makes the law a radical site. By articulating sexual rights as interconnected with other social justice issues, sexual minority groups in India also began to transform the language of rights and law. Perhaps this is where law's persisting allure lies—not in the concrete promise of rights but in its transformative potential and the ability of that potential to rekindle social justice, inclusion, and democracy.

This expanded idea of social justice does not mean that sexual minorities can seamlessly form alliances with each other. There are many obstacles and challenges to such alliance building. For example, in the process of making a case for affirmative action in education and employment, some transgender groups have represented sex work as an abject form of labor that they are forced into because of the historical discrimination and stigma attached to nonnormative gender. While the demand for equal employment opportunities is legitimate and important, if not articulated carefully this desire can also reproduce middle-class aspirations that marginalize sex work and frame it as the most undesired form of labor. This could go against the struggles of sex workers (both ciswomen and transwomen) who have been consistently fighting for their labor rights. Transgender rights struggles that do not consider these intersections could reproduce the same inequalities they seek to fight.

A 2015 matrimonial ad further illustrated the challenges of forming alliances among various sexual minority groups. In the first ever gay matrimonial ad, the mother of a prominent gay activist sought a vegetarian groom for her son, and in the style of a typical matrimonial ad, she also indicated her caste preference (even while stating that caste is not a bar). The advertisement was hailed by some as a sign of progress, but it also came under significant criticism from the queer community, who saw it as a perfect example of "homonormativity," where the desire for same-sex relationships is articulated within dominant heteronormative institutions and frameworks. More particularly for the Indian context, they critiqued the ways in which the advertisement reinforced caste-based norms of marriage.[33] It was noted that in India only 6 percent of marriages are intercaste; the fact that the advertisement does not challenge this indicates how deep-seated caste ideologies can permeate the LGBTQ movement.[34] The debate around the matrimonial advertisement showcased the fault lines within LGBTKQHI politics.

Thus, a comparative approach to sexual minority politics does not simply reproduce the desire for solidarity politics but is attentive to political visions and strategies that bridge or emphasize differences among and within minority groups. In contexts where sexual diversity rather than sexual identity politics has been made central to political struggles, radical solidarities among sex workers and LGBQK and transgender/hijras groups have been made possible. This is exemplified by groups such as Voices in New Delhi, Telangana Hijra Intersex Transgender Samiti in Hyderabad, and Karnataka Sexual Minorities Forum and Karnataka Sex Workers' Union, both from the state of Karnataka. These groups have pursued non-identity-based politics consciously and built solidarities among various minority groups. In 2014 when the Karnataka police detained 167 members of the transgender community (mostly hijra-identified individuals) under the Karnataka Beggary Act, the Karnataka Sexual Minorities Forum along with other civil societal groups fought this mass detention.[35] They called it a violation of fundamental freedoms of movement guaranteed by the constitution. Most recently, the Karnataka Sexual Minorities Forum, Karnataka Sex Workers' Union, and other civil society organizations have voiced their discontent with the state media's representation of lesbian marriages. Furthermore, these long-standing collaborations have helped these various groups mobilize against the Indian government's recent attempt to pass the problematic anti-trafficking and Transgender Rights Protection bills, articulating these bills as assaults on the idea of the welfare state. A joint statement on these two bills by the Coalition for Sex Worker and Sexual Minority Rights succinctly captures this politics of solidarity: "Both the Bills (Transgender Bill and Trafficking Bill 2018) are fundamentally motivated by a criminalizing impulse. The state instead of taking on welfarist/developmentalist functions chose to focus on incarcerating the poor and marginalized, including sex workers, bonded laborers, contract workers, domestic workers, construction workers, transgender persons, interstate, intra-state and international migrant workers."[36] These solidarity struggles move away from thinking of sexuality only as identity to also articulate it along with class, caste, and other social identities. It is this intersectional politics and the awareness of the interconnected nature of rights that will ultimately sharpen sexual politics in India—not just limit it to only upper-caste, middle-class, English-speaking gays—by rearticulating these politics and making hijras, kothis, and sex workers the reference points for these struggles.

Transnational Lessons from India

In a globalized world where sexual rights have also become an important part not only of global human rights discourses but also of international relations, what lessons can we draw from the struggles of sexual minorities in India? What impact might the Indian struggles have on other similar social movements? Even while situating Indian rights struggles in their particular historical and social context, we can still draw some broad lessons from the social movement successes in India that would be useful for other contexts as well. Perhaps the most immediate impact could be on former British colonies, which have Section 377 in their penal code. In declaring Section 377 unconstitutional, the Indian legal precedent could prove to be an effective tool for activists in former British colonies such as Singapore, Malaysia, Bangladesh, and Pakistan that have the same exact section on their books. Even though these countries are governed by different laws and constitutions, the exemplary example that Indian social movements have set in broadening the debate around

Section 377—especially in articulating it not just as a homosexual law but also as one that impacts heterosexual citizens' sexual expression—can have wider resonance in other contexts as well. The impact of the Indian success has already been felt in Kenya, where LGBTQ groups are also fighting British-era sodomy laws. Soon after the Indian Supreme Court's decision, the Kenyan High Court allowed both pro- and anti-gay-rights groups to make submissions in the court to discuss the relevance of the Indian decision on Kenya's laws.[37]

Recently, the South Asian subcontinent has made tremendous strides in the recognition of gender nonnormativity. Pakistan, Bangladesh, Nepal, and India have all recognized nonbinary gender identities. While this is a huge gain for gender-nonconforming individuals in the subcontinent, there are still several obstacles in implementing these policies and bringing social transformation to these groups.[38] A recent study pointed out that despite the fact that Pakistan recognized a third gender identity for gender-nonconforming individuals, because of the lack of material benefits associated with the third gender category, there has been very little enthusiasm on the part of the community to register as third gender. Similarly, in Bangladesh, despite the fact that the government officially recognized hijras in 2013, the perception of hijras as people who are impotent because of genital differences undermines these progressive reforms. While similar challenges exist in India, transgender and hijra groups there are challenging state bureaucratization and marginalization through welfare discourses. Moreover, they were able to articulate discrimination based on a binary understanding of gender as on par with caste-based discrimination. This has helped them to seek affirmative action in education and employment (even though it is being disputed by the state). These developments in South Asia also call for alliances among gender dissidents in the subcontinent, as an opportunity to mutually learn from and support each other's struggles.

At a theoretical level, the Indian case indicates that the state is not simply antagonistic toward sexually marginalized groups and that particular state institutions can be steered effectively to rally for the rights of the marginalized communities. The HIV/AIDS epidemic effectively created an opening in the state, enabling sexual minorities to act as appendices of the state, further complicating the idea of a state external to the communities it governs. Even when sexual minorities resisted the state, it was not always to negate its power. Rather it was also to amplify the state's responsibility for social justice by upholding constitutionally guaranteed values. The sexual minority struggles in India show that by strengthening the idea of constitutional morality, they could fight against traditionalist and conservative forces that have tried to undermine their rights in the name of popular morality.

The Indian struggles also underscore that without the active participation of marginalized groups and powerful social movement building, there cannot be positive legal change. While the Indian feminist movement had already taught us an invaluable lesson, the sexual minority struggles further strengthen this idea. In this sense, rights claims and emancipatory politics are not contrasting approaches for social struggles. They can be two sides of the same coin. Rights are not invoked solely for harm reduction; communities place great faith in the power of rights to be socially transformative tools. The new dynamic of sexual rights and social change in India is undoubtedly a reason for celebration. At the same time, we must also continue to interrogate the ways in which movements mobilize around rights to make them accountable for social change and transformation.

ACKNOWLEDGMENTS

This book would not have been possible without the intellectual and emotional support of mentors, colleagues, friends, and family. Through over a decade of working on this book I have accrued debt to numerous institutions, organizations, and individuals. Even though a simple "thank-you" may not be enough to repay this debt, I will make an attempt to express my heartfelt gratitude to remind myself of the amazing community of scholars and friends I am surrounded by.

First of all, without the exciting and vibrant legal and political struggles challenging assumptions about sex and gender in contemporary India, this book would have been unthinkable. I feel humbled to have witnessed some of these struggles firsthand and to have learned about them through conversations with numerous people in New Delhi, Bangalore, Kolkata, Rajahmundry, Chennai, and Mumbai. I would like to thank all the organizations and individuals I met during my field research who generously gave me their time for this project. Without their support, this book would not have been possible. Bharosa Trust, DMSC (Durbar Mahila Samanwaya Committee), Godavari Mahila Samakya, Voices Against 377, Delhi Queer Pride Committee, Lawyers Collective, Naz Foundation India, Naz Foundation International, UNDP (United Nations Development Programme), Pahal, Savera, Kinnar Bharati, Mitra Trust, Humsafar Trust, Pehchan-India HIV/AIDS Alliance, Sangama, Alternative Law Forum, Anekha, Karnataka Sexual Minorities Forum, Telengana Hijra Intersex Transgender Samiti, and several other organizations opened their spaces in numerous ways to me. Special thanks to Aryankrishnan Ramakrishnan, Dr. Jayshree Anand, Bharati Dey, Sushant, Dr. Samarjit Jana, Jaya Sharma, Pramada Menon, Meena Seshu, Radhika Chandiramani, Madhu Mehra, Anjali Gopalan, Akshay Khanna, Nandinee Bandhopadhya, Bishaka Lashkar, Sumit Baudh, Tripti Tandon, Ponni Arasu, Gautam Bhan, Earnest Noronha, Rudrani, Aditya Bandopadhyaya, Krishna, Pami, Raju, Rahul, Dr. Venkatesan

Chakrapani, Pallav Patankar, Gowthaman Ranganathan, Living Smile Vidya, Vyjayanti Mogli, Bittu. K, Krishna, Rudrani, Simran Shaikh, and Abhina Aher, all of whom took time out of their busy schedules to talk to me and share their insights and experiences.

I am grateful for my graduate school training at UW–Madison for preparing me to undertake such ambitious and challenging research. I was fortunate to have Myra Marx Ferree as my advisor and mentor there. Myra is an extraordinary mentor; she was also my number one advocate. Her unwavering support did not deter her from giving honest and critical feedback, and she always pushed me to be the best. Even so many years after leaving graduate school, she was willing to read and comment on drafts of the book proposal and chapters. Without her belief in my project, this book would not have come to fruition. At UW–Madison I was also lucky to have support from my incredible dissertation committee: Julie D'Acci, Gay Seidman, Jane Collins, Anne Enke, and Joseph Elder. Julie D'Acci, Gay Seidman, Jane Collins, Mara Loveman, Samer Alatout, Maria Lepowsky, and other faculty members at UW–Madison were very crucial in shaping my intellectual trajectory and success in the program. I am also immensely grateful to Myra for creating a biweekly writing group for her students. The writing group was not only a forum for accountability and feedback but also a safe space that sustained me during the sometimes-grueling graduate school life. I offer my deep gratitude to Myra and other members of the writing group, including Angela Barian, Ayesha Khurshid, Peter Brinson, Jessica Brown, Hae Yeon Choo, Wendy Christensen, Laura Heideman, Susan Rottmann, Sarah Warren.

My time at Harvard as a College Fellow between 2010 and 2012 gave me space to start conceiving of this project as a book. My colleagues at the Committee for Women's, Gender, and Sexuality Studies have shown so much faith in this project. I am especially grateful to Afshane Nazmabadi, Caroline Light, Linda Schlossberg, Robin Bernstein, and Amy Parker for their support and collegiality. Caroline Light and Linda Schlossberg also became my writing companions during weekly on-site writing sessions. I was also lucky to have students like Tara Suri and Jia Hui Lee; their intellectual curiosity and openness to learning always reminded me of why I love my profession. I was also incredibly lucky to have the Andrew Mellon Postdoctoral Fellowship (2012–2014) at USC. Alice Echols, Sharon Hays, and Rhacel Parreñas were incredible feminist mentors. I am particularly grateful for Rhacel, who took me under her wing and plugged me into intellectual networks beyond USC. I thank her for inviting me to participate in the "Intimate Industries in Asia" workshop at Pomona College, as well as the opportunity to participate in the New Directions in Feminist Research workshop. Both workshops helped me to broaden my understanding of sexual economies, and I thank the participants of both these workshops for their feedback and support.

Texas A&M has been my academic home for the past five years, and I am immensely grateful for this opportunity. Without the collegiality and support of my mentors and colleagues in the Department of Sociology and the Women's and Gender Studies Program, this book would not have come to fruition. I am lucky to have a department chair like Jane Sell, whose commitment to seeing junior faculty succeed makes everything easier. She always found ways to get me resources that would help in writing the book. At the Women's and Gender Studies Program I am particularly grateful to Claire Katz, Joan Wolf, Marian Eide, Tasha Dubriwny, and Mindy Bergman for their vision and leadership. I am extremely grateful to Jane Sell, Verna Keith, Jyotsna Vaid, and Vanita Reddy for their incredible mentorship and support. Nancy Plankey-Videla, Joseph Jewell, Dan Humphrey, and Heili Pals always stepped in when I needed advice and support. Vanita Reddy, Dan Humphrey, Carmela Garritano, and Melanie Hawthorne generously provided feedback on my book proposal. Vanita Reddy also read drafts of the book chapters and even stepped in as a copy editor during crunch time. I am ever grateful for her support and mentorship.

I am also lucky to have feminist mentors and supportive communities beyond these institutions. The Future of Minority Studies (FMS) institute, "Queer Politics in a Transnational Context," at Cornell in the summer 2009 had a big role in shaping me as a transnational scholar. I am immensely grateful to Jacqui Alexander and Minnie Bruce Pratt for their nurturance, intellectual energy, and teaching me how to sit with difficult questions. I thank Nadia Ellis, Eng-Beng Lim, Gabeba Baderoon, Erica Lorraine, and other colleagues and friends at the institute for sharing critical thoughts, scholarship on queer politics and pedagogy, and many fun-filled exchanges. Bandana Purkayastha, Manisha Desai, Mangala Subramaniam, Vrushali Patil, and other colleagues at SWS (Sociologists for Women in Society) showed how rewarding it is to be part of a nurturing scholarly community. I want to particularly thank Bandana Purkayastha for her unwavering commitment to creating intellectual safe spaces for women of color. From my first encounter with Jyoti Puri at the South Asia Studies Conference in Madison in 2007 to numerous ASA conferences and other forums, she consistently engaged with my project and gave me valuable input and feedback. Jyoti taught me how to be intellectually rigorous and generous at the same time. Sharmila Rudrappa invited me to present my work at UT Austin and has always been supportive of my work. She also mentored me through the ADVACE scholar-mentor program. I would like to thank Tanya Golash-Boza and Ayu Saraswati at Creative Connections for giving me the opportunity to participate in their writing retreats in Peru and Indonesia. These retreats reinforced for me that the best intellectual work is produced through caring and supportive communities, contemplative practices, and connection with nature.

Without the financial support of ASA's Martin Levin Dissertation Fellowship (2007), National Science Foundation's Dissertation Improvement Grant (2010), and Texas A&M's Glasscock Center for the Humanities Faculty Research Fellowship (2015), I would not have had the financial means to undertake the research for this book. I am also grateful for the Sociology and Women's and Gender Studies Program at Texas A&M for giving me teaching releases in Spring 2015 that helped me to go back to India to conduct additional research for the book.

At NYU Press I would like to thank Monica Casper, Lisa Jean Moore, and Ilene Kalish for taking an interest in the project and putting me in touch with Clara Platter. Clara's trust in the project made everything possible. Her guidance and support made this process bearable and less tedious. I would also like to thank the three anonymous reviewers for taking time to read the manuscript and offer me valuable feedback. I am also very fortunate to have found Jenny Gavacs as my development editor. If not for her input and guidance I would still be struggling with structure and direction for this book. She not only read through numerous iterations of the manuscript but offered her encouragement and support when I needed it the most. Desirae Embree contributed her editorial skills and put up with my last-minute requests for copyediting.

Friends in India and the United States have contributed to this book in direct and indirect ways and have kept me afloat during challenging times. I am deeply grateful to Sudipta Mukhopadhyay for sharing her home and making me feel welcome in New Delhi. She also shared her wide network of friends and NGO contacts, which helped me to start the research. Bindu Menon, Sunandan K. N., Bindu K. C., and Sharmila Sreekumar also opened their homes to me and supported me with their beaming intellectual energy and great conversations. Aryan Ramakrishnan's friendship and comradery sustained me in many doubt-filled and uncertain moments during my field work. Ifat Hamid, Mukta Gosh, Gargi Banerjee, Suresh Rajan, Sushant, and other friends in New Delhi never let me feel home sick. Numerous friends in Madison made graduate school a fun, lively, and nurturing experience. Hae Yeon Choo, Ayesha Khurshid, Wendy Christensen, Joe Gabriel, and Kyurim Kyoung sustained me with good food, conversations, and the emotional support that was needed to get through both graduate school and frigid winters. I leaned on Devin Ryder, Paula Garbarino, Shweta Majumdar, Katie Hasson, Aparna Sharma, and Kellea Miller for friendship and support during my time in Boston and LA. Special thanks to Sungyon Lee and Vanita Reddy for opening their beautiful homes to me in College Station. My friends in Austin—Vanita Reddy, Matt Daniel, Elizabeth Jackson, Sharmila Rudrappa, Amy Moreland, and Melanie Cofield—make me feel grounded there.

My parents, Seshadri Rao and Siva Kumari, provide me with unconditional love and support that makes everything seem possible. They instilled in me the value of hard work and an appreciation for the good life. Knowing that they will be always be by my side gives me confidence to take bold leaps in life. My niece Ujwala Naidu adds brightness to my life, and her presence is a gift. Her enthusiasm to be one of the first readers of this book actually motivated me to complete it. Her sense of fairness and justice makes me very hopeful for the next generation. I also want to thank my sister Lavanya Naidu and my nephew Praveen Naidu for their love and support. Even though my paternal grandmother Manikyamma and maternal grandfather Raja Gopal Rao did not live to see the completion of the book, I continue to feel their love and presence in my life. My Chicago family—Srinivas Kadiam, Madhavi Pollisetti, Rela, Romi, Claire Stewart, Val Stewart, Adam Apostolovich, Louis and Charlie—share joy and holiday cheer with me. Graham Stewart stands by me each day and fills my life with love, lightness, and laughter—all the essential ingredients necessary for focused writing. He joyfully participates in activities that sustain me, from planting trees to hiking Machu Picchu. But more than that, he silently sat with me in our study, working on his latest mapping software while I worked on the book manuscript. Through his everyday presence he strengthened my belief that love is profoundly felt in small acts of kindness and generosity. I am ever grateful for the gift of his love.

Without the support of my feminist sisters Hae Yeon, Ayesha, and Vanita, I would not have come this far. Finding Vanita has been one of the high points of my time at TAMU. She seamlessly balances her role in my life as a mentor, friend, and collaborator, offering me candid advice on book writing and publishing but also standing with me as a friend and witness. I am also lucky that we get to take many US and world adventures together. Ayesha's generosity and kindness are boundless and she always inspires me to be a better person. Meeting Hae Yeon in graduate school was like winning the friendship lottery. I could not have asked for a better friend and intellectual companion. Over a decade and a half of friendship, she has seen me through so much, bearing witness to my personal and professional struggles and successes. I am also lucky that she wrote her book before I did, as she was always there to hold my hand and guide me through this process. I have often relied overmuch on her generosity and support, but she never complains. I am lucky to be sailing the sea of life with these friends by my side.

Abbreviations

ABVA: AIDS Bhedbhav Virodhi Andolan
AIDS: acquired immune deficiency syndrome
ALF: Alternative Law Forum
CBO: community-based organization
DMSC: Durbar Mahila Samanwaya Committee
GMS: Godavari Mahila Samakya
HIV: human immunodeficiency virus
HSS: HIV sentinel surveillance
IDU: injecting drug user
IPC: Indian Penal Code
ITPA: Immoral Traffic Prevention Act
LC: Lawyers Collective
MSM: men who have sex with men
MWCD: Ministry of Women and Child Development
NACO: National AIDS Control Organization
NACP: National AIDS Control Program
NALSA: National Legal Services Agency
NBA: Narmada Bachao Andolan
NGO: nongovernmental organization
PUCL-K: People's Union for Civil Liberties Karnataka
SACS: State AIDS Control Societies
SANGRAM: Sampada Gramin Mahila Sanstha
SC: Supreme Court
STI: sexually transmitted infection
TAC: treatment action campaign
TI: targeted intervention
UNDP: United Nations Development Programme
VAMP: Veshya Anyay Mukti Parishad

APPENDIX B

Timeline for Anti-Sodomy-Law Contestations

1994 ABVA petition in the Delhi High Court

2001 Naz Petition in the Delhi High Court

2002 First challenge to the Naz petition filed by Joint Action Council Kannur (JACK) arguing that the law is required to prevent HIV from spreading

2004 Delhi High Court dismisses the Naz petition on technical grounds

2006 Supreme Court sends the petition back to the Delhi High Court for consideration

2006 Second counterpetition filed by B. P. Singhal, who challenges the Naz petition on the grounds of Indian culture and tradition

2006 Voices Against 377 joins as a copetitioner, adding strength to the Naz petition

2009 Delhi High Court Judgment in *Naz Foundation v. NCT of Delhi* delivered; the judgment declares Section 377 unconstitutional

2009 First Special Leave Petition (SLP) filed by Suresh Koushal challenging the Naz Foundation Judgment

2009 15 other SLPs filed, challenging the Naz judgment

2009–2011 Several interventions filed by various petitioners supporting Naz judgment

2013 Supreme Court in Suresh Kumar Koushal reverses the Naz decision and upholds the constitutionality of Section 377

2013 Curative Petition filed

2018 Supreme Court lists the matter to be heard by a five-judge constitutional bench

2018 Supreme Court declares Section 377 unconstitutional

NOTES

INTRODUCTION

1 "377 and Counting at the Bridge" (2018), www.youtube.com/watch?v=1jpjX5IFyoY.

2 Kapur (2005).

3 Jameela (2007) and Kotiswaran (2011).

4 For a discussion on law and juridical power, see Tadros (1998). Even though Foucault does not elucidate the relationship between biopower and law, scholars like Tadros argue that law is not juridical in Foucauldian sense but operates in a field of power relations within which it is only a directing force.

5 Foucault (1978, 139).

6 While Foucault talks about subjectivity, he provides very little discussion on agency. For more on conceptions of power, subjectivity, and agency, see Allen (2002).

7 While sex workers are not typically included under the umbrella of sexual minorities, I place them under this category as they challenge the normative expectation that sex should be available for free in marriage or a committed relationship. Within the hierarchical ordering of sexuality, sex workers are outside what Gayle Rubin (1984) calls the "charmed circle" (accepted and privileged sexual practices) of sexuality.

8 See Narrain and Bhan (2005), Kapur (2005), and Puri (2016b) for anti-sodomy-law struggles and Kotiswaran (2011) and Shah (2014) for sex worker mobilization and rights. Kapur's *Erotic Justice* is the only other work that compares sex worker and LGBT struggles for decriminalization. But my work is different in that I engage with the shifting relationship between state and marginalized groups in the context of the international health crisis.

9 See Logie et al. (2012) and Swendeman et al. (2009).

10 Ghosh (2005).

11 For a discussion on hybrid strategies that integrate social justice and public health approaches, see Currier and McKay (2017).

12 For a macro perspective on the impact of HIV/AIDS on sexual identities, see Altman (2001, 2008) and Parker et al (2004).

13 Law (2001, 126).

14 For a discussion on sex worker organizing in the Dominican Republic, see Kempadoo (2005); for a discussion on sex worker organizing in Brazil, see Longo (2005); and for a discussion on organizing in Senegal, see Tandia (2005).

15 Rubin (1984).

16 Khan (2001).

17 Even though there are other MSM categories such as *panthis* (the masculine partners of *kothis*), these groups do not constitute a self-identifying, coherent constituency and are not commonly targeted by HIV prevention activities. In general, panthis are featured in HIV/AIDS programs only in tandem with kothis.

18 Kothis vary in the way they express their femininity and perform their gender. Some like to dress up like women and see themselves primarily as women desiring men. Some may never cross-dress and look very masculine and still identify as kothi. One of the primary ways in which kothis identify themselves is through sexual acts with their partners; they see themselves as the receiving partners in the sexual act.

19 See Reddy (2005) for a discussion on overlaps between kothi and *hijra* identification.

20 See Dutta (2012).

21 Foucault (1978, 1991); Bernstein and Schaffner (2005); Puri (2016b).

22 Puri (2016b, 11).

23 Puri (2016b, 11).

24 Foucault (1978, 1991).

25 Foucault (1978).

26 Foucault (1978, 1991).

27 Whereas "biopower" and "biopolitics" are often used interchangeably, "biopower" often refers to the operationalization of power at the individual level, whereas "biopolitics" operates at the level of the population and brings life explicitly into the area of politics.

28 Foucault (1978).

29 Sharma (2006, 78).

30 Ferguson and Gupta (2002).

31 Ferguson and Gupta (2002, 996).

32 Naples and Desai (2002); Poster and Zakia (2002); Swati Ghosh (2005); Moghadam (2005).

33 See Stoler (1995); Butler (1996); Fraser (1996); and Hekman (1996).

34 Agamben (2005); Butler (1996); Biehl (2004); Comaroff (2007).

35 See also Agamben (2005).

36 Chatterjee (2006, 60).

37 Kapur (2005).

38 See Petryna (2002); Rose (2001); Rose and Novas (2004).

39 For discussion on Chernobyl, see Petryna (2002); and for discussion on HIV/AIDS activism, see Epstein (1996).

40 Robins (2006); Comaroff (2007).

41 Epstein (1996).

42 Biehl (2004); Robins (2006); Comaroff (2007).

43 Biehl (2004).

44 Dehesa and Mukherjea (2012, 197).

45 Golder (2011, 292).

46 See Brown (1995); Butler (2004); Žižek (2005).

47 Golder (2015).

48 Puri (2016b, 8).

49 Rubin (1984); Alexander (1994).

50 The public nuisance law (Section 268) includes any act of commission or omission "which causes any common injury, danger or annoyance to the public or to the people in general who dwell or occupy property in the vicinity, or which must necessarily cause injury, obstruction, danger or annoyance to persons who may have occasion to use any public right."

51 Wahab (2012, 487).

52 The term "unnatural offenses" is left undefined in the Indian Penal Code, as these offenses are seen as "loathsome." Alok Gupta (2006) points to how the ambiguity in the wording of the term "unnatural" left it purely to the imagination of judges to determine what kinds of acts qualified as unnatural. According to Gupta, this definition has been broadened from anal and oral sex to thigh sex and mutual masturbation in India.

53 Puri (2016b).

54 Jyoti Puri found a case law of ninety-nine cases through a legal database search and discovered that Section 377 has mostly been used to persecute cases of rape against women and boys that otherwise don't fall under the purview of rape laws. Puri argues that the intent and practice of the law are different in that Section 377's intended goal of persecuting unnatural sex transforms in practice into a law that punishes heinous crimes focusing on crimes committed by heterosexual men, that is, nonconsensual sexual acts on women, girls, and boys. For more, see Puri (2016b).

55 For a discussion on prosecution under Section 377, see Gupta (2002), Bhaskaran (2004), and Puri (2016b).

56 Narrain (2004, 149).

57 Puri (2016b).

58 See D'Cunha (1992) and Kotiswaran (2001). Some of the reasons for this disproportionate arrest of sex workers are offered by Kotiswaran. One major explanation is that there is a nexus between police and brothel keepers that prevents the police from enforcing the law on brothel keepers.

59 PUCL-K (2003, 50).

60 Kotiswaran (2001, 169).

61 In addition to the ITPA, other criminal provisions in the Indian Penal Code regulate underage trafficking, and the sale of persons can also be invoked to criminalize prostitution and trafficking; additional provisions in police laws and special local laws also make sex workers subject to public nuisance and public obscenity prohibitions. These general laws may be used more frequently than the ITPA in some regions. For more on this, see Kotiswaran (2011).

62 While the Criminal Tribes Act itself was repealed, it was exported into the police
codes of different states in India and continues to exist there. Two examples of
this continuation of the colonial criminalization of gender nonconformity are
the Karnataka Police Act and the Hyderabad Police Act. Section 36 (A) of the
Karnataka Police Act (1963) gives power to police officials to register names and
places of "eunuchs" residing in their jurisdiction. "Preparation and maintenance
of a register of the names and places of residence of all [persons] residing in the
area under his charge and who are reasonably suspect of kidnapping or emascu-
lating boys or of committing unnatural offences or any other offence or abetting
the commission of such offences."

63 The colonial state's intervention in gender and sexuality has been a matter of immense scholarly discussion in India. Postcolonial scholars have shown that colonial intervention in India significantly changed a wide range of gender and sexual
practices that did not often adhere to the heterosexual and monogamous matrix
of power. Colonial and social movement reform led to debates around child
marriages, widow remarriage, age of consent, and a host of other practices that
made sexuality very central to these projects. While social reformers often tried
to maintain a separation between spiritual and material dimensions of the nation
to resist colonial intervention, as Nivedita Menon (2007) points out, when it came
to nonnormative sex there was very little disagreement between nationalists and
colonialists. While much of the debate around this time regarded middle-class
women's sexuality, discussions around the regulation of religious prostitution and
women's erotic singing point to the ways in which colonial and nationalist politics
tried to muffle alternative sexual expressions. For a conversation on sexuality and
colonial social reform, see Kannabiran (1995), Nair (1996), Rege (1995), Vanita
and Kidwai (2000), Vanita (2002), and Ashwini (2009). The autonomous women's
movement in India in the 1970s for the first time brought issues of sexual violence
into public debate and sought to reform existing rape laws. Even though sexuality
was central to autonomous women's organizing, it figured mostly as danger. It was
not until the 1990s that sexual minority politics started to emerge and that sexuality began to be articulated as not only danger but also pleasure. For a discussion
on postcolonial sexual politics, see John and Nair (1998).

64 For example, see Bernstein (2010, 2012); Parreñas (2011); Agustin (2007); Kapur
(2005); Jordan (2002).

65 Bernstein (2012, 242).

66 VAMP reported a raid conducted in 2005 by an NGO funded by American
evangelicals in which thirty-five women were arrested and detained for medical examination (Ahmed and Seshu 2012). It also reported that only four of the
women were underage, two of whom were merely living with relatives in the area
and had no connection to sex work. Further, the women received no apology or
compensation for their loss of income, and the organization has continued to
conduct raids periodically.

67 Until recently, India had been on the Tier 2 Watchlist of the Trafficking in Persons Report, indicating that the nation was not making a significant effort to combat trafficking. India was therefore at risk of Tier 3 placement, which would cause it to lose nonhumanitarian, non-trade-related foreign assistance from the United States. For more on this, see Kotiswaran (2012).

68 O'Flaherty and Fisher (2008).

69 Waites (2009); Correa, Petchesky, and Parker (2008).

70 While the concept of sexual orientation was first articulated in international law in 1992, it took longer for gender identity to be recognized. The breakthrough came with the release of the Yogyakarta Principles on the application of international human rights law to sexual orientation and gender identity in 2007. The conceptual linkages between sexual orientation and gender identity were well established, and the follow-up Human Rights Council resolution in 2014 also "called on the Office of the High Commissioner to update the previous report of the High Commissioner on sexual orientation and gender identity." For more on this, see Correa, Petchesky, and Parker (2008).

71 Perumal Murugan's 2001 novel *One Part Woman* is about a married couple, Kali and Ponna, who are taunted for being childless by their families and neighbors. Their only recourse is participating in the annual chariot festival for the god Ardhanareeshwara. Murugan's book came under attack from right-wing forces who claimed that it represented an attack on religious sentiment and defamed women. Due to violent threats, Murugan was forced to withdraw unsold copies of the book and announce his retirement from writing. Later this controversy led to a series of litigation, with Murugan winning the case in Madras High Court. The court withdrew criminal complaints against him and the ban on his book.

CHAPTER 1. "HIV IS OUR FRIEND"

1 Jameela (2007).

2 SANGRAM (2018).

3 While panthis are included in some programs for HIV/AIDS intervention, it is mostly through kothis that panthis are identified. Panthi masculinity often affords them more protections when compared to kothis, whose sexuality is tied to their gender identity as feminine partners in the sexual act. Kothis are the penetrated partners and desire masculine-identified men who are the penetrators in the sexual act. Even though there are other MSM categories, these groups do not constitute self-identifying, coherent constituencies and are not commonly targeted by HIV prevention activities (Boyce 2007). In general, panthis are featured in HIV programs only in tandem with kothis.

4 Lakkimsetti (2014).

5 In 2017, the Indian parliament passed the Human Immunodeficiency Virus (HIV) and Acquired Immune Deficiency Syndrome (AIDS) Bill. Although it has been criticized, the bill strengthens the rights of people suffering from HIV and AIDS.

In addition to focusing on prevention, the bill makes antiretroviral treatment a legal right of HIV/AIDS patients. It also prohibits discrimination against people living with and affected by HIV in employment, education, and politics. Another important feature of the bill is that it prohibits testing, medical treatment, and research without informed consent. This is in striking contrast to a 1989 bill that gave medical authorities arbitrary power to test and confine people who test HIV-positive. For more, see Ministry of Law and Justice (2017).

6 Human Rights Watch (2002).

7 The Indian government is not exceptional in denying the impact of the AIDS epidemic or refusing essential services to communities during the initial phase of the epidemic. As Richard Parker (2011) points out, within almost every community and country that has confronted HIV, the initial tendency on the part of the governments has been denial. And it was the grassroots activists from communities that were directly affected by the epidemic that responded to it and pressed the government to take action.

8 Groups like ABVA (AIDS Bhedbhav Virodhi Andolan) in New Delhi organized several protests against the government's policies on testing, confidentiality, and discrimination linked to AIDS. One example of this occurred in August 1991; ABVA organized a sit-in in front of the All India Medical Institute, a premier health care organization, to protest a doctor's refusal to attend to an HIV-positive pregnant woman. ABVA also found solidarity with activist groups in other countries that protested this action at Indian embassies in the United States and Europe. In addition, ABVA published citizen reports, including one on "Women and AIDS-Denial and Blame." For more on these early struggles by activist groups to make the Indian state accountable, see ABVA (1991).

9 NACO (2016–2017).

10 NACO (2016–2017).

11 According to NACO, bridge populations are people who through their close proximity to high-risk groups are at a great risk of contracting HIV. Clients and partners of sex workers, truckers, and migrant laborers are often interpreted as bridge populations.

12 NACO (2016).

13 Foucault (1978).

14 India has a planned economy, and soon after independence the country adopted five-year plans. The five-year plans provide a framework for the government to set its economic and developmental goals.

15 HIV sentinel surveillance (HSS) is a vital surveillance system component to monitor the levels and trends of the HIV epidemic among different population groups in the country. Data from HSS are also used to estimate the HIV burden in the country. Surveillance is conducted through anonymous testing in antenatal clinics and STI clinics. In 2010–2011 HSS was conducted at 1,359 sentinel sites—696

antenatal clinic (ANC) sites, 184 STD sites, and 479 sites among high-risk groups and bridge populations. Department of AIDS Control (2014).

16 Durbar Mahila Samanwaya Committee (2004, 28).

17 UNAIDS (2000, 58).

18 NACO (2007, 16).

19 Home-based sex workers usually operate from houses they rent temporarily from friends or neighbors. They do not openly identify as sex workers, as they continue to have and live with families. Unlike working at a brothel with intermediaries such as brothel owners and managers, in these settings women operate their business on their own, drawing on their own networks. Sex work in India is mostly unorganized, although there are major red-light districts in New Delhi, Mumbai, and Kolkata.

20 The six states in which the Avahan program operated were Tamil Nadu, Karnataka, Andhra Pradesh, Maharashtra, Nagaland, and Manipur.

21 Bill & Melinda Gates Foundation (2008, 9).

22 Bill & Melinda Gates Foundation (2008, 10).

23 Bill & Melinda Gates Foundation (2008, 31).

24 Since the design of NACP III started in 2005, NACO has been able to hold wider consultations with development partners and working groups that have looked into various themes of the program.

25 Sgaier et al. (2013).

26 NACO (2007, 16).

27 United Nations Development Programme (2010, 4).

28 NACO (2007, 16).

29 Mehta (2012).

30 These partners are Alliance India, Humsafar Trust, SAATHI, Sangama, Alliance India Andhra Pradesh, and SIAAP.

CHAPTER 2. CHALLENGING "BARE LIFE"

1 PUCL-K (2003, 24).

2 Agamben (1998).

3 PUCL-K (2003, 50).

4 Human Rights Watch (2002).

5 Sangha (2013).

6 Kothis are one of the most disempowered groups. Because their feminized behavior does not conform to the normative masculinity, they are stigmatized by their family members as "not man enough" (thereby bringing shame on the family) and hence fit for abjection. By contrast, panthis (the active male partner of both kothis and hijras) have a masculinist identity and as a result are unlikely to be targets of stigma and discrimination.

7 PUCL-K (2003, 31–32).

8 Sinha (2004).

9 Banerji (1974, 1984).

10 The other reason why men are not targeted through this program is because of the history of mass sterilization of men during a dark period in Indian politics, when Prime Minister Indira Gandhi imposed a state of emergency (1975–1977) and suspended all fundamental citizen rights. During this period, mass sterilization camps were established and men from lower socioeconomic backgrounds were subjected to forced sterilization. To divert attention from that history, population policies since the 1970s have exclusively targeted women through aggressive population control policies. For a discussion on India's population policies and forced sterilization, see Chatterjee and Riley (2001) and Rudrappa (2015).

11 Whereas IUDs and sterilization are seen as nationally oriented, condoms are perceived as individually oriented and hence have less credibility.

12 For more discussion on condoms and consumerism, see Mazzarella (2001, 2013).

13 Human Rights Watch (2002, 4).

14 Human Rights Watch (2002, 15).

15 Human Rights Watch (2002, 16).

16 Other sections under which the NGO staff were arrested included Sections 120B (conspiracy to commit an offense), 109 (abetment), and 292 (sale, etc. of obscene material).

17 Human Rights Watch (2002, 19).

18 "Game of Homosexuality" (2001).

19 Rajalakshmi (2001, italics added).

20 "Game of Homosexuality" (2001).

21 For example, Ashley Currier (2010, 2012) discusses how nationalist parties in Namibia such as the South West African People's Organization (SWAPO) have constructed same-sex sexualities as Western, un-African, and un-Christian and have demanded the removal of homosexual behavior and identities from the Namibian national imaginary. She uses the term "political homophobia" to refer to how state leaders denigrate sexual diversity, same-sex sexualities, gender variance, and non-heterosexual persons. Similarly, Amar Wahab (2016) discusses the increasing influence of transnational evangelism that has precipitated a state-religious complex of what he calls "anticipatory political homophobia" in Ugandan. For a discussion on how social movements challenge political homophobia in South Africa, see Stychin (1996).

22 Gupta (2006, 4820).

23 Human Rights Watch (2002).

24 Human Rights Watch (2002, 13).

25 Human Rights Watch (2002, 22).

26 Human Rights Watch (2002, 28).

27 Durbar Mahila Samanwaya Committee (2004, 28).

28 Robins (2006, 314).

29 Lemke (2011, 10).

CHAPTER 3. EMPOWERED CRIMINALS

1 For more, see D'Cunha (1992) and Kotiswaran (2001).

2 Sex worker organizations not only demand the repeal of objectionable clauses in the ITPA, such as punishment for soliciting in public, but also call for the repeal of the law itself. Their argument is that other provisions in the Indian Penal Code can be used to punish trafficking, underage rape, harassment, and other crimes that are often associated with sex trafficking and that the separate prostitution law serves only to regulate women's sexuality and uphold patriarchal ideas that women's sexual labor belongs to men and to marriage.

3 Letter to the Parliamentary Standing Committee on Human Resource Development by Ashodaya Sex Workers Collective, Mangalore, 2006, italics added.

4 Jameela (2007, 116).

5 The conference organizers invited communities that are traditionally involved in dancing and other activities to have a broad dialogue about entertainment as a form of work. The attendees also included bar dancers who were recently displaced from their work in the city of Mumbai, where in 2005 the state of Maharashtra banned women from dancing in dance bars. For a discussion of the regulation of dance bars, see Lakkimsetti (2016b, 2017), Kotiswaran (2010), and Agnes (2007).

6 National Consultation on Sex Work, HIV and the Law (November 2007), document circulated by the Lawyers Collective (on file with the author) and can be found on www.lawyerscollective.org.

7 The term "unnatural offenses" is left undefined in the Indian Penal Code, as these offenses are seen as "loathsome." Alok Gupta (2006) points to how the ambiguity in the wording of "unnatural" left it purely to the imagination of the judges to determine what kind of acts qualify as unnatural. According to Gupta, this definition has been broadened in India from anal and oral sex to thigh sex and mutual masturbation.

8 Puri (2016b).

9 Puri found a case law of ninety-nine cases through a legal database search and found that Section 377 has mostly been used to persecute cases of rape against women and boys that otherwise don't fall under the purview of rape laws. Puri argues that the intent and practice of the law are different in that Section 377's intended goal of persecuting unnatural sex transforms in practice into a law that punishes heinous crimes focusing on crimes committed by heterosexual men, that is, nonconsensual sexual acts on women, girls, and boys. For more, see Puri (2016b).

10 Narrain (2007); Puri (2016b).

11 From 2004 to 2008 Naz's Milan Program was among India's first programs working with MSM and kothis on HIV/AIDS prevention.

12 Human Rights Watch (2002).

13 I gathered from my conversation with activist groups in New Delhi that the decision to file the petition in the Delhi High Court was taken because ABVA had already filed a petition in the Delhi High Court in 1994 and also because the Naz Foundation, which was willing to file the petition, was based in New Delhi. Moreover, the decision was also politically expedient as approaching the SC as a first option would involve a huge political risk: as the SC is an apex court, its decision is final. An unfavorable decision would have ended the activists' legal strategy. In contrast, approaching Delhi High Court was less risky; an unfavorable decision from this court would allow the activists to revise their argument and either approach the SC to challenge the decision or file a similar petition in another high court.

14 The Naz petition sought revisions to Section 377 rather than the complete repeal of the sodomy law because of the fact that the rape laws in India define rape narrowly as penovaginal penetration. Section 377 is the only law that can be used to punish bodily violations of women and minors (including boys) that fall under anal or oral penetration. Section 377 is often used concurrently with Section 376 (rape law) and other provisions of the Indian Penal Code.

15 *Naz Foundation v. Govt. of NCT of Delhi and Ors*, WP (C) No. 7455/2001, High Court of Delhi at New Delhi.

16 *Naz Foundation v. Govt. of NCT of Delhi and Ors*, WP (C) No. 7455/2001, High Court of Delhi at New Delhi, 13, italics added.

17 *Naz Foundation v. Govt. of NCT of Delhi and Ors*, WP (C) No. 7455/2001, High Court of Delhi at New Delhi, 17, italics added.

18 In December 1995, the Indian Ministry of Health and Family Welfare and the Indian Law Institute with the cooperation of UNDP, WHO, and other national and international groups organized the International Conference on AIDS—Law and Humanity in New Delhi. The conference focused on the need for a united approach to HIV/AIDS-related legal issues that would protect society against the spread of HIV and respect the dignity and fundamental human rights of HIV-infected persons and those suspected of being infected and their families and friends. The conference participants adopted the New Delhi Declaration and Action Plan on AIDS. The plan's principles are designed to guide policy makers in developing laws and strategies to help fight HIV/AIDS.

19 Quoted in Human Rights Watch (2002, 27).

20 *Naz Foundation v. Govt. of NCT of Delhi and Ors*, Writ Petition (C) No. 7455 of 2001, Reply Affidavit on Behalf of Respondents 4 and 5, July 17, 2006, 3.

21 *Naz Foundation v. Govt. of NCT of Delhi and Ors*, Writ Petition (C) No. 7455 of 2001, Reply Affidavit on Behalf of Respondents 4 and 5, July 17, 2006, 3.

22 *Naz Foundation v. Govt. of NCT of Delhi and Ors*, Writ Petition (C) No. 7455 of 2001, Counter Affidavit on Behalf of Respondent 5, September 2003, 4.

23 *Naz Foundation v. Govt. of NCT of Delhi and Ors*, Writ Petition (C) No. 7455 of 2001, Counter Affidavit on Behalf of Respondent 5, September 2003, 4.

24 *Naz Foundation v. Govt. of NCT of Delhi and Ors*, Writ Petition (C) No. 7455 of
   2001, Counter Affidavit on Behalf of Respondent 5, September 2003, 6.

25 *Naz Foundation v. Govt. of NCT of Delhi and Ors*, Writ Petition (C) No. 7455 of
   2001, Counter Affidavit on Behalf of Respondent 5, September 2003, 7.

26 The 172nd law commission review in 2000, reviewing the rape laws, recommended the repeal of Section 377.

27 *Naz Foundation v. Govt. of NCT of Delhi and Ors*, Writ Petition (C) No. 7455 of
   2001, High Court of Delhi, New Delhi, July 2, 2009, 73.

28 The Supreme Court is the highest appellate court; all higher courts in India must
   abide by its rulings. Usually a small bench of two or three judges decides cases;
   occasionally a case can be referred to a larger bench of five judges.

CHAPTER 4. TOLERABLE IDENTITIES, INTOLERABLE SEX ACTS

1 *Suresh Kumar Koushal and Another v. Naz Foundation and Others*, Civil Appeal
   No. 10972 of 2013, Supreme Court of India, New Delhi, December 11, 2013, 77.

2 *National Legal Services Authority v. Union of India and Others*, Writ Petition
   (Civil) No. 604 of 2013, Supreme Court of India, New Delhi, April 15, 2014, 5.

3 In 2004, Kokila, a twenty-one-year-old hijra from the southern city of Bangalore,
   was raped by several men. When she attempted to seek redress by the police, she
   was verbally abused, physically tortured, arrested, and forced to remain naked
   for many hours. Instead of taking her violations seriously, the police arrested her
   under Section 377. For more details on this case, see International Lesbian, Gay,
   Bisexual, Trans and Intersex Association (2017).

4 Puri (2016b).

5 See Brown (1995).

6 Golder (2015).

7 Golder (2011, 292).

8 Puri (2016b).

9 Voices Against 377, "Public Action Against Section 377 in New Delhi" (press
   release), on file with the author.

10 Voices Against 377 (2005, 21).

11 The reason to not include the queer women's affidavit came from the fear that if
   queer women's issues were raised it might lead to a backlash. There was a case in
   Sri Lanka where lesbian women who were not included in the law were included
   later. Hence, there were charged debates within the organizations about the inclusion of women in legal petitions.

12 Voices' decision to join the legal case came about when an explicitly right-wing
   petition was filed in the Delhi High Court by Mr. B. P. Singhal. In 2001 JACK
   India filed a petition challenging the Naz petition; this petition was ironically arguing that Section 377 does not impede HIV/AIDS prevention. They also argued
   that the Naz petition was an international conspiracy and that NGOs like the Naz
   Foundation were receiving massive amounts of funding from international agencies to disrupt Indian society. But it was Singhal's petition that brought explicitly

homophobic and Hindu right-wing arguments to the legal debate. Singhal argued that homosexuality was a Western contamination and hence foreign to India. After Singhal's petition was filed, LGBTQ groups in India felt that it would be a good strategy to file briefs in support of Naz's original petition and thus amplify activist voices in the legal debate. Voices thus represents a broad coalition of human rights and child rights groups.

13 *Naz Foundation v. Government of NCT of Delhi and Others*, Writ Petition (C) No. 7455 of 2001, High Court of Delhi at New Delhi, July 2, 2009, 91.

14 Kannabiran (2009).

15 *Suresh Kumar Koushal and Another v. NAZ Foundation and Others*, Civil Appeal No. 10972 of 2013, Supreme Court of India, New Delhi, December 11, 2013, 77.

16 A curative petition (which was articulated in 2002 by the SC), through which an SC decision might be challenged, is presided over and decided by a bench comprising the three most senior judges of the SC, along with the two judges who originally deliberated on the decision under challenge. Prior to 2002, all SC decisions were subject only to a review petition whereby the very same judges who had adopted the decision assessed whether their decision had any errors.

17 The Indian Constitution states that for cases involving a substantial question of law as to the interpretation of the Constitution, the minimum number of judges required to sit on the bench is five. In practice, the court has often failed to comply with this provision when deciding cases questioning the interpretation of the Constitution—the Suresh Kumar Koushal case, for instance, would have been a prime candidate for being heard by a constitutional bench.

18 This does not mean that there is no disagreement around the centrality of Section 377 among sexual minority groups. There is charged debate among LGBTKQHI groups about the nature of the movement and whether Section 377 should be given a privileged place in it. But after the Supreme Court judgment in 2013, some of this criticism fizzled out, as the court's decision indicated the difficulty in challenging the law. One camp feels that Section 377 should not be confined to legal battles and that any social movement building should focus on the rights of a broader spectrum of LGBTKQHI groups and sexual minorities. However, other groups feel that Section 377 is not going to truly impact the lives of sexual minorities even if it is repealed.

19 See Dutta (2013).

20 NALSA was formed in 1987 under the Legal Services Authorities Act. Its main goal is to provide free legal services to marginalized groups. Articles 14 and 22(1) of the Indian Constitution require for the state to ensure equality before law. The principal objective of NALSA is to provide free and competent legal services to the weaker sections of the society and to ensure that opportunities for securing justice are not denied to any citizens by reason of economic or other disadvantage. NALSA's functions also include spreading legal literacy and awareness as well as undertaking social justice litigations.

21 NALSA (2016).

22 Unlike the US Supreme Court, where all judges preside over a case, for India's Supreme Court a small bench of two or three judges decides most cases. This is due to the fact that the SC has a large number of cases to decide. Only matters that pertain to constitutional interpretation are heard before a larger bench.

23 The SC recognizes the right to determine and express one's gender and grants legal status to a "third gender." Lawyers Collective (2016).

24 *NALSA v. Union of India*, 15.

25 In 1871, the British colonial state introduced the Criminal Tribes Act, giving the government extensive powers to arrest and monitor the movement of these tribes. Hijras were included under the category of criminal tribes. The act included the registration of eunuchs and their property as well as penalties for registered hijra appearing in female clothes or dancing in public or for hire. It gave power to magistrates to remove male children under sixteen who were living with registered hijras and to prosecute them and authorized officials to require information as to registered property, a stipulation that aimed to interfere with hijra inheritance and succession patterns and prohibited eunuchs from being named in wills or receiving gifts. For a discussion on the Criminal Tribes Act and hijras, see Hinchy (2017).

26 Among the first few cases recorded in British India, *Queen Empress v. Khairati* (1884) is cited widely by queer scholars. Khairati was initially arrested for singing in women's clothes and was subjected to a physical examination by a civil surgeon. The examination revealed distortion of his anus and other evidence of "unnatural intercourse." While Khairati denied the allegations, the session judge concluded that Khairati was a habitual sodomite. The case was later dismissed by the Allahabad High Court, as the earlier conviction lacked the details of the offense of sodomy, that is, the time, place, and person with whom the offense was committed. While Khairati's case was dismissed, it attracted scholarly attention as evidence of the increasing role of medical jurisprudence regarding offenses against the body. For more discussion on this case and colonial archives, see Arondekar (2009).

27 *NALSA v. Union of India*, 14.

28 "377 and Counting at the Bridge" (2018), www.youtube.com/watch?v=1jpjX5IFyoY.

29 *Dr. Akkai Padmashali & Ors v. Union of India & Ors*, Writ Petition (C) No. 572 of 2016, 42 (M).

30 One of the things that the tabled bill does is introduce a problematic definition of "transgender." It defines a transgender person as neither wholly female nor wholly male, or a combination of female or male, or neither female nor male, and whose sense of gender does not match with the gender assigned to the person at the time of birth. This includes transmen and transwomen, persons with intersex variations, and genderqueer persons. Including intersex as gender-nonconforming is

a problem that several activist groups brought to the attention of the ministry. The Ministry of Social Justice and Empowerment (MSJE) has clearly brought to the bill a popular narrative of trans people as phantasmagoric beings who are half man and half woman, or neither male nor female. This definition is biologically determinist and would apply more to people with intersex variations who identify as genderqueer or a section of trans people who identify as third gender, but not the whole spectrum. There is no mention of trans people who identify as male or female in the bill. While NALSA gives individuals a choice to identify as a man, a woman, or third gender/transgender, the bill provides only one option—transgender.

31 Halley (1993).

CHAPTER 5. INTERCONNECTED RIGHTS

1 "Reactions to Section 377 Verdict" (2018).

2 On December 23, 2012, a three-member committee headed by J. S. Verma, former chief justice of the Supreme Court, was constituted to recommend amendments to Indian criminal law so as to provide for quicker trials and enhanced punishment for sexual assault.

3 Among the recommendations made by sex workers to the committee are providing directives to the police to immediately register cases of sexual assault and violence irrespective of occupation and that sexual assault during police raids or forced sex during arrests and detention should be considered as aggravated sexual assault and that appropriate and timely action should be taken against police officers engaging in this behavior. Feminists India (2013).

4 National Network for Sex Workers (2013).

5 Sections 370 and 370A of the Indian Penal Code already penalize trafficking and the sexual exploitation of trafficked victims, respectively. Critics argue that the new bill will cause unnecessary confusion, as the relationship of this bill to existing legal frameworks is unclear. Another critique is that the bill provides the police with excessive powers and creates bureaucratic institutions with no accountability. For a discussion and critique of the bill, see Kotiswaran (2016).

6 The recent anti-trafficking bill proposed by MWCD is seen as a response to a 2016 Global Slavery Index, where India was depicted as significantly responsible for the persistence of "modern slavery." It was reported that out of 45.8 million "modern slaves" around the world, 18.3 million were in India. See Kotiswaran (2016).

7 Colonial governors elsewhere in Asia and Africa used the language of Section 377 in dozens of statutes criminalizing so-called unnatural offenses. Among the countries that retained Section 377 were Bangladesh, Pakistan, and Singapore.

8 In addition to the NALSA judgment, in 2015 a private member bill introduced by Tiruchi Siva was unanimously passed in the upper house of parliament. Among other things, the bill proposed setting up national commissions for

protecting transgender rights and coordinating the activities of all government departments to intervene in any proceedings involving allegations of violations of the rights of transgender persons pending before a court with the approval of such court that would be responsible for handling grievances and atrocities. In addition, it also recommends establishing Transgender Rights Courts to adjudicate criminal cases regarding transgender people. Despite the unanimous support in the upper house, the government undermined this bill by drafting its own bill in 2016.

9 In contrast to the right to self-identity granted by the SC, the Transgender Persons (Protection of Rights) Bill (2018) makes the identification process bureaucratic. It recommends setting up District Screening Committees that would have the power to issue gender identity certificates. The committees would be constituted by a chief medical officer, a district social welfare officer, a psychologist or psychiatrist, a representative of the transgender community, and an additional officer deemed appropriate by the government.

10 The bill states that whoever compels or entices a transgender person to indulge in the act of begging will be subject to a minimum of ten years' rigorous imprisonment and up to life imprisonment. Critics of the bill point out that it should make a distinction between coerced labor and limited choices as the result of structural barriers to other employment options. The bill is also problematic because it defines family in a very narrow sense as people related by blood or marriage or through legal adoption. This completely ignores the fact that hijra kinship networks are very important for the survival of the community.

11 One example of a transprotectionist attitude is 2017 remarks by Ramdas Athawale, the junior minister for social justice. Newspapers reported that during a workshop on developing sensitivity toward transgender people, the minister advised the transcommunity not to wear saris. By making this remark the minister not only violated individuals rights to dress of choice but also naturalized saris as belonging to ciswomen. Rao (2017).

12 Quoted in Golder (2015, 159).

13 Unlike other scholars who critique the privacy arguments put forward in the Section 377 case, there is enough evidence in the Navtej Singh Johar judgment to prove that privacy rights are expanded in the context of the debate around Section 377. Privacy is not associated with a place but also encompasses the right to make decisions about whom one chooses to be intimate with. Decisional privacy or privacy of choice has been established both in the Johar judgment and in the recent judgment on privacy (*Puttaswamy v. Union of India*) by the Supreme Court.

14 While scholars like Joseph Massad (2002) and Jasbir Puar (2007) take this first position, the second position is represented by Adam, Duyvendak, and Krouwel (1999).

15 Also see similar discussion on the Lebanese context by Moussawi (2015).

16 Wilson (2002, 253).

17 Kaviraj (2005, 294).

18 Kaviraj (2005, 293).

19 Kaviraj (2005, 295).

20 Individuals like B. P. Singhal and some state representatives argued that repealing Section 377 would open the floodgates of delinquency. Moreover, they also argued that Indian society was not ready for such a change as it does not approve of homosexuality. By using popular morality as an argument against decriminalization, these voices undermine the constitutionally guaranteed rights to equality and freedom.

21 For Dr. Ambedkar, the architect of the Indian Constitution, "constitutional morality" was not a natural sentiment but needed to be cultivated consciously. Ambedkar felt that in the absence of democratic traditions (he was especially concerned about caste inequalities) the constitution and rule of law would protect Indian democracy. The Indian Constitution is a lengthy and elaborate document, and Ambedkar's justification was that the absence of a democratic tradition required constitutional provisions to be written out in much greater detail than was necessary in more mature democracies where there was greater consensus on how democratic institutions should function (Beteille, 2008).

22 *Naz Foundation v. Government of NCT of Delhi and Others*, Writ Petition (C) No. 7455 of 2001, High Court of Delhi at New Delhi, July 2, 2009.

23 Kannabiran (2009).

24 *Navtej Singh Johar & Ors v. Union of India*, Writ Petition (C) No. 76 of 2016, Supreme Court of India, September 6, 2018, 268.

25 *Navtej Singh Johar & Ors v. Union of India*, 2018, 82.

26 For a more detailed discussion on constitutional morality, see Beteille (2008).

27 The Directive Principles of State Policy held out a promise that the state would attempt to maintain a minimum standard of living for all citizens. Democratic socialist principles are seen as one of the important pillars of Indian politics.

28 *NALSA v. Union of India*, para. 126.

29 On September 27, 2018, the Indian Supreme Court declared Section 497 (adultery law) of the Indian Penal Code unconstitutional. The court ruled that the criminal offense of having a sexual relationship with a woman without her husband's consent was archaic and deprived women of agency. This decision was hailed as one of several socially progressive rulings by the court and came a few weeks after the sodomy law was declared unconstitutional.

30 *State (Govt. of NCT of Delhi) v. Pankaj Chaudhary and Ors*, Criminal Appeal No. 2298 of 2009, Supreme Court of India, October 30, 2018.

31 The Narmada Bachao Andolan (NBA) is seen as an icon of nonviolent, grassroots protest against destructive development. NBA has protested the construction of mega-dams on the River Narmada without the consultation of people who are displaced by these projects. The group has also fought against the disruption and displacement of millions of people without just and adequate compensation.

32 Kothari (2017).
33 Gupta (2015).
34 Karthikeyan (2015).
35 Ranganathan (2014).
36 Coalition of Sex Workers and Sexual Minorities' Rights (2018).
37 Reuters (2018).
38 For a discussion of the legal recognition of a third gender category in Pakistan, see Nisar (2018). For a discussion of the paradoxes of legal recognition in Bangladesh, see Hossain (2017).

REFERENCES

ABVA. 1991. "Less Than Gay: A Citizens' Report on the Status of Homosexuality in India." New Delhi: ABVA.

Adam, Barry D., Jan Willem Duyvendak, and André Krouwel. 1999. "Gay and Lesbian Movements beyond Borders? National Imprints of a Worldwide Movement." In *The Global Emergence of Gay and Lesbian Politics*, edited by Adam, Duyvendak, and Krouwel, 344–371. Philadelphia: Temple University Press.

Agamben, Giorgio. 1998. *Home Sacer: Sovereign Power and Bare Life*. Stanford, CA: Stanford University Press.

———. 2005. *State of Exception*. Translated by Kevin Attell. Chicago: University of Chicago Press.

Agnes, Flavia. 2007. "State Control and Sexual Morality: The Case of the Bar Dancers of Mumbai." In *Enculturing Law: New Agendas for Legal Pedagogy*, edited by Matthew John and Sitharamam Kakarala, 158–175. New Delhi: Tulika Books.

Agustin, Laura. 2007. *Sex at the Margins: Migration, Labor, Markets and the Rescue Industry*. New York: Zed Books.

Ahmed, Aziza, and Meena Seshu. 2012. "We Have the Right Not to Be 'Rescued': When Anti-trafficking Programs Undermine the Health and Well-Being of Sex Workers." *Anti-Trafficking Review* 1:149–168.

Alexander, Jacqui M. 1994. "Not Just (Any) Body Can Be a Citizen: The Politics of Law, Sexuality and Postcoloniality in Trinidad and Tobago and the Bahamas." *Feminist Review* 48 (1): 5–23.

———. 1997. "Erotic Autonomy as a Politics of Decolonization: An Anatomy of Feminist and State Practice in the Bahamas Tourist Economy." In *Feminist Genealogies, Colonial Legacies, Democratic Futures*, edited by M. Jacqui Alexander and Chandra Talpade Mohanty, 63–100. New York: Routledge.

———. 2005. "Transnationalism, Sexuality, and the State: Modernity's Traditions at the Height of Empire." In *Pedagogies of Crossing: Meditations on Feminism, Sexual Politics, Memory and the Sacred*, 181–256. Durham, NC: Duke University Press.

Allen, Amy. 2002. "Power, Subjectivity, and Agency: Between Arendt and Foucault." *International Journal of Philosophical Studies* 10 (2): 131–149.

Altman, Dennis. 2001. *Global Sex*. Chicago: University of Chicago Press.

———. 2008. "AIDS and the Globalization of Sexuality." *Social Identities* 14 (2): 145–160.

Arondekar, Anjali. 2009. *For the Record: On Sexuality and the Colonial Archive in India*. Durham, NC: Duke University Press.

Bacchetta, Paola. 1999. "When the (Hindu) Nation Exiles Its Queers." *Social Text* 17 (4): 141–167.

Banerji, D. 1974. "Family Planning in India: The Outlook for 2000 AD." *Economic and Political Weekly* 9 (48): 1984–1989.

Bernstein, Elizabeth. 2010. "Militarized Humanitarianism Meets Carceral Feminism: The Politics of Sex, Rights, and Freedom in Contemporary Antitrafficking Campaigns." *Signs* 36 (1): 45–71.

———. 2012. "Carceral Politics as Gender Justice? The 'Traffic in Women' and Neoliberal Circuits of Crime, Sex, and Rights." *Theory and Society* 41 (3): 233–259.

Bernstein, Elizabeth, and Laurie Schaffner, eds. 2005. *Regulating Sex: The Politics of Intimacy and Identity*. New York: Routledge.

Beteille, Andre. 2008. "Constitutional Morality." *Economic and Political Weekly* 43 (40): 35–42.

Bhan, Gautam. 2018. "For All That We May Become: On the Section 377 Verdict." *Hindu*, September 7. www.thehindu.com.

Bhaskaran, Suparna. 2004. *Made in India: Decolonization, Queer Sexualities, Transnational Projects*. London: Palgrave Macmillan.

Biehl, Joao. 2004. "The Activist State: Global Pharmaceuticals, AIDS, and Citizenship in Brazil." *Social Text* 22:105–132.

Bill & Melinda Gates Foundation. 2008. "Avahan—The India AIDS Initiative: The Business of HIV Prevention at Scale." https://docs.gatesfoundation.org.

Boellstroff, Tom. 2005. *The Gay Archipelago: Sexuality and Nation in Indonesia*. Princeton, NJ: Princeton University Press.

Bose, Brinda, and Subhabrata Bhattacharya, eds. 2005. *The Phobic and the Erotic: The Politics of Sexualities in Contemporary India*. Calcutta: Seagull Books.

Boyce, Paul. 2007. "'Conceiving *Kothis*': Men Who Have Sex with Men in India and the Cultural Subject of HIV Prevention." *Medical Anthropology* 26 (2): 175–203.

Brown, Wendy. 1995. *States of Injury: Power and Freedom in Late Modernity*. Princeton, NJ: Princeton University Press.

Butler, Judith. 1996. "Sexual Inversions." In *Feminist Interpretations of Michel Foucault*, edited by Susan J. Hekman, 59–76. University Park: Pennsylvania State University Press.

———. 2004. *Undoing Gender*. New York: Routledge.

Chatterjee, Nilanjana, and Nancy E. Riley. 2001. "Planning and Indian Modernity: The Gendered Politics of Fertility Control." *Signs* 26 (3): 811–845.

Chatterjee, Partha. 1989. "The Nationalist Resolution of the Women's Question." In *Recasting Women: Essays in Colonial History*, edited by Kumkum Sangari and Sudesh Vaid, 233–253. New Delhi: Kali for Women.

———. 2000. "Two Poets and Death: On Civil and Political Society in the Non-Christian World." In *Questions of Modernity*, edited by Timothy Mitchell, 35–48. Minneapolis: University of Minnesota Press.

———. 2006. *Politics of the Governed: Reflections on Popular Politics in Most of the World*. New York: Columbia University Press.

Coalition of Sex Workers and Sexual Minorities' Rights. 2018. "Oppose Transgender Persons (Protection of Rights) Bill, 2018 and Trafficking of Persons (Prevention, Protection and Rehabilitation) Bill, 2018." Press release, December 20. http://orinam.net.

Cohen, Lawrence, 2005. "Kothi Wars: AIDS Cosmopolitanism and the Morality of Classification." In *Sex in Development: Science, Sexuality, and Morality in Global Perspective*, edited by Vincanne Adams and Stacy Leigh Pig, 269–303. Durham, NC: Duke University Press.

Comaroff, Jean. 2007. "Beyond the Politics of Bare Life: AIDS, (Bio)Politics, and the Neoliberal Order." *Public Culture* 19 (1): 197–219.

Correa, Sonia, Rosalind Petchesky, and Richard Parker. 2008. *Sexual Health and Human Rights*. London: Routledge.

Cruz-Malave, Arnaldo, and Martin F. Manalansan IV, eds. 2002. *Queer Globalizations: Citizenship and the Afterlife of Colonialism*. New York: New York University Press.

Currier, Ashley. 2010. "Political Homophobia in Postcolonial Namibia." *Gender & Society* 24 (1): 110–129.

———. 2012. "The Aftermath of Decolonization: Gender and Sexual Dissidence in Postindependence Namibia." *Signs* 37 (2): 441–467.

Currier, Ashley, and Tara McKay. 2017. "Pursuing Social Justice through Public Health: Gender and Sexual Diversity Activism in Malawi." *Critical African Studies* 9 (1): 71–90.

Dave, Naisargi N. 2012. *Queer Activism in India: A Story in the Anthropology of Ethics*. Durham, NC: Duke University Press.

Davidson, Julia O'Connell, and Jacqueline Sanchez Taylor. 2005. "Travel and Taboo: Heterosexual Sex Tourism to the Caribbean." In *Regulating Sex: The Politics of Intimacy and Identity,* edited by Elizabeth Bernstein and Laurie Schaffner, 83–101. New York: Routledge.

D'Cunha, J. 1992. "Prostitution Laws: Ideological Dimensions and Enforcement Practices." *Economic and Political Weekly* 27 (17): WS34–WS44.

Dehesa, Rafael de la. 2010. *Queering the Public Sphere in Mexico and Brazil: Sexual Rights Movements in Emerging Democracies*. Durham, NC: Duke University Press.

Dehesa, Rafael de la, and Ananya Mukherjea. 2012. "Building Capacities and Producing Citizens: The Biopolitics of HIV Prevention in Brazil." *Contemporary Politics* 18 (2): 186–199.

Delacoste, Frederique, and Priscilla Alexander, eds. 1987. *Sex Work: Writing by Women in the Sex Industry*. Pittsburg: Cleis.

Department of AIDS Control. 2014. "State HIV Epidemic Fact Sheet." New Delhi: Department of AIDS Control.

Doezema, Jo. 2001. "Ouch! Western Feminists' 'Wounded Attachment' to the 'Third World Prostitute.'" *Feminist Review* 67:16–38.

Durbar Mahila Samanwaya Committee. 2004. "The Fallen Learn to Raise." 3rd ed. Kolkata: Durbar Mahila Samanwaya Committee.

Dutta, Aniruddha. 2012. "An Epistemology of Collusion: *Hijras, Kothis* and the Historical (Dis)continuity of Gender/Sexual Identities in Eastern India." *Gender and History* 24 (3): 825–849.

———. 2013. "Legible Identities and Legitimate Citizens: The Globalization of Transgender and Subjects of HIV-AIDS Prevention in Eastern India." *International Feminist Journal of Politics* 15 (4): 494–514.

Epstein, Steven. 1996. *Impure Science: AIDS, Activism and the Politics of Knowledge.* Berkeley: University of California Press.

Feminists India. 2013. "Aastha Parivaar-Federation of Sex Workers in Maharastra Submission to Justice Verma Commission." http://feministsindia.com.

Ferguson, James, and Akhil Gupta. 2002. "Spatializing States: Toward an Ethnography of Neoliberal Governmentality." *American Ethnologist* 29 (4): 981–1002.

Foucault, Michel. 1977. *Discipline and Punish: The Birth of the Prison.* New York: Vintage.

———. 1978. *The History of Sexuality,* vol. 1: *An Introduction.* Translated by Robert Hurley. New York: Vintage.

———. 1991. "Governmentality." In *The Foucault Effect: Studies in Governmentality,* edited by Graham Burchell, Colin Gordon, and Peter Miller, 87–105. Chicago: University of Chicago Press.

Fraser, Nancy. 1996. "Michel Foucault: A 'Young Conservative'?" In *Feminist Interpretations of Michel Foucault,* edited by Susan J. Hekman, 59–77. University Park: Pennsylvania State University Press.

"Game of Homosexuality in the Name of AIDS Prevention." 2001. *Pioneer* (Lucknow), August 22.

Ghosh, Swati. 2005. "Surveillance in Decolonized Social Space: The Case of Sex Workers in Bengal." *Social Text* 23 (2): 55–69.

Golder, Ben. 2011. "Foucault's Critical (Yet Ambivalent) Affirmation: Three Figures of Rights." *Social & Legal Studies* 20 (3): 283–312.

———. 2015. *Foucault and the Politics of Rights.* Stanford, CA: Stanford University Press.

Gopinath, Gayatri. 2005. *Impossible Desires: Queer Diasporas and South Asian Public Cultures.* Durham, NC: Duke University Press.

Gore, Ellie. 2018. "Reflexivity and Queer Embodiment: Some Reflections on Sexualities Research in Ghana." *Feminist Review* 120:101–119.

Grewal, Inderpal, and Caren Kaplan. 2001. "Global Identities: Theorizing Transnational Studies of Sexuality." *GLQ* 7 (4): 663–679.

Gupta, Alok. 2002. "Trends in the Application of Section 377." In *Humjinsi: A Resource Book on Lesbian, Gay and Bisexual Rights in India,* edited by Bina Fernandez, 66–74. Mumbai: Indian Centre for Human Rights and Law.

———. 2006. "Section 377 and the Dignity of Indian Homosexuals." *Economic and Political Weekly* 41 (46): 4815–4823.

Gupta, Saurabh. 2015. "Mumbai Mother Places Matrimonial Ad for Her Gay Son, Seeks a Groom." *NDTV,* May 21. www.ndtv.com.

Halley, Janet. 1993. "Reasoning about Sodomy: Act and Identity in and After *Bowers v. Hardwick.*" *Virginia Law Review* 79:1721–1780.

Hekman, Susan J. 1996. "Introduction." In *Feminist Interpretations of Michel Foucault*, edited by Hekman, 1–12. University Park: Pennsylvania State University Press.

Hinchy, Jessica. 2017. "The Eunuch Archive: Colonial Records of Non-normative Gender and Sexuality in India." *Culture, Theory and Critique* 58 (2): 127–146.

Hossain, Adnan. 2017. "The Paradox of Recognition: Hijra, Third Gender and Sexual Rights in Bangladesh." *Culture, Health & Sexuality* 19 (12): 1418–1431.

Human Rights Watch. 2002. "Epidemic of Abuse: Police Harassment of HIV/AIDS Workers in India." New York: Human Rights Watch.

International Lesbian, Gay, Bisexual, Trans and Intersex Association. 2017. "Ongoing Police Violence Against Hijras in India." https://ilga.org.

Jameela, Nalini. 2007. *Autobiography of a Sex Worker*. Translated by J. Devika. Chennai: Westland.

John, Mary E., and Janaki Nair, eds. 1998. *A Question of Silence? The Sexual Economies of Modern India*. New Delhi: Kali for Women.

Jordan, Ann. 2002. "Human Rights or Wrongs? The Struggle for a Rights-Based Response to Trafficking in Human Beings." *Gender & Development* 10 (1): 28–37.

Kannabiran, Kalpana. 1995. "Judiciary, Social Reform and Debate on 'Religious Prostitution' in Colonial India." *Economic and Political Weekly* 30 (43): 59–69.

Kannabiran, Kalpana. 2009. "From 'Perversion to Right to Life with Dignity.'" *Hindu*, July 6. www.thehindu.com.

Kapur, Ratna. 2005. *Erotic Justice: Law and the New Politics of Postcolonialism*. London: Glasshouse.

———. 2009. "Out of the Colonial Closet, But Still Thinking 'Inside the Box': Regulating 'Perversion' and the Role of Tolerance in De-radicalising the Rights Claims of Sexual Subalterns." *NUJS* 2 (3): 381–396.

Karthikeyan, Rangamalika. 2015. "The Casteist Gay-Groom Ad Is a Hard Lesson for Civil Rights Activists." *News Minute*, May 20. www.thenewsminute.com.

Kaviraj, Sudipta. 2005. "On the Enchantment of the State: Indian Thought on the Role of the State in the Narrative of Modernity." *European Journal of Sociology* 46 (2): 263–296.

———. 2012. *The Trajectories of the Indian State*. Hyderabad: Orient Blackswan.

Keck Margaret E., and Kathryn Sikkink. 1998. *Activists beyond Borders: Advocacy Networks in International Politics*. Ithaca, NY: Cornell University Press.

Kempadoo, Kamala. 2005. "COIN and MODEMU in the Dominican Republic." In *Global Sex Workers: Rights, Resistance, and Redefinition*, edited by Kamala Kempadoo and Jo Doezema, 260–266. New York: Routledge.

Khagram, Sanjeev, James Riker, and Kathryn Sikkink. 2002. *Restructuring World Politics: Transnational Social Movements, Networks, and Norms*. Minneapolis: University of Minnesota Press.

Khan, Shivananda. 2001. "Culture, Sexualities, and Identities: Men Who Have Sex with Men in India." *Journal of Homosexuality* 40 (3–4): 99–115.

Khanna, Akshay. 2013. "Three Hundred and Seventy Seven Ways of Being—Sexualness of the Citizen in India." *Journal of Historical Sociology* 26 (1): 120–142.

Kothari, Jayna. 2017. "The Right to Privacy: The Promise for Full Recognition of Transgender Rights." Orinam, August 28. http://orinam.net.

Kotiswaran, Prabha. 2001. "Preparing for Civil Disobedience: Indian Sex Workers and the Law." *Boston College Third World Law Journal* 21 (2): 161–242.

———. 2010. "Labours in Vice or Virtue? Neo-liberalism, Sexual Commerce, and the Case of Indian Bar Dancing." *Journal of Law and Society* 37 (1): 105–122.

———. 2011. *Dangerous Sex, Invisible Labor: Sex Work and the Law in India*. Princeton, NJ: Princeton University Press.

———. 2012. "Vulnerability in Domestic Discourses on Trafficking: Lessons from the Indian Experience." *Feminist Legal Studies* 20 (3): 245–262.

———. 2016. "Empty Gestures: A Critique of India's New Trafficking Bill." *Open Democracy*, June 22. www.opendemocracy.net.

Lakkimsetti, Chaitanya. 2014. "'HIV Is Our Friend': Prostitution, Power and State in Postcolonial India." *Signs: Journal of Women in Culture and Society* 40 (1): 201–226.

———. 2016a. "Empowered Criminals and Global Subjects: Gender and the Paradox of Transnational Advocacy in India." *Qualitative Sociology* 39:375–396.

———. 2016b. "'From Dance Bars to the Streets': Moral Dispossession and Eviction in Mumbai." *Positions: Asia Critique* 24 (1): 205–230.

———. 2017. "'Home and Beautiful Things': Aspirational Politics of Sex in Dance Bars in India." *Sexualities* 20 (4): 463–481.

Law, Lisa. 2001. *Sex Work in Southeast Asia: The Place of Desire in a Time of AIDS*. Routledge: New York.

Lawyers Collective. 2016. www.lawyerscollective.org.

Lemke, Thomas. 2005. "'A Zone of Indistinction': A Critique of Giorgio Agamben's Concept of Biopolitics." *Outlines: Critical Practice Studies* 7 (1): 3–13.

———. 2011. *Biopolitics An Advanced Introduction*. New York: New York University Press.

Lind, Amy, and Christine Keating. 2013. "Navigating the Left Turn: Sexual Justice and the Citizen Revolution in Ecuador." *International Feminist Journal of Politics* 15 (4): 515–533.

Logie, Carmen, Peter Newman, Venkatesan Chakrapani, and Murali Shunmugam. 2012. "Adapting the Minority Stress Model: Associations between Non-conformity Stigma, HIV-Related Stigma and Depression among Men Who Have Sex with Men in South India." *Social Science & Medicine* 74:1261–1268.

Longo, Paulo Henrique. 2005. "The Pegacao Program: Information, Prevention and Empowerment of Young Male Sex Workers in Rio de Janeiro." In *Global Sex Workers: Rights, Resistance, and Redefinition*, edited by Kamala Kempadoo and Jo Doezema, 231–239. New York: Routledge.

Manalansan, Martin F. 2003. *Global Divas: Filipino Gay Men in the Diaspora*. Durham, NC: Duke University Press.

Massad, Joseph. 2002. "Re-orienting Desire: The Gay International and the Arab World." *Public Culture* 14:361–385.

Mazzarella, William. 2001. "Citizens Have Sex, Consumers Make Love: Marketing KamaSutra Condoms in Bombay." In *Asian Media Productions*, edited by Brian Moeran, 168–196. Honolulu: University of Hawai'i Press.

———. 2013. "Cultural Politics of Branding: Promoting 'KamaSutra' in India." In *Consumer Culture, Modernity and Identity*, edited by Nita Mathur, 204–238. Thousand Oaks, CA: Sage.

McClintock, Anne. 1992. "Screwing the System: Sex Work, Race, and the Law." *Boundary* 19 (2): 70–95.

———. 1995. *Imperial Leather: Race, Gender and Sexuality in the Colonial Context*. New York: Routledge.

Mehta, Sonal. 2012. "Making Pehchan: Why the Global Fund Matters for Sexual Minorities." *Huffington Post*, November 15. www.huffingtonpost.com.

Menon, Nivedita. 2004. *Recovering Subversion: Feminist Politics beyond the Law*. Champaign: University of Illinois Press.

———. 2007. *Sexualities*. New Delhi: Women Unlimited.

Ministry of Law and Justice. 2017. The Human Immunodeficiency Virus and Acquired Immune Deficiency Syndrome (Prevention and Control) Act. *Gazette of India*, April 21. http://naco.gov.in.

Moghadam, Valentine. 2005. *Globalizing Women: Transnational Feminist Networks*. Baltimore: Johns Hopkins University Press.

Moussawi, Ghassan. 2015. "(Un)critically Queer Organizing: Towards a More Complex Analysis of LGBTQ Organizing in Lebanon." *Sexualities* 18 (5–6): 593–617.

NACO. 2007. "Targeted Interventions Under NACP III." https://naco.gov.in.

———. 2016. "Funds and Expenditures." http://naco.gov.in.

———. 2016–2017. "Annual Report 2016–17." http://naco.gov.in.

Nair, Janaki. 1994. "The Devadasi, Dharma and the State." *Economic and Political Weekly* 29 (50): 3157–3159.

———. 1996. *Women and Law in Colonial India*. New Delhi: Kali for Women.

NALSA. 2016. "Introduction." https://nalsa.gov.in.

Naples, Nancy, and Manisha Desai, eds. 2002. *Women's Activism and Globalization: Linking Local Struggles and Transnational Politics*. New York: Routledge.

Narrain, Arvind. 2004. "The Articulation of Rights around Sexuality and Health: Subaltern Queer Culture in India in the Era of Hindutva." *Sexuality, Human Rights, and Health* 7 (2): 142–164.

———. 2007. "Rethinking Citizenship: A Queer Journey." *Indian Journal of Gender Studies* 14 (1): 61–71.

Narrain, Arvind, and Gautam Bhan. 2005. *Because I Have a Voice: Queer Politics in India*. New Delhi: Yoda Press.

National Network for Sex Workers. 2013. "Ordinance Criminalizes Sex Workers: Sex Workers Appeal to President to Reject Ordinance." Press release. https://maggiemc-neill.files.wordpress.com.

Nguyen, Vinh-Kim. 2004. "Antiretroviral Globalism, Biopolitics, and Therapeutic Citizenship." In *Global Assemblages: Technology, Politics, and Ethics as Anthropological Problems,* edited by Aihwa Ong and Stephen J. Collier, 124–144. Malden, MA: Blackwell.

———. 2010. *The Republic of Therapy: Triage and Sovereignty in West Africa's Time of AIDS.* Durham, NC: Duke University Press.

Nisar, Muhammad. 2018. "(Un)becoming a Man: Legal Consciousness of the Third Gender Category in Pakistan." *Gender & Society* 32 (1): 59–81.

O'Flaherty, Michael, and John Fisher. 2008. "Sexual Orientation, Gender Identity and International Human Rights Law: Contextualizing the Yogyakarta Principles." *Human Rights Law Review* 8 (2): 207–248.

Ong, Aihwa. 2003. "Zones of New Sovereignty in Southeast Asia." In *Globalization Under Construction: Governmentality, Law, and Identity*, edited by Richard Warren Perry and Bill Maurer, 39–70. Minneapolis: University of Minnesota Press.

Parker, Richard. 2011. "Grassroots Activism, Civil Society Mobilization, and the Politics of the Global HIV/AIDS Epidemic." *Brown Journal of World Affairs* 17 (2): 21–37.

Parker, Richard, Diane di Mauro, Beth Filiano, Jonathan Garcia, Miguel Muñoz-Laboy, and Robert Sember. 2004. "Global Transformations and Intimate Relations in the 21st Century: Social Science Research on Sexuality and the Emergence of Sexual Health and Sexual Rights Frameworks." *Annual Review of Sex Research* 15:362–398.

Parreñas, Rhacel. 2011. *Illicit Flirtations: Labor, Migration, and Sex Trafficking in Tokyo.* Palo Alto, CA: Stanford University Press.

Patton, Cindy. 2002. *Globalizing AIDS.* Minneapolis: University of Minnesota Press.

Petryna, Adriana. 2002. *Life Exposed: Biological Citizens after Chernobyl.* Princeton, NJ: Princeton University Press.

Poster, Winifred, and Salime Zakia. 2002. "Limits of Microcredit: Transnational Feminism and USAID Activities in the United States and Morocco." In *Women's Activism and Globalization: Linking Local Struggles and Transnational Politics*, edited by Nancy Naples and Manisha Desai, 185–215. New York: Routledge.

Povinelli, Elizabeth A., and George Chauncey. 1999. "Thinking Sexuality Transnationally." *GLQ* 5 (4): 439–449.

Puar, Jasbir. 2007. *Terrorist Assemblages: Homonationalism in Queer Times.* Durham, NC: Duke University Press.

———. 2015. "Homonationalism as Assemblage: Viral Travels, Affective Sexualities." *Revista Lusofona de Estudos Culturais* 3 (1): 319–337.

PUCL-K. 2003. "Human Rights Violations Against the Transgender Community: A Study of *Kothi* and *Hijra* Sex Workers in Bangalore, India." Karnataka: PUCL-K.

Puri, Jyoti. 2002. "Concerning Kamasutras: Challenging Narratives of History and Sexuality." *Signs* 27 (3): 603–639.

———. 2014. "Sexualizing the State: Sodomy, Civil Liberties, and the Indian Penal Code." In *Contesting Nation: Gendered Violence in South Asia. Notes on the Post-Colonial Present*, edited by Angana Chatterji and Lubna Chowdhury. New Delhi: Zubaan Books.

———. 2016a. "Sexualizing Neoliberalism: Identifying Technologies of Privatization, Cleansing, and Scarcity." *Sexuality Research and Social Policy* 13 (4): 308–320.

———. 2016b. *Sexual States: Governance and the Struggle over the Anti-sodomy Law in India*. Durham, NC: Duke University Press.

Rajalakshmi, T. K. 2001. "Targeting NGOs." *Frontline* 10 (18): 1–14.

Ranganathan, Gowthaman. 2014. "Arbitrary Detention of Hijras in Bangalore: Communities Demand Justice. Orinam, November 26. http://orinam.net.

Rao, Balakoteshwara. 2017. "Transgenders Should Not Wear Sari: Ramadas Athawale." *Times of India*, August 1. https://timesofindia.indiatimes.com.

"Reactions to Section 377 Verdict: Jamaat-e-Islami Hind Expresses Dismay." 2018. *Hindu*, September 6. www.thehindu.com.

Reddy, Gayatri. 2005. *With Respect to Sex: Negotiating Hijra Identity in South India*. Chicago: University of Chicago Press.

Rege, Sharmila. 1995. "The Hegemonic Appropriation of Sexuality: The Case of the Lavani Performer of Maharastra." *Contributions to Indian Sociology* 29 (1–2): 23–38.

Reuters. 2018. "In Legal Battel over Gay Sex, Kenyan Court to Consider Indian Ruling." NBC News, September 28. www.nbcnews.com.

Robins, Steven. 2006. "From 'Rights' to 'Ritual': AIDS Activism in South Africa." *American Anthropologist* 2:312–323.

Rose, Nikolas. 1996. "The Death of the Social? Refiguring the Territory of Government." *Economy and Society* 25:327–356.

———. 2001. "The Politics of Life Itself." *Theory, Culture & Society* 18 (6): 1–30.

Rose, Nikolas, and Carols Novas. 2004. "Biological Citizenship." In *Global Assemblages: Technology, Politics, and Ethics as Anthropological Problems*, edited by Aihwa Ong and Stephen J. Collier, 439–463. Malden, MA: Blackwell.

Rubin, Gayle. 1984. "Thinking Sex: Notes for a Radical Theory of the Politics of Sexuality." In *Social Perspectives in Lesbian and Gay Studies*, edited by Peter M. Nardi and Beth E. Schneider, 100–133. New York: Routledge.

Rudrappa, Sharmila. 2015. *Discounted Life: The Price of Global Surrogacy in India*. New York: New York University Press.

Sangha, Sadhana Mahila. 2013. "Violence Against People in Sex Work in India: Submission to the Special Rapporteur on Violence Against Women—Ms. Rashida Manjoo." www.ohchr.org.

SANGRAM. 2018. "Raided: How Anti-trafficking Strategies Increase Sex Workers' Vulnerability to Exploitative Practices." India: SANGRAM.

Schotten, Heike. 2016. "Homonationalism: From Critique to Diagnosis. Or, We Are All Homonational Now." *International Feminist Journal of Politics* 18:351–370.

Sgaier, Sema K., et al. 2013. "How the Avahan HIV Prevention Programs Transitioned from the Gates Foundation to Government of India." *Health Affairs* 32 (7).

Shah, Svati. 2014. *Street Corner Secrets: Sex, Work, and Migration in the City of Mumbai*. Durham, NC: Duke University Press.

Shahani, Nishant. 2017. "Patently Queer: Late Effects and the Sexual Economies of India." *GLQ* 23 (2): 195–220.

Sharma, Aradhana. 2006. "Crossbreeding Institutions, Breeding Struggle: Women's Employment, Neoliberal Governmentality, and State (Re)formation in India." *Cultural Anthropology* 21 (1): 60–95.

Sheikh, Danish. 2013. "The Road to Decriminalization: Litigating India's Anti-sodomy Law." *Yale Human Rights and Development Law Journal* 16 (1): 104–132.

Sinha, Suveen K. 2004. "The Nowhere Men: The Gory Murder of Two Gay Men in Delhi Exposes the Darkness, and Despair, Prevalent in the Community." *Outlook*, August 30. www.outlookindia.com.

Sothern, Matthew. 2007. "HIV and Body Space: Aids and the Queer Politics of Future Negation in Aotearoa New Zealand." In *Geographies of Sexualities: Theory, Practices and Politics*, edited by Kathy Browne, Jason Lim, and Gavin Brown, 181–194. Farnham: Ashgate.

Stoler, Ann Laura. 1995. *Race and the Education of Desire: Foucault's History of Sexuality and the Colonial Order of Things*. Durham, NC: Duke University Press.

Stychin, Carl. 1996. "Constituting Sexuality: The Struggle for Sexual Orientation in the South African Bill of Rights." *Journal of Law and Society* 23 (4): 445–483.

Sweet, Michael J. 2002. "Eunuchs, Lesbians, and Other Mythical Beasts: Queering and Dequeering the *Kama Sutra*." In *Queering India: Same-Sex Love and Eroticism in Indian Culture and Society*, edited by Ruth Vanita, 77–84. New York: Routledge.

Swendeman, Dallas, Ishika Basu, Sankari Das, Smarajit Jana, and Mary Jane Rotheram-Borus. 2009. "Empowering Sex Workers in India to Reduce Vulnerability to HIV and Sexually Transmitted Diseases." *Social Science & Medicine* 69:1157–1166.

Tadros, Victor. 1998. "Between Governance and Discipline: The Law and Michel Foucault." *Oxford Journal of Legal Studies* 18 (1): 75–103.

Tambe, Ashwini. 2009. *Codes of Misconduct: Regulating Prostitution in Late Colonial Bombay*. Minneapolis: University of Minnesota Press.

Tandia, Oumar. 2005. "Prostitution in Senegal." In *Global Sex Workers: Rights, Resistance, and Redefinition*, edited by Kamala Kempadoo and Jo Doezema, 240–245. New York: Routledge.

Tarrow, Sidney. 2001. "Transnational Politics: Contention and Institutions in International Politics." *Annual Review of Political Science* 4 (1): 1–20.

UNAIDS. 2000. "Female Sex Worker HIV Prevention Projects: Lessons Learnt from Papua New Guinea, India and Bangladesh." Geneva: UNAIDS.

United Nations Development Programme. 2010. "Hijras/Transgender Women in India: HIV, Human Rights and Social Exclusion." New York: United Nations Development Programme.

Vanita, Ruth, ed. 2002. *Queering India: Same-Sex Love and Eroticism in Indian Culture and Society*. New York: Routledge.

Vanita, Ruth, and Saleem Kidwai. 2000. *Same-Sex Love in India: Readings from Litera-ture and History*. New York: Palgrave Macmillan.

Voices Against 377. 2005. "Rights for All: Ending Discrimination against Queer Desire under Section 377." New Delhi: Voices Against 377.

Wahab, Amar. 2012. "Homophobia as the State of Reason: The Case of Postcolonial Trinidad and Tobago." *GLQ* 18 (4): 481–505.

———. 2016. "'Homosexuality/Homophobia Is Un-African?' Un-mapping Transna-tional Discourses in the Context of Uganda's Anti-Homosexuality Bill/Act." *Journal of Homosexuality* 63 (5): 685–718.

Waites, Matthew. 2009. "Critiques of 'Sexual Orientation' and 'Gender Identity' in Human Rights Discourse: Global Queer Politics beyond the Yogyakarta Principles." *Contemporary Politics* 15 (1): 137–156.

Wilson, Ara. 2002. "The Transnational Geography of Human Rights." In *Truth Claims: Representation and Human Rights*, edited by Mark Philip Bradley and Patrice Petro, 251–265. New Brunswick, NJ: Rutgers University Press.

Yue, Audrey. 2008. "Gay Asian Sexual Health in Australia: Governing HIV/AIDS, Racializing Biopolitics and Performing Conformity." *Sexualities* 11 (1–2): 227–244.

Žižek, Slavoj. 2005. "Against Human Rights." *New Left Review* 35:115–131.

INDEX

ABVA. *See* AIDS Bhedbhav Virodhi
Andolan
adultery laws, 138, 172n29
Agamben, Giorgio, 25, 54, 74
Ahar, Abhina, 129
AIDS Bhedbhav Virodhi Andolan
(ABVA), 88–89, 127, 162n8, 166n13
AIDS Prevention Bill (1989), 33
ALF. *See* Alternative Law Forum
All India Sex Worker Conference (2007),
80–82
Alternative Law Forum (ALF), 107–8, 122,
140–41
Ambedkar, B. R., 137, 172n21
anti-sodomy law (Section 377): ABVA
activism against, 88–89, 127, 166n13; activism implications for all rights-based
struggles, 26, 103–8, 111–12, 122, 124–25,
127, 131–32, 139–41, 168n18; BJP position on, 97, 110; British colonial state
origins in, 18, 88, 122, 144–45, 169n26;
heterosexual acts covered under, 18,
88, 91, 95, 104, 145, 159n54, 165n9; HIV/
AIDS activism impact on, 87–100, 123,
134; HIV/AIDS prevention hampered
by, 90–96; international pressures for
repeal of, 23, 96; Koushal judgment upholding, 26–27, 101–2, 108–11; Lucknow
incident impact for, 64–68, 69, 73,
89–90, 93, 112; NACO petition against,
93–96, 98–99; NALSA judgment
contradictions with, 102–3, 121, 123–24,
126; Naz petitions and judgments for
repeal of, 73, 89–92, 94, 96–97, 105,
107, 108, 111, 122, 137, 141, 166nn13–14,
167n12; police harassment and violence
with, 54, 63–66, 68, 90–94, 108–9,
128; prosecution under, 18, 109; Queer
Pride March addressing, 106–8; queer
women impacted by, 18, 102, 104–6,
123, 167n11; rape laws relation to, 1, 18,
95, 159n54, 166n14; right-wing politics
shift in debate on, 140–41; for sexual
minorities, implications of, 1–2, 4, 18–
19, 23, 26–27, 54, 64–68, 76, 92, 101–8,
122, 168n18; social movements mobilization in fight against, 19, 101, 103–8,
112, 122, 124–24, 128, 131–32; state positions/
divisions on, 92–99; transgender/hijra
threat under, 1–2, 102; unconstitutionality ruling (2009) on, 26, 76, 96, 99,
107, 110, 111, 136–37; unconstitutionality
ruling (2018) on, 2, 27, 101, 127, 137, 144;
Voices campaign against, 103–7, 122,
136–137, 139–40, 167n12
anti-sodomy laws, global, 23, 90, 144–45,
170n7
Athawale, Ramdas, 171n11
Australia, HIV/AIDS policies in, 5
Autobiography of a Sex Worker (Jameela),
82
Avahan India AIDS Initiative (Avahan),
44–46, 163n20

Bandhopadhya, Aditya, 111–12
Bandyopadhyay, Nandinee, 29
Bangladesh, 144–45, 170n7, 173n38
begging laws, 132–34, 171n10

belonging. *See* citizenship and belonging

Bhan, Gautam, 127

Bharatiya Janata Party (BJP), 97, 110

Bharosa Trust, 63–68, 69

Biehl, Joao, 13

Bill & Melinda Gates Foundation, 35, 44

"biological citizenship," 15–16

biopower/biopolitics: Agamben on, 74; citizenship and belonging with, 10–17, 77, 128; Foucault on, 3, 11, 157n4; HIV/ AIDS, 3–4, 15–16, 25, 44, 47–48, 51–52, 73–74, 77, 102–3, 123, 125, 131; juridical power conflict with and shift to, 3, 15, 21, 30, 55, 62–63, 64, 69, 74, 123; life and death management implications with, 13, 14, 70; marginalized populations experience of, 12–13, 15, 77; police violence and, 70–73, 74; project outcome variances with, 125–26; rights-based struggles and victories relation to, 4, 7, 74–75, 102–3; sex work/workers engagement with, 4, 70–73, 79–80; state power relation to, 3, 74–75, 100; terminology distinctions for, 158n27

birth control education, 63

BJP. *See* Bharatiya Janata Party

Brazil, HIV/AIDS activism in, 15–16

British colonial state: anti-sodomy law origins with, 18, 88, 122, 144–45, 169n26; gender and sexuality interventions of, scholarship on, 160n63; hijras regulation under, 20, 160n62, 169n25

Butler, Judith, 13

caste. *See* class status/caste

CBOs. *See* community actors/ community-based organizations

Chandra, Pushkin, 62

Chatterjee, Partha, 13–14

child sexual abuse, 95

Chowdhury, Renuka, 78, 85–87

citizenship and belonging: biopower projects role in, 10–17, 77, 128; hijras

struggle for benefits of, 32–33; HIV/ AIDS programs relation to, 15–16, 77

class status/caste: for kothis, 8, 10, 31; marriage and, 143; in mass sterilizations of men in 1970s, 164n10; rights-based struggles inclusion of, 16, 143, 144, 145; for sex workers, 19–20

Comaroff, Jean, 13

community actors/community-based organizations (CBOs): governmentality role of, 12, 51–52, 128–29; government funding for, 114, 117; in HIV/ AIDS programs in India compared with US, 15; HIV/AIDS programs involvement of, 15, 25, 35, 39, 45–51, 73, 122, 129; interviews with, 6; MSM/gay support from, 46, 48–50; NACO emphasis on, 48–51; peer educators role in mobilizing, 48, 51; Pehchan project on involvement of, 48–50, 122, 129; state power role of, 10–11, 12, 51–52, 73; transgender/hijra rights support from, 113–14, 117. *See also* nongovernmental organizations; *specific organizations*

condoms: awareness lacking about, 63, 164n11; criminalization with distribution of, 26, 62–63; distribution of and education on, 26, 36–38, 40, 42–43, 51, 56, 57, 63–64, 68; to prisoners, 88–89

Constitution, Indian: adaptability of, 137–38; Ambedkar vision of, 137, 172n21; anti-sodomy law rulings based on conflict with, 2, 26, 27, 76, 96, 99, 101, 107, 110, 111, 127, 136–37, 144; Directive Principles of State Policy of, 138, 172n27; identities compared to sex acts supported under, 102–3, 121, 123–24, 126; inclusion tenet in, 107; popular morality superseded by morality of, 27, 136–38, 172n20; provision for questioning interpretations of, 168n17, 169n22

constitutional morality, 27, 136–38, 146, 172nn20–21

criminalization/decriminalization. *See* laws and criminalization
Criminal Tribes Act (1871), 20, 160n62, 169n25
Currier, Ashley, 164n21

dancing, 20, 82, 119, 165n5
decriminalization. *See* laws and criminalization
development projects, destructive, 139, 170n31
Dey, Bharati, 71–72
Directive Principles of State Policy, 138, 172n27
Durbar Mahila Samanwaya Committee (DMSC), 37–40, 69–72, 80–82

empowerment: transnational governmentality and women's, 12–13; women, sex worker collective impact on, 70–73, 80–81, 86–87
evangelism, 160n66, 164n21

family planning policies, 63
feminist perspectives: rights discourse from, 102–3; of sex work and trafficking conflation, 22; on transnational governmentality, 12–13

Ferguson, James, 12
Fire (film), 23–24
Foucault, Michel, 157n6; on "arts of government," 73; on biopower/biopolitics, 3, 11, 157n4; on governmentality, 11, 35; on political strategy, 133; on power and resistance relation, 100; rights discourse and, 16, 103; on sexuality, 11, 13

Gandhi, Indira, 164n10
Gandhi, Rahul, 97
Gates Foundation, 35, 44
gay groups. *See* kothis; MSM/gay groups

gender identity: British colonial regulations of, 20, 160nn62–63, 169n25; international recognition of, 161n70, 173n38; kothis, 8, 158n18, 161n3; NALSA judgment shortcomings on, 169n30; self-definition rights for, 9–10, 116–17, 171n9
gender minorities. *See* LGBTKQHI groups; LGBTQ groups; sexual and gender minorities; *specific gender groups*
Global Fund, 35, 48–50, 122, 129
globalization, 4, 12, 113, 134, 144
Godavari Mahila Samakya (GMS), 55–56, 72
Golder, Ben, 16, 103
Gopalan, Anjali, 89, 111
governmentality: of community actors and NGOs, 12, 51–52, 128–29; defining, 11–12, 35; of HIV/AIDS programs, 35, 51–52, 79–80; transnational, 12–13, 30, 35
Grover, Anand, 81–82, 90
Gupta, Akhil, 12
Gupta, Alok, 159n52, 165n7

Halley, Janet, 123–24
heterosexuality, 23–24, 105, 160; anti-sodomy law covering acts of, 18, 88, 91, 95, 104, 145, 159n54, 165n9; HIV/AIDS epidemic role of, 34; HIV/AIDS policies focusing on, 66
hijras: anti-sodomy law threat to, 1–2, 102; begging criminalization implications for, 132–33; British colonial regulation of, 20, 160n62, 169n25; CBOs support of, 113–14, 117; citizenship benefits exclusion for, 32–33; classification of, 46, 113; cultural role and visibility of, 32; HIV/AIDS policies and programs inclusion of, 3, 9, 14–15, 46, 117; kothi gender identification compared with, 8;

hijras (cont.)

kothis relationship with, 8–9; NALSA judgment on rights of, 1, 7, 26, 101–2, 112–17, 126, 132–33, 138, 169n30; police violence against, 19, 32, 33, 61–62, 143; rights-based struggles and victories for, 1, 4, 7, 24, 26–27, 101–2, 112–17, 126, 132–33, 138, 145, 169n30, 170n8, 171nn9–11, 173n38; self-identification right for, 116–17; state/police surveillance of, 20; state programs/welfare available for, 114, 116, 117; stigmatization and discrimination of, 10, 20, 32–33, 125, 145

Hindu right-wing politics: constitutional morality in context of, 27, 137; nonnormative sexuality attacks in, 21, 23–24, 97; on transgender rights, 24

HIV/AIDS activism: of ABVA, 88–89, 162n8, 166n13; anti-sodomy law impacted through, 87–100, 123, 134; for HIV-positive individuals, 162n8; on ITPA, 83–87; police harassment and arrests with, 64–69; for prisoners, 88–89; in South Africa, 15–16; state action role of, 162nn7–8

HIV/AIDS epidemic: heterosexual sex role in, 34; in India compared globally, 34, 89; MSM/gay group mobilization in 1980s, 23; NALSA judgment using context of, 113, 114–15, 117, 118, 123; police violence toward sexual minorities revealed with, 25–26, 70; in sex workers mobilization, role of, 5, 29; sex workers statistics on, 46; state relations with sexual minorities impacted by, 2–4, 5–6, 14–15, 21, 29–30, 33–34, 50–52, 62, 92, 129, 134–35, 136, 145–46; state response to, 3, 13, 14, 29–30, 33–34, 162n7

HIV/AIDS policies and programs: anti-sodomy law impact for, 90–96; in Australia, 5; Avahan, 44–46, 163n20;

as biopower projects, 3–4, 15–16, 25, 44, 47–48, 51–52, 73–74, 77, 102–3, 123, 125, 131; citizenship and belonging with, 15–16, 77; community actors/ organizations role in, 15, 25, 35, 39, 45–51, 73, 122, 129; governmentality of, 35, 51–52, 79–80; heterosexual sex focus for, 66; "high-risk" groups distinction and targeting in, 7, 14–15, 25, 34–36, 38, 39–40, 47, 162n11; on HIV-positive individual rights, 161n5, 162n8; international donors to, 35, 44; kothi inclusion in, 9, 26, 31, 161n3; MSM/gay groups benefiting from, 5, 76, 102; MSM/gay groups inclusion and treatment in, 3, 14–15, 26, 31, 46, 66–67, 158n17; NACP I (1994–1999), 35–36; NACP II (1999–2006), 39–40, 44, 46; NACP III (2007–2012), 45–46, 48, 49–51, 163n24; NACP IV (2012–2017), 48–49; NGOs role in, 35, 44, 46, 51, 91; numbers-driven goals critique of, 50; peer educators in, 5, 21, 26, 30, 37, 38–43, 47, 51, 55–56, 62, 70–71, 80–81; peer-to-peer interventions in, 40–43; police violence addressed in, 70; police violence and harassment experienced in, 21, 26, 53, 54–55, 56, 62–70, 74, 89–90; prevention and behavior focus shift in, 3, 30, 34; sexuality laws and criminalization impact on, 4, 21, 23, 26, 53, 54–55, 56, 62–65, 69–70, 74, 79–80, 84–85, 89–96; sexual minorities impacted globally by, 5, 15–16; sexual minorities stigmatization role in, 33–34; sex worker laws impact for, 4, 79–80, 84–85; sex workers participation/ peer education in, 37, 38–43, 55–56, 70–71, 79–80; sex workers treatment in, 3, 14–15, 22, 25, 35, 36–40; sex work/worker knowledge lacking in, 36–38; sex work/workers benefits

from, 3, 14–15, 25, 71–73, 76, 79–80;
state/police surveillance and, 4, 47–
48, 50, 162n15; STIs testing/treatment
in, 38, 40–43, 44, 47, 162n15; suppression approach in early, 30, 33–34;
transgender/hijra groups inclusion
and treatment in, 3, 9, 14–15, 46, 117;
in US, 15–16, 34, 89. *See also* National
AIDS Control Organization
HIV sentinel surveillance (HSS), 162n15
homophobia: HIV/AIDS activists impacted by, 66–68; in Namibia, 164n21;
police violence role of, 60; political,
66, 95–96, 102, 164n21
HSS. *See* HIV sentinel surveillance
human rights: LGBTQ designation
in global campaigns on, 9, 134–35;
transnational framework for, 21–22,
23, 24–25, 161n70. *See also* rights-based
struggles and victories
Humsafar Trust, 46, 92

identity rights: economic and sex work
rights compared with, 134; global recognition of, Indian successes impacting, 145; sex acts rights compared with,
102–3, 121, 123–24, 126. *See also* gender
identity; rights-based struggles and
victories
Immoral Traffic Prevention Act (ITPA):
Chowdhury role in, 78, 85–87;
enforcement of, 19, 77; HIV/AIDS
activism on, 83–87; MSM/gay/kothi
activism against, 26; NACO on, 83–
87; Nordic model of client criminalization in, 77–78, 86–87; sex work
and trafficking conflated under, 77,
78, 81–82, 84, 129–31, 159n61, 165n2;
sex worker protests against, 26, 27, 76,
79–82, 83, 86–87, 165n2; sex worker
rescue and rehabilitation approach
of, 19–20, 77, 86–87; state positions/
contradictions on, 83–87; transgender

and male sex workers covered under,
20; WCD reforms proposal for, 76,
78–82, 85–86
International HIV/AIDS Alliance, 46

Jaitley, Arun, 97
Jameela, Nalini, 82
Jana, Smarajit, 37–38, 70–71
juridical power: biopower conflict with
and shift from, 3, 15, 21, 30, 55, 62–63,
64, 69, 74, 123; Foucault on, 3. *See also*
laws and criminalization

Karnataka, 60–61, 143–44, 160n62
Karnataka Police Act (1963), 160n62
Kaviraj, Sudipta, 135–36
Kothari, Jayna, 141–42
kothis: class status for, 8, 10, 31; gay designation contrast with, 9–10; gender
identification for, 8, 158n18, 161n3;
hijra gender identification compared
with, 8; hijras relationship with,
8–9; HIV/AIDS programs inclusion
and mobilization of, 9, 26, 31, 161n3;
ITPA protests from, 26; panthis as
masculine partners in, 8, 31, 158n17,
161n3, 163n6; police violence on, 19,
31, 60; stigmatization and discrimination of, 10, 163n6; support groups,
research within, 6. *See also* LGBT-
KQHI groups
Kotiswaran, Prabha, 20, 159n58
Koushal judgment (2103): anti-sodomy
law upheld with, 26–27, 101–2, 108–11;
NALSA judgment compared with, 116,
121–24, 125

LABIA, 105–6, 112
Law, Lisa, 5
laws and criminalization: adultery, 138,
172n29; begging, 132–34, 171n10; contradictions within sexual minority, 83–87,
92–97, 102–3, 121, 123–24, 126, 132–34;

laws and criminalization (*cont.*)
HIV/AIDS programs impacted by sexual minority, 4, 21, 23, 26, 53, 54–55, 56, 62–65, 69–70, 74, 79–80, 84–85, 89–96; on HIV-positive individuals, 161n5, 162n8; LC work on sexual and gender minority, 80–81, 83, 90, 116; MSM/gay groups struggles against, 31, 87–100; NACO role in repealing sexual minority, 21, 83–87, 93–96, 98–99; NALSA and Koushal judgments on, compared, 116, 121–24, 125; NALSA judgment shortcomings for, 117–21, 132–33, 169n30; police violence relation to, 54, 59–60, 63–66, 68, 90–94, 108–9, 128; privacy judgment impact for, 141–42; public nuisance, 17, 20, 54, 128, 159n50, 159n61; queer women threat from, 18, 102, 104–6, 123, 167n11; rape laws relation to anti-sodomy, 1, 18, 95, 159n54, 166n14; sexual assault, amendments to, 170n2; sexual minorities rights-based victories transforming language of, 139–44; sex work, 4, 7, 19–20, 21, 26, 30–31, 59–60, 70–71, 76–82, 100, 129–30, 134–35, 138, 142, 165n2; sex work and trafficking conflated in, 22, 77, 78, 81–82, 84, 129–31, 134, 159n61, 165n2; state/police surveillance role in, 14, 18, 20; "unnatural offenses" classification in, 1, 17–18, 66, 68, 88, 91, 121, 128, 140–41, 159n52, 160n62, 165n7, 169n26, 170n7; WCD work in repealing sexual minority, 76, 78–82, 85–86. *See also* anti-sodomy law; Immoral Traffic Prevention Act; Koushal judgment; National Legal Services Agency judgment
Lawyers Collective (LC), 80–81, 83, 90, 116
Legal Services Authorities Act, 168n20
Lemke, Thomas, 74

lesbians. *See* queer women
LGBTKQHI groups, 6, 7; anti-sodomy law reform impact for, 26, 168n18; LGBTQ designation compared with, 9; social movement strength for, 131–32; Voices coalition of, against anti-sodomy law, 103–7, 122, 136–37, 139–40, 167n12. *See also specific identities*
LGBTQ groups: human rights global designation of, 9, 134–35; LGBTKQHI designation compared to, 9; transphobia within, 10. *See also specific identities*
literacy, 63–64, 168n20
Lucknow incident (2001), 64–68, 69, 73, 89–90, 93, 112

marginalized populations, 17; biopower/biopolitics experience for, 12–13, 15, 77; constitutional morality fight implications for, 27, 136–38, 172n20; state relations for, 13–14, 135–38. *See also* sexual and gender minorities; *specific groups*
marriage, same-sex, 2, 19, 92, 104–5, 127, 143
Ministry of Social Justice and Empowerment (MSJE), 115–16, 132, 169n30
Ministry of Women and Child Development (MWCD), 130
morality: constitutional morality superseding popular, 27, 136–38, 172n20; public health programs debates on, 95–96
MSJE. *See* Ministry of Social Justice and Empowerment
MSM/gay groups: Avahan program targeting of, 44–45; classification of, 113; community and international support for, 46, 48–50; criminalization struggles and activism of, 31, 87–100; HIV/AIDS policies and programs on, 3, 14–15, 26, 31, 46, 66–67, 158n17; HIV/AIDS programs benefits for, 5, 76, 102;

HIV/AIDS role in 1980s mobilization of, 23; HIV prevalence in, 46; ITPA protests from, 26; Lucknow incident impact for, 64–68, 69, 73, 89–90, 93, 112; marriage rights for, 2, 19, 92, 127, 143; police rape within, 60; police treatment of murder of, 62; police violence toward, 60, 90, 94; sexual identities within, 8. *See also* kothis

Murugan, Perumal, 24, 161n71

Muslims, 24, 140–41

MWCD. *See* Ministry of Women and Child Development

NACO. *See* National AIDS Control Organization

NACP. *See* National AIDS Control Program

NALSA. *See* National Legal Services Agency

Namibia, 164n21

Narmada Bachao Andolan (NBA), 139, 170n31

National AIDS Control Organization (NACO): anti-sodomy law opposition of, 93–96, 98–99; community ownership emphasis of, 48–51; function and authority of, 6, 34; "high-risk" categorization by, 7, 34–36, 39–40, 162n11; international donors to, 35, 44; on ITPA, 83–87; Pehchan project partnership with, 48–50, 122, 129; on police violence, 69; program implementation process for, 35; sexual minorities decriminalization support from, 21, 83–87, 93–96, 98–99; TI program of, 39–40, 49–50; transgender rights support from, 113. *See also* peer educators

National AIDS Control Program (NACP): phase I (1994–1999), 35–36; phase II (1999–2006), 39–40, 44, 46; phase III (2007–2012) of, 45–46, 48, 49–51, 163n24; phase IV (2012–2017), 48–49

National Legal Services Agency (NALSA) judgment (2014): agency origins and mission behind, 168n20; anti-sodomy law contradiction with, 102–3, 121, 123–24, 126; background and judiciary efforts for, 114–15; HIV/AIDS context behind, 113, 114–15, 117, 118, 123; Koushal judgment compared with, 116, 121–24, 125; shortcomings of, 117–21, 132–33, 169n30; transgender and hijra rights under, 1, 7, 26–27, 101–2, 112–17, 126, 132–33, 138, 169n30; transnational support of, 113, 122

National Network of Sex Workers, 72, 130

Naz Foundation India (Naz): anti-sodomy law repeal petition process for, 73, 89–92, 94, 96–97, 105, 107, 108, 111, 122, 137, 141, 166nn13–14, 167n12; founding of, 89; MSM/gay groups support from, 46; peer educators at, 7, 53; police harassment and violence experience for, 62–63, 89–90; sexual and gender minority relations at, 9–10; Voices as copetitioners with, 105

Naz Foundation International (NFI), 46, 64–68

NBA. *See* Narmada Bachao Andolan

New Delhi Queer Pride Committee protests (2015), 110–11

NFI. *See* Naz Foundation International

nongovernmental organizations (NGOs), 6, 160n66; governmentality of, 12, 51–52, 128–29; HIV/AIDS program involvement of, 35, 44, 46, 51, 91; police harassment and violence towards, 66–69. *See also specific organizations*

Noronha, Earnest, 113, 114–15

One Part Woman (Murugan), 24, 161n71

Pakistan, 144–45, 170n7, 173n38

panthis, 8, 31, 158n17, 161n3, 163n6

Parker, Richard, 162n7

Patankar, Pallav, 92

peer educators: in community mobilization, 48, 51; condom distribution and education by, 36–37, 38, 42–43, 56, 57, 63–64; in HIV/AIDS programs, 5, 21, 26, 30, 37, 38–43, 47, 51, 55–56, 62, 70–71, 80–81; legal protection tactics for, 64; at Naz, 7, 53; police relations shift for, 71–72, 74; police violence against, 26, 53, 55, 56, 63–64, 69, 74; responsibilities of, 36–37, 38, 40–43, 55–56; sex workers as, 37, 38–43, 55–56, 70–71, 79–80; state relationship shift for, 62, 74; STIs information role of, 38, 40–43

peer-to-peer interventions, 40–43

Pehchan project, 48–50, 122, 129

People's Union for Civil Liberties Karnataka (PUCL-K), 60–61

police: brothel owners nexus with, 159n58; condoms confiscated and destroyed by, 62–63; peer educators role in shifting relations with, 71–72, 74; sexual minorities reporting crime to, 61–62; sexual minorities romantic relationships with, 61; sex worker collectives impacting relations with, 71–72. *See also* state/police surveillance

police violence and harassment: anti-sodomy law role in, 54, 63–66, 68, 90–94, 108–9, 128; biopolitics and, 70–73, 74; criminalization of sexual minorities role in, 54, 59–60, 63–66, 68, 90–94, 108–9, 128; HIV/AIDS policies addressing, 70; HIV/AIDS programs experience of, 21, 26, 53, 54–55, 56, 62–70, 74, 89–90; homophobia role in, 60; on kothis, 19, 31, 60; on LGBTKQHI groups, 60–62; on MSM/gay groups, 60, 90, 94; NACO on, 69; Naz experience of, 62–63, 89–90; peer educators experience of, 26, 53, 55, 56, 63–64, 69, 74; sex worker collectives experience of, 68–69; of sex workers, 19–20, 30,

38, 55, 56, 59–60, 68–69, 159n58; stigma role in, 60; transgender/hijra groups experience of, 19, 32, 33, 61–62, 143

population policies, 164n10

postcolonial scholarship, 13–14, 160n63

prisoners, HIV/AIDS programs for, 88–89

privacy rights, 76, 102, 105, 131–32, 138, 141–42, 171n13

prostitution. *See* Immoral Traffic Prevention Act; sex work/workers

public health programs, 9, 38, 95–96. *See also* HIV/AIDS policies and programs

public nuisance law, 17, 20, 54, 128, 159n50, 159n61

PUCL-K. *See* People's Union for Civil Liberties Karnataka

Puri, Jyoti, 10, 18, 135, 159n54

Queen Empress v. Khairati (1884), 169n26

Queer Pride March (2009), 106–8

queer scholarship, 17, 102–3, 169n26

queer women, 4, 9, 18, 102, 104–6, 112, 123, 167n11

Ranganathan, Gowthaman, 107–8, 109–10

Rao, Prasada, 93

rape: anti-sodomy law relation to laws on, 1, 18, 95, 159n54, 166n14; by police of sexual minorities, 60; sex worker laws on, 129, 138

research sources and process, 6–10

rights-based struggles and victories: anti-sodomy law protests implications for all, 26, 103–8, 111–12, 122, 124–25, 127, 131–32, 139–41, 168n18; biopower projects impact for, 4, 7, 74–75, 102–3; caste-based injustices inclusion in, 16, 143, 144, 145; citizenship and belonging in, 32–33; constitutional morality invoked in, 27, 136–38, 146; feminist perspective on, 102–3; global, Indian sexual minority victories impact for, 144–46; globalization impact for, 4, 113,

134, 144; identity rights compared to sex acts in, 102–3, 121, 123–24, 126; interconnectedness of, 139–44; Koushal and NALSA judgments contrasted in, 116, 121–24, 125; Lucknow incident impact for, 64–68, 69, 73, 89–90, 93, 112; of Muslims, 140–41; NALSA judgment shortcomings for, 117–21, 132–33, 169n30; privacy, 76, 102, 105, 131–32, 138, 141–42, 171n13; public nuisance laws impact for, 17, 20, 54, 128, 159n50, 159n61; for same-sex marriage, 2, 19, 92, 127, 143; sex worker, 8, 21–22, 36–37, 68–69, 70–73, 76, 80–82, 86–87, 129–31, 134, 142, 143–44, 165n2; sex worker collectives working on, 70–73, 80–84, 86–87; social justice responsibility of state and, 27, 136–38, 146; state power relation with, 17, 102–3; of transgender/hijra groups, 1, 4, 7, 24, 26–27, 101–2, 112–17, 126, 132–33, 138, 145, 169n30, 170n8, 171nn9–11, 173n38

rights discourse/scholarship, 16, 17, 19, 102–3

right-wing politics: constitutional morality in context of, 27, 137, 146; nonnormative sexuality suppression/attacks by, 21, 23–25, 97, 161n7; sexuality criminalization views shift in, 140–41; on transgender rights, 24

Rose, Nikolas, 15

Rubin, Gayle, 7, 157n7

SACS. See State AIDS Control Societies

Sampada Gramin Mahila Sanstha (SANGRAM), 36–37, 68–69

SC. See Supreme Court, India

Section 377. See anti-sodomy law

Seshu, Meena, 36–37

sex acts: anti-sodomy law on heterosexual, 18, 88, 91, 95, 104, 145, 159n54, 165n9; identity rights compared to, 102–3, 121, 123–24, 126

sexual abuse, 95, 170n2. See also rape

sexual and gender minorities: alliances between, 27, 142–44; anti-sodomy law implications for, 1–2, 4, 18–19, 23, 26–27, 54, 64–68, 76, 92, 101–8, 122, 168n18; "bare life" meaning for, 54, 59, 74; caste role in rights-based struggles for, 16, 143, 144, 145; constitutional morality fight implications for, 27, 136–38, 146; defining, 7; global impact of rights-based struggles of, 144–46; HIV/AIDS epidemic impact on state relations with, 2–4, 5–6, 14–15, 21, 29–30, 33–34, 50–52, 62, 92, 129, 134–35, 136, 145–46; HIV/AIDS epidemic revealing violence toward, 25–26, 70; HIV/AIDS policies and stigmatization of, 33–34; HIV/AIDS work impact globally for, 5, 15–16; LC work with/for, 80–81, 83, 90, 116; Lucknow incident view into rights-based struggles for, 64–68, 69, 73; NACO support in decriminalization of, 21, 83–87, 93–96, 98–99; at Naz, relations between, 9–10; police relations for, 61–62, 71–72, 74; police violence and harassment for, 19–20, 26, 30–33, 38, 53–56, 59–66, 68–69, 74, 89–94, 108–9, 128, 143, 159n58; self-identification rights for, 9–10, 116–17, 171n9; sex workers as mobilization pioneers for, 73; sex workers place/role in, 7, 73, 157nn7–8; social justice goals relation to rights of, 27, 136–44, 146; state/police surveillance of, 14, 18, 20; state power navigation by, 11, 21, 29, 54, 100, 136; state programs incorporation of, 4–5, 14–15; stigma of, anti-sodomy law increasing, 92; stigma role in violence against, 60; terminology used globally for, 9; in transnational human rights framework, 21–22, 23, 24–25, 161n70. See also specific topics and groups sexual and gender minorities rights and laws. *See* laws and criminalization; rights-based struggles and victories

sexuality: British colonial interventions in, scholarship on, 160n63; criminalization of "unnatural," 1, 17–18, 66, 68, 88, 91, 121, 128, 140–41, 159n52, 160n62, 165n7, 169n26, 170n7; Foucault on, 11, 13; right-wing regulation of, 21, 23–25, 97, 161n70; sex worker experience of, 81–82; state power relation with, 10–11, 102–3, 105; struggles, contemporary social context for, 21–25; women's movements view shift on, 160n63

sexually transmitted infections (STIs) testing/treatment, 38, 40–43, 44, 47, 162n15

Sexual States (Puri), 10

sex worker collectives: DMSC, 37–40, 69–72, 80–82; GMS, 55–56, 72; number and scope of, 72–73; police harassment experience of, 68–69; police relations impacted by, 71–72; rights-based and empowerment work of, 70–73, 80–84, 86–87; SANGRAM, 36–37, 68–69; VAMP, 22, 68–69, 160n66

Sex Work in Southeast Asia (Law), 5

sex work/workers: All India Sex Worker Conference on, 80–82; Avahan program targeting of, 44–45; "bare life" meaning for, 59; biopolitics participation of, 4, 70–73, 79–80; class status for, 19–20; criminalization role in violence experienced by, 59–60; criminalization struggles and activism of, 4, 7, 19–20, 21, 26, 30–31, 59–60, 70–71, 76–82, 100, 129–30, 134–35, 138, 142, 165n2; high-risk categorization of, 7, 35, 36, 38; HIV/AIDS impact for awareness and mobilization of, 5, 29; HIV/AIDS policies and programs treatment of, 3, 14–15, 22, 25, 35, 36–40; HIV/AIDS program benefits for, 3, 14–15, 25, 71–73, 76, 79–80; HIV/AIDS program participation/peer education of, 37, 38–43, 55–56, 70–71, 79–80; HIV prevalence in, 46; home-based, 40, 163n19; Indian politics impacted by, 4; ITPA protests from, 26, 27, 76, 79–82, 83, 86–87, 165n2; labor-rights perspective for, 8, 22, 82, 129–31, 134, 142, 165n2; as mobilization pioneers, 73; peer-to-peer interventions with, 40–41; police violence and harassment of, 19–20, 30, 38, 55, 56, 59–60, 68–69, 159n58; rape laws for, 129, 138; rescue and rehabilitation approach to, 19–20, 22, 31, 77, 86–87, 130, 160n66; rights-based struggles for, 8, 21–22, 36–37, 68–69, 70–73, 76, 80–82, 86–87, 129–31, 134, 142, 143–44, 165n2; sexual desire experience for, 81–82; sexual minorities place/role of, 7, 73, 157nn7–8; state programs exclusion of, 30; stigma of, 7, 8, 30–31; STIs testing/treatment services for, 38, 40–43, 44; terminology and language differences for, 8; therapeutic/service work benefits in, 82; trafficking conflated with, 22, 77, 78, 81–82, 84, 129–31, 134, 159n61, 165n2; transgender and male, ITPA covering, 20; transnational human rights framework for, 21–22; violence from clients and pimp/brothel, 30, 56–59. *See also* Immoral Traffic Prevention Act

Sharma, Aradhana, 12–13

Sheikh, Danish, 140–41

Singapore, 144, 170n7

Singhal, B. P., 167n12, 172n20

Siva, Tiruchi, 170n8

slavery, modern, 170n6

social justice, 27, 136–44, 145–46

sodomy laws. *See* anti-sodomy law

Sonagachi project, 37–39, 70–71

South Africa, HIV/AIDS activism in, 15–16

State AIDS Control Societies (SACS), 34, 91

state economy framework, 162n14

state/police surveillance: HIV/AIDS programs role of, 4, 47–48, 50, 162n15; sexual minority criminalization role in, 14, 18, 20; of transgender/hijra groups, 20

state power: biopolitical impacts on, 3, 74–75, 100; community actors role in, 10–11, 12, 51–52, 73; constitutional morality role in evolution of, 27, 136–38, 146; Foucault on resistance relation to, 100; globalization impacts on, 12; HIV/AIDS programs role in, 4, 47–48; over life and death, 13, 14, 25–26, 54, 70; rights-based struggles relation with, 17, 102–3; sexuality relation with, 10–11, 102–3, 105; sexual minorities navigation of, 11, 21, 29, 54, 100, 136; transnational governmentality role in, 12–13, 35

state programs/welfare: sexual minorities incorporation in, 4–5, 14–15; sex workers exclusion from, 30; for transgender groups, 114, 116, 117. *See also* HIV/AIDS policies and programs

state relations: marginalized groups idealization of, 13–14, 135–38; peer educators impact for, 62, 74; with sexual minorities, HIV/AIDS impact on, 2–4, 5–6, 14–15, 21, 29–30, 33–34, 50–52, 62, 92, 129, 134–35, 136, 146

state violence. *See* police violence and harassment

sterilization, male, 164n10

STIs testing/treatment. *See* sexually transmitted infections testing/treatment

Supreme Court, India (SC), 167n28; constitutional interpretation process for, 168n17, 169n22; curative petition for challenging decision of, 109, 168n16. *See also* anti-sodomy law; Koushal judgment; laws and criminaliza-tion; National Legal Services Agency judgment

surveillance. *See* state/police surveillance

Tamil Nadu, 113–14

targeted intervention (TI) program, 39–40, 49–50

Toonen v. Australia (1994), 23

trafficking: India place globally in, 161n67, 170n6; sex work conflated with, 22, 77, 78, 81–82, 84, 129–31, 134, 159n61, 165n2

Trafficking in Persons Report, 22, 161n67

Trafficking of Persons Bill (2018), 130, 170nn5–6

transgender groups: anti-sodomy law activism from, 1–2, 7, 115; anti-sodomy law threat to, 1–2, 102; CBOs supporting rights of, 113–14, 117; classification of, 46, 113, 169n30; global rights recognition for, 145, 173n38; "high-risk" categorization of, 7; Hindu right-wing politics impact for, 24; HIV/AIDS policies and programs inclusion of, 3, 9, 14–15, 46, 117; Indian politics impacted by activism from, 4; MSJE support of, 115–16, 132, 169n30; NACO support of, 113; NALSA judgment on rights of, 1, 7, 26–27, 101–2, 112–17, 126, 132–33, 138, 169n30; Pehchan activism for, 48–50, 122, 129; police violence and harassment of, 19, 32, 33, 61–62, 143; privacy judgment impact for, 141–42; rights-based struggles and victories for, 1, 4, 7, 24, 26–27, 101–2, 112–17, 126, 132–33, 138, 145, 169n30, 170n8, 171nn9–11, 173n38; self-identification right for, 116–17; sex worker laws for, 20; state/police surveillance of, 20; state programs/welfare for, 114, 116, 117; support groups for, research within, 6; Tamil Nadu pioneer in rights for, 113–14; UNDP support of, 113, 114, 115, 122, 123. *See also* hijras

Transgender Persons Bill, 132, 171n9
transnational governmentality, 12–13, 30, 35
transnational human rights framework, 21–22, 23, 24–25, 161n70
transphobia, 10, 133
Tripathi, Laxmi Narayan, 1–2, 115

UN. See United Nations
UNDP. See United Nations Development Programme
United Nations (UN), 23, 90
United Nations Development Programme (UNDP), 35, 113, 114, 115, 122, 123
United States (US): anti-sodomy law repeal in, 90; HIV/AIDS approach in, 15–16, 34, 89

VAMP. See Veshya Anyay Mukti Parishad
Verma, J. S., 170n2
Veshya Anyay Mukti Parishad (VAMP), 22, 68–69, 160n66
violence. See police violence and harassment; rape

violence, sex worker client and pimp, 30, 56–60
Voices Against 377 (Voices), 103–7, 122, 136–37, 139–40, 167n12

Wahab, Amar, 18, 164n21
WCD. See Women and Child Development Ministry
WHO. See World Health Organization
women: dance bar prohibitions on, 165n5; population control policies targeting, 164n10; queer, 4, 9, 18, 102, 104–6, 112, 123, 167n11; right-wing attacks on, 24; sexuality evolution for, 160n63; sex worker collective empowerment for, 70–73, 80–81, 86–87; transnational governmentality and empowerment for, 12–13
Women and Child Development Ministry (WCD), 76, 78–82, 85–86
World Health Organization (WHO), 37–38, 88, 166n18

Yogyakarta Principles, 23, 161n70
Yue, Audrey, 5

ABOUT THE AUTHOR

Chaitanya Lakkimsetti is Assistant Professor of Sociology and Women's & Gender Studies at Texas A&M University.